A Commentary on the Pearl of Great Price

A Jewel Among the Scriptures

Jerald R. Johansen

International Standard Book Number
0-88290-269-5

Library of Congress Catalog Card Number
84-62621

Horizon Publishers Catalog and Order Number
1019

Printed and Distributed in the
United States of America
by

Horizon
Publishers
& Distributors, Incorporated

50 South 500 West   P.O. Box 490
Bountiful, Utah 84010-0490

Acknowledgments

A special thanks is given to the Church Education System Publications Review Committee. Dr. Benjamin Martinez is a member of that committee and also a colleague of mine at the Ogden LDS Institute of Religion. Brother Martinez reviewed the manuscript initially and was very encouraging about the material. He gave some helpful suggestions and valuable critique. It was then submitted to Brother Gerald Lund, Chairman of the Committee, who assigned the manuscript to two other members of the committee. It was given to Brother J. Lewis Taylor of the Salt Lake Institute of Religion, and to Brother Richard E. Jackson, Teacher Support Consultant of the Ogden Area Seminaries. Both of these men carefully read the manuscript checking for accuracy of doctrine. They also red-lettered and penciled in helpful suggestions. Both felt the work would be very helpful to Seminary and Institute teachers as well as students of the Pearl of Great Price. Dr. Joe Christensen, Associate Commissioner of Church Education, also read the manuscript and gave encouragement and helpful suggestions.

A special thanks to the Ogden Institute secretaries, Beverly Tervort, Ellen Herzog, and Di Lindeman, for assisting in the typing of the manuscript. Also my thanks to Horizon Publishers & Distributors, Inc., and Duane Crowther for accepting the work and being willing to publish this book.

Finally my love and thanks to my wife, Lenore, who believed in me and who encouraged me to continue to write in spite of opposition and disappointment along the way—and to my children: Diane, Alan, Blake, Valerie, Mark, and Laura who always knew "Dad could do it!"

Introduction

The author has been with The LDS Department of Seminaries and Institutes of Religion for almost twenty-seven years. Most of these years have been as a teacher of college-age youth. To teach the gospel of Jesus Christ, as found in the standard works of The Church of Jesus Christ of Latter-day Saints, has been a sacred privilege. There have been times when the Spirit of the Lord has helped both the teacher and the students to "climb exceedingly high mountains" with the prophets and to get at least a glimpse of the inspiration they received and were trying to share with us.

In many respects, the Pearl of Great Price, because of its small size, allows us in one college term to go into more depth and to analyze and consider the individual passages more carefully than we are able to do with some of the longer books of scripture. We have been able to "drink deeper at the spring"—to savor the meaning of the passages and not to be under quite as much pressure to cover the breadth that the other works have in sheer number of pages. There is great power in this small book. It is concentrated power, condensed power—Spiritual Power.

Over the years the author has kept notes and written lesson plan after lesson plan on this great book. Doing so has not become tedious and has not become old. It has been a new and exciting process each time these great truths are reviewed with the students. The lesson plans have been re-written every quarter, and the process started to become a longer one of writing out the thoughts and concepts, not just outlining them. Someone has said that "writing crystalizes thinking." This seemed to be the case in writing out the thoughts to be presented in the Pearl of Great Price classes.

In the process of writing out these thoughts, the desire became very great to preserve the material in book form for the students and to make chapters of the major ideas to be developed. Therefore, before and after class—with every spare minute—the notes and lesson plans unfolded into the present work. It has been an enjoyable and, at times, an exhilarating experience to take the oral presentation and put it all in writing. It changes a bit in this process, for we often speak and talk differently than we write, but the present writing is as close as the author and teacher would speak these concepts.

This book is thus written to all my former students of the Pearl of Great Price, and also to all those of the future I may teach. It is written to my own wife and family and all of my brothers and sisters in the Church who may find it helpful—to my colleagues in the Seminary and Institute programs and to all those in the Church school system who may find it helpful in learning and teaching the Pearl of Great Price. If anyone not of our faith should read it and be touched by this "jewel among scriptures" and be led by it to embrace the fullness of the gospel of Jesus Christ—even that same gospel which was taught to our common father, Adam—I would be humbly grateful.

This book is almost exclusively a commentary and analysis of the books of Moses and Abraham found in the Pearl of Great Price. The "Joseph Smith History," which follows these books in the Pearl of Great Price, where Joseph Smith tells of his own story of the restoration and the first vision, is basic, and preliminary, for anyone who reads this material for the first time.

No extensive commentary is given in this book on "Joseph Smith—Matthew," which is also found in the Pearl of Great Price. This is an extract from the translation or revision of the Bible as revealed to Joseph Smith, the prophet, in 1831 of Matthew 23:39, and chapter 24. Since the book of Moses and the book of Abraham are basically the story of mankind's first two thousand years on earth, an additional chapter on this revelation seemed to the author too great a jump in the flow and theme of this work. This does not mean to imply that this portion is not important: It is a vital scripture for these latter days as the Savior foretells the signs of his second coming and "of the end of the world—or the destruction of the wicked, which is the end of the world." (JST, Matthew 24:4).

Anyone interested in learning more about the Prophet Joseph Smith's inspired translation of the Bible is referred to Robert J. Matthew's excellent book, *Joseph Smith's Translation of the Bible—"A Plainer Translation,"* published by BYU Press of Provo, 1975, or his dissertation entitled, "A Study of the Inspired Revision of the Bible," BYU, 1968. The Joseph Smith translation of the Bible is published by the Reorganized Church of Jesus Christ of Latter Day Saints, Herald Publishing House in Independence, Missouri. Some of the excerpts from the Prophet Joseph Smith's translation of the Bible can be found in the Appendix of the Bible published by The Church of Jesus Christ of Latter-day Saints, Salt Lake City, Utah, 1979.

The author has, in this writing, tried to use from the Joseph Smith translation Biblical quotes whenever possible.

Contents

Chapter One

A Preface—
Overview of the Pearl of Great Price

Again, the kingdom of heaven is like unto a merchant man, seeking goodly pearls:

Who, when he had found one pearl of great price, went and sold all that he had, and bought it.'' (Matthew 13:45, 46.)

The Pearl of Great Price—a "Jewel" Among Scriptures

The Pearl of Great Price is a "jewel" among scriptures. Of the four standard works of The Church of Jesus Christ of Latter-day Saints, it is the smallest in size yet is no less significant in its message than are the Bible, the Doctrine and Covenants, and the Book of Mormon.

This scripture teaches us that the first man, Adam, and the other ancient patriarchs and prophets received, by revelation from the Lord, the plan of salvation (Moses 6:62). These people, in the first dispensation on earth, were given the gospel of Jesus Christ in its plainness and in its fullness. They were then told to teach the gospel to their children and to all men everywhere (Moses 6:57).

The Pearl of Great Price contains some of the clearest and most profound statements in any scripture on the great Council in Heaven where the Gods pre-planned the earth. It tells us about ". . . the intelligences that were organized before the world was" (Abraham 3:22). It tells us where we were before we were born on earth, our purpose for being here, and what our final destination will be if the commandments of the Lord are kept (Abraham 3:26).

Many "Plain and Precious Things Were Taken Away from the Bible"

As soon as Joseph Smith began to translate the Book of Mormon, he learned that many "plain and precious things" were taken from the Bible, and that this record had lost many of the covenants of the Lord, and ". . . they had taken away from the gospel of the Lamb many parts which are plain and most precious; . . ."—they had lost some of the "pearls of great price (see 1 Nephi 13:26-29). Joseph Smith also learned from the Book of Mormon that he would bring forth "other books" in addition to the Book of Mormon and that "these last records . . . shall establish the truth of the first, which are of the twelve apostles of the Lamb, and shall make known the plain and precious things which have been taken away from them" (1 Nephi 13:39-40).

As early as June 1830, after the publication of the Book of Mormon, the Lord revealed to Joseph Smith a conversation that He (the Lord) had with Moses concerning the book which Moses was to write about the creation of the world. The Lord informed Moses:

> . . . Thou shalt write the things which I shall speak.
> And in a day when the children of men shall esteem my words as naught and take many of them from the book which thou shalt write, behold, I will raise up another like unto thee [Joseph Smith]; and they shall be had again among the children of men—among as many as shall believe." (Moses 1:40-41.)

Thus, in some of the earliest revelations, Joseph Smith was told that not only was the Bible imperfect, but also that at least some of the missing parts would be restored by the latter-day prophet.

In Translating the Bible Joseph Smith Restores Parts of Moses

Joseph Smith's work on restoring many of the plain and precious truths of the Bible became a springboard for many revelations now in the Pearl of Great Price. Chapter two in this work will expand upon this concept and also tell us how the Pearl of Great Price came to be in its present form.

Climbing "Exceedingly High Mountains"—a Figurative Expression

When we read the Pearl of Great Price we are "climbing exceedingly high mountains" with the prophets. This is a figurative expression used by the writers of the scriptures—it means that such prophets are seeing some things from God's perspective: they are getting a "God's-eye view." For example it was not just Mt. Horeb or Mt. Sinai that Moses climbed. His climb up "an exceedingly high mountain" may not have been unlike the experience the apostle Paul had when he said:

> I knew a man in Christ above fourteen years ago, (whether in the body, I cannot tell; or whether out of the body, I cannot tell: God knoweth;) such an one caught up to the third heaven.
> How that he was caught up into paradise, and heard unspeakable words, which it is not lawful for a man to utter. (2 Corinthians 12:2, 4.)

Modern man has seen the earth from the moon, but how many have seen the earth from the perspective of Kolob—of heaven—of the celestial world—from God's perspective? Such a "climb up an exceedingly high mountain" would indeed be a "pearl of great price" if the experience could be shared. Moses had great panoramic visions of the world. He gave us word symbols to try to share with us his experiences. Some of these words, in the Pearl of Great Price, are in the book of Moses.

Abraham Gazed at the Heavens Through the Urim and Thummim

The great prophet Abraham saw and felt the same things Moses recorded. In fact Abraham saw God's perspective of the earth and the heavens through the aid of the Urim and Thummim before Moses did since Abraham lived before Moses. If we were to study the Pearl of Great Price chronologically, rather than by book, we would begin with the book of Abraham before the book of Moses.

As Abraham gazed at the heavens, through the Urim and Thummim, he saw far more than man has yet seen with modern telescopes. Abraham wrote these experiences first in his own language. Later they were written in the Egyptian language, and now those experiences have been translated into English and other languages so that we may read and ponder these great things.

The Bible gives us some of the revelations the Lord gave to Abraham, but the Pearl of Great Price, in the book of Abraham, greatly expands the writings and revelations the Lord gave to him. The book tells of the mission Abraham had in the land of Egypt, and of the revelations he shared with a few of the Egyptians.

Joseph Smith: Matthew

Following the book of Abraham, in the current publication of the Pearl of Great Price by The Church of Jesus Christ of Latter-day Saints, is a small excerpt called "Joseph Smith: Matthew." This is an extract from the work of Joseph Smith's translation of the Bible as revealed to him in 1831; it is a revision of Matthew 23:39 and also of chapter 24. Jesus told the apostles in the New Testament of the impending destruction of Jerusalem. He also discoursed on the Second Coming of the Son of Man and the destruction of the wicked.

Since the restoration of the gospel in these latter days was to prepare for the Second Coming of the Lord, i.e., "Prepare ye, prepare ye for that which is to come, for the Lord is nigh" (D&C 1:12), this revelation originally given to the ancient apostles is again given in clarity and it is included in the Pearl of Great Price.

Joseph Smith: History

Another book, or excerpt, in the Pearl of Great Price is called "Joseph Smith: History." Joseph Smith had an affinity with Moses and Abraham. He shared and understood their experiences on the "exceedingly high mountain." He could understand both Moses and Abraham: he was a prophet like unto them.

Elder Gordon B. Hinckley of the First Presidency said of Joseph Smith's First Vision: "It is the greatest event in the history of the world since the resurrection of Jesus Christ." Although there are several written accounts of Joseph Smith's First Vision, the account as published in the Pearl of Great Price is the account accepted as scripture. This great vision of Joseph Smith, the circumstances surrounding it, and events which surrounded the coming forth of the Book of Mormon with the heavenly visitation of the angel Moroni, are rightly included in the current publication of the Pearl of Great Price.

The Articles of Faith, which were written by Joseph Smith to briefly explain our beliefs to the world, are also found in the concluding pages of the Pearl of Great Price. On March 1, 1842, Joseph Smith records in his journal:

> At the request of Mr. John Wentworth, Editor and Proprietor of the *Chicago Democrat*, I have written the following sketch of the rise, progress, persecution, and faith of the Latter-day Saints, of which I have the honor, under God, of being the founder. . . . (History of the Church, Vol. 4, pp. 535-541.)

The Articles of Faith were part of this letter to Mr. Wentworth.

No commentary is made in this work on the Articles of Faith. Elder James E. Talmage has written an exhaustive study on the Articles of Faith, a book which has become a "Mormon Classic." Anyone interested in knowing more about the meaning and background of the Articles of Faith as well as having an understanding of the doctrine is referred to this excellent work.

A Chronological Overview of the Pearl of Great Price

The Pearl of Great Price unfolds the creation story of earth and man. It covers about the first 2,000 years of man's existence on earth. However, through such revelations as were given Enoch, we get glimpses of the history of the world even to "the coming of the Son of Man, in the last days, to dwell on the earth in righteousness for the space of a thousand years" (Moses 7:65).

The Pearl of Great Price tells, in some detail, how Adam and Eve received the "fullness" of the gospel and how they were "glad" for the good news. It tells how Adam came to understand the importance of faith in God, in prayer; even the first prayer, and of the principle of obedience and the ordinance of sacrifice. It tells how Adam and Eve learned the principle of repentance and the meaning of the Atonement; how they learned the significance and meaning of the ordinance of baptism and receiving the Holy Ghost which quickened "the inner man." It also tells us that Adam received the priesthood "after the order of him who was without beginning of days or end of years, from all eternity to all eternity" (Moses 6:67). In this way he became a "son of God" and the Pearl of Great Price tells how, through following his example, all mankind can become sons and daughters of God.

The Pearl of Great Price tells how Adam and Eve tried to share the gospel with their own children—many of whom were parents themselves. It tells how these grown children rejected the gospel. Thus the first apostasy took place in the days of Adam and Eve. Adam and Eve prayed for a son, "that he may not reject his words" and Cain came to them in answer to that prayer. Cain rejected the gospel and became a son of perdition, the originator of "secret combinations." (Such combinations are secret pacts with Satan, or any of his hosts, to commit murder, or lie, or steal, or commit adultery, or get gain in evil ways.)

The Pearl of Great Price gives us the origin of the black race—the "roots beyond roots" of this people. It tells us that the black race has a heritage reaching back to the early history of civilization. "Jubal, who was the father of all such as handle the harp and organ. . . . Tubal Cain, an instructor of every artificer in brass and iron." (Moses 5:45, 46.)

The Pearl of Great Price contains the writings of Enoch, one of the most influential prophets who ever lived. It tells how he established "Zion" and that the whole people of Zion were "of one heart and one mind, and dwelt in righteousness; and there was no poor among them" (Moses 7:18).

Enoch was caught up to "an exceedingly high mountain" and saw things from God's perspective. He saw the God of heaven weep and asked, "How is it thou canst weep, seeing thou art holy, and from all eternity to all eternity?" Enoch discovered why God wept and does weep and Enoch also wept. Enoch asked when the earth would rest and when the Lord would come. The Lord gave Enoch a panoramic vision of the world down through time. Enoch saw our day, the restoration of the gospel in the latter days; he saw events before Christ's second coming; finally, he saw the "day of rest" following the Second Coming. Enoch's writings and visions are some of the great "pearls" of the Pearl of Great Price.

Through Enoch's eyes we see the flood that caused "the end of all flesh . . . for the earth is filled with violence, and behold I will destroy all flesh from off the earth" (Moses 8:30). The Pearl of Great Price tells us about the survivors of the flood. It tells us that the seed of Cain was also preserved from the flood because Ham married Egyptus, a descendant of Cain. We learn that "from this descent sprang all the Egyptians" (Abraham 1:22).

We learn from the Pearl of Great Price that Abraham was born into a world in which Egyptian influence was predominant. Abraham was of the tenth generation from Noah. Ten noted characters lived from Noah to Abraham. The Pearl of Great Price tells us that Abraham's own father was an apostate from the truth. It tells of conditions of civilization at the time of Abraham: how many of the people's hearts were set to do evil; how civilization had retrogressed to where human sacrifices were performed "in offering up their children unto their dumb idols" (Abraham 1:7). Abraham tells how he opposed such measures and how he himself was almost killed by one

of the Egyptian priests in a most cruel manner. He also tells of his miraculous rescue by an angel of the Lord (Abraham 1:15).

Abraham prayed to the Lord and the Lord appeared to him and told
him to leave Haran and told him he was going "to make of thee a minister
to bear my name in a strange land" (Abraham 2:6). His father stayed in Ur
and turned again to his idolatry.

The Pearl of Great Price then tells of Abraham's mission call and his
mission preparation before he went into Egypt. The Lord used the Urim
and Thummim to teach Abraham about the planets and stars. He taught
Abraham to express these truths in the language of the Egyptians. Abraham
learned the fullness of the gospel and he attempted to teach this fullness to
the Egyptians. The Pearl of Great Price tells how Abraham's beautiful wife,
Sarai, was lusted after by the Pharaoh and how Abraham had to tell the
Pharaoh she was his sister in order to save his own life and preserve his
wife's virtue and also to gain the time he needed to teach the gospel to the
Egyptians.

Abraham's sojourn in Egypt was abruptly interrupted when the Pharaoh
discovered that he had been courting Abraham's wife instead of his sister.
Abraham was ordered to leave Egypt but he was given safe conduct out of
the country.

What did Abraham leave in Egypt? Apparently he left his notes or his
notes copied by someone. Abraham, or perhaps some of his believers buried
the notes, or copies of Abraham's writings, in the folds of linen covering
Egyptian mummies.

The Saga of the Book of Abraham

The facinating saga of the record of Abraham along with eleven mummies traveling from the tombs of Egypt to America is a most interesting
story. Four of the mummies along with Egyptian papyri were brought by a
Mr. Chandler to Joseph Smith in Kirtland, Ohio, in 1835. Joseph Smith
showed an unusual interest in the papyri, and the mummies and papyri
were purchased by several members of the Church and given to the prophet.
Joseph Smith worked diligently, in every spare moment, to translate the
Egyptian papyri but it was not until March, 1842, that the first excerpt
was published in *Times and Seasons*. This excerpt, in our present Pearl of
Great Price, is the book of Abraham.

Notice, however, was given by John Taylor, editor of the *Times and
Seasons* in 1842, that further extracts from the book of Abraham would be
forthcoming but they never came. A year and four months after the notice
given in the *Times and Seasons* Joseph Smith lay dead, but the fascinating
questions surrounding the Egyptian papyri go on.

One of the last chapters in this book deals with what happened to the
mummies and papyri after the death of the Prophet Joseph Smith. It retells

about the surprising discovery by a non-Mormon scholar, the giving of the papyri to Church scholar, Hugh B. Nibley of Brigham Young University, and a brief synopsis of the message of the Joseph Smith papyri that came into the hands of the Church. Brother Nibley states that the papyri given to the Church is *not the papyri from which Joseph Smith translated the book of Abraham, but that it is just as important.* The papyri which the Church now has contains an Egyptian Endowment, an endowment which is, according to Dr. Nibley, "a very good imitation."

There is some relationship between the temple endowment and the Egyptian papyri. The last chapter deals with how The Church of Jesus Christ of Latter-day Saints received the temple endowment as it is given in the temples today. It suggests that at least the Egyptian papyri acted as a catalyst in helping Joseph Smith receive the temple endowment. How much of a role it played is not known and may never be known.

The Pearl of Great Price Not Complete

The Pearl of Great Price is a book that is not complete in and of itself. It does contain the fullness of the gospel, but to be fully understood it needs to be read in conjunction with all of the standard works of the Church. The book of Moses could properly belong in the Bible and thus it should be read with the Bible, and vice versa, and this is also true of the book of Abraham. Both the Book of Mormon and the Doctrine and Covenants amplify, and give fuller meaning to, doctrines found in the Pearl of Great Price.

We need all of the standard works to appreciate any one of them. We need to read all of the scriptures as one to see how they interlock and testify of the same things. When the Savior visited the Nephites on this American continent he "expounded all the scriptures in one, which they had written" (3 Nephi 23:14). We need to study the Pearl of Great Price in this same way. Indeed we need to study all of our scriptures in this way.

Intriguing Questions About the Pearl of Great Price

We do not have all the answers yet to the many intriguing questions the Pearl of Great Price raises, such as:

•Where, then, are the papyri from which Joseph Smith translated the book of Abraham?

•Why do we not have further extracts from the book of Abraham?

•Why do we not have the writings of Joseph of Old that were part of the original papyri?

•Did Joseph Smith receive the temple endowment partially from the catalytic effect of the Egyptian papyri? How much of it?

•If Abraham taught the Egyptians the fullness of the gospel and they are all "descendants from Ham and Egyptus" did a prior dispensation also allow blacks to have the fullness, including the priesthood and endowments?

•Are we ready, as a people, to accept the full impact of the latter-day revelation to take the fullness of the gospel and the priesthood and temple endowment to all people "without regard for race or color"?

A thorough study of the Pearl of Great Price can more fully prepare us for the "mission of Abraham."

Chapter Two

How We Got the Pearl of Great Price

The Plain and Simple Truths of the Gospel

Let us go back in Church history to the night of September 21, 1823, when the angel Moroni appeared to Joseph Smith and said:

> . . . There was a book deposited, written upon gold plates, giving an account of the former inhabitants of this continent, and the source from whence they sprang. He also said that the fulness of the everlasting Gospel was contained in it, as delivered by the Savior to the ancient inhabitants. (Joseph Smith—History 1:34.)

The essence of the gospel—the plain and simple truths of the gospel— the doctrine of the Savior that could be considered the "fullness of the ever- lasting gospel as delivered by the Savior" is recorded in the Book of Mormon in these words:

> And this is my doctrine, and it is the doctrine which the Father hath given unto me; . . . and I bear record that the Father commandeth all men, every- where, to repent and believe in me.
> And whoso believeth in me, and is baptized, the same shall be saved; and they are they who shall inherit the kingdom of God.
> And whoso believeth not in me, and is not baptized, shall be damned.
> . . . And whoso believeth in me believeth in the Father also; and unto him will the Father bear record of me, for he will visit him with fire and with the Holy Ghost.
> Verily, verily, I say unto you, that this is my doctrine, and whoso buildeth upon this buildeth upon my rock, and the gates of hell shall not prevail against them.
> And whoso shall declare more or less than this, and establish it for my doctrine, the same cometh of evil, and is not built upon my rock. (3 Nephi 11:32-35, 39-40.)

These are the plain and simple truths of the gospel of Jesus Christ as given by the Savior Himself to the ancient inhabitants of the American continents. They are the plain and simple truths He gave to the people in Palestine, the truths once recorded clearly and plainly in the Bible. Faith in Jesus Christ, repentance, baptism, and receiving the Holy Ghost by the laying on of hands by those who have proper priesthood authority—this is the essence of the doctrine of Jesus Christ.

A Parable About the Apostasy

If these principles are so plain and simple, why have these truths of the gospel of Jesus Christ been distorted, made complicated, and even lost by the Christian world? How did the Israelites of the Old Testament, who were looking forward to the coming of the Savior with this simple message, miss it when it was declared?

Hear it again in one of the parables of the Savior:

> Behold, there was a certain householder, who planted a vineyard, and hedged it round about, and digged a winepress in it; and built a tower, and let it out to husbandmen, and went into a far country.
>
> And when the time of the fruit drew near, he sent his servants to the husbandmen, that they might receive the fruits of it.
>
> And the husbandmen took his servants, and beat one, and killed another, and stoned another.
>
> Again, he sent other servants, more than the first; and they did unto them likewise.
>
> But last of all, he sent unto them his son, saying, They will reverence my son.
>
> But when the husbandmen saw the son, they said among themselves, This is the heir, come, let us kill him, and let us seize on his inheritance.
>
> And they caught him, and cast him out of the vineyard, and slew him.
>
> And Jesus said unto them, When the lord therefore of the vineyard cometh, what will he do unto those husbandmen?
>
> They say unto him, He will destroy those miserable, wicked men, and will let out the vineyard unto other husbandmen, who shall render him the fruits in their seasons.
>
> Jesus said unto them, Did ye never read in the scriptures, The stone which the builders rejected, the same is become the head of the corner; this is the Lord's doings, and it is marvelous in our eyes.
>
> Therefore say I unto you, The kingdom of God shall be taken from you, and given to a nation bringing forth the fruits thereof.
>
> For whosoever shall fall on this stone, shall be broken; but on whomsoever it shall fall, it will grind him to powder. (JST, Matthew 21:35-46.)

God, the Father, is the householder. The vineyard he planted and prepared carefully is the world. Mankind in general are the husbandmen who were placed on this earth to take care of it and to care for each other. Free agency was given to man and then the Lord God left mankind to use that agency and to care for his world. The winepress could be an analogy of the Savior who would one day shed his blood for all mankind. The tower represents, perhaps, the gospel of Jesus Christ that was given to man—even to the first man. The first principles of the gospel—faith in Jesus Christ, repentance, baptism, and the gift of the Holy Ghost—were the principles taught to the first people on earth and they represent the hedge. The fruits of the gospel and of the Spirit of the Holy Ghost are love, joy, peace, long-suffering, gentleness, goodness, faith, meekness, and temperance. (See Galatians 5:22-23.) When the householder sent his servants, His prophets, to the earth to "receive the fruits" of the gospel which had been given to the world, an apostasy had taken place—works of darkness had prevailed upon the earth among all the sons of men. Among the husbandmen there were secret combinations between men and the devil. Their "rotten fruits" were murder, intrigue, lust and greed, hatred, and the lack of love, one to another. Early man rejected the prophets, beat them, killed them, stoned them.

Then the householder, God the Father, sent His Only Begotten Son, Jesus Christ, to the earth. They killed the Son, the Heir—they crucified the Son of the householder—the Son of God: "Verily, I say unto you, I am the stone, and those wicked ones reject me. I am the head of the corner. These Jews shall fall upon me, and shall be broken." (JST, Matthew 21:51-52.)

History records that some Jews were crushed and broken under the power of Rome and scattered throughout the world. New Testament history records that some Jews—disciples of Christ—took the gospel to the Gentiles when the Jews, as a whole, rejected it. For a time the Gentiles accepted the gospel and bore "fruit," but, once again, they apostatized and corrupted the "vineyard."

> The earth also is defiled under the inhabitants thereof; because they have transgressed the laws, changed the ordinance, broken the everlasting covenant.
> Therefore hath the curse devoured the earth, and they that dwell therein are desolate. (Isaiah 24:5-6.)

Thus the plain and precious truths of the gospel of Jesus Christ are lost from the world until God, the householder, "will let again his vineyard unto other husbandmen, even in the last days, who shall render him the fruits in their seasons" (JST, Matthew 21:55).

The Restoration

The restoration of the gospel in these latter-days has taken place. We are the husbandmen charged with caring for the vineyard for the last time before the Savior comes in His glory. We are commanded to bring forth the fruits of the gospel.

The scriptures—the Word—the written testimony of the gospel can assist us in bringing forth those fruits. Joseph Smith learned that the plain and precious truths of the gospel of Jesus Christ, which had once been written in the Bible, had become lost and perverted. As Joseph Smith translated the Book of Mormon, he also learned from it.

The words of Nephi tell Joseph, and all of us, what happened to the precious truths of the Bible:

> And the angel said unto me: Knowest thou the meaning of the book? And I said unto him: I know not.

And he said: Behold it proceedeth out of the mouth of a Jew. And I, Nephi, beheld it; and he said unto me: The book that thou beholdest is a record of the Jews, which contains the covenants of the Lord, which he hath made unto the house of Israel; and it also containeth many of the prophecies of the holy prophets; and it is a record like unto the engravings which are upon the plates of brass, save there are not so many; nevertheless, they contain the covenants of the Lord, which he hath made unto the house of Israel; wherefore, they are of great worth unto the Gentiles.

And the angel of the Lord said unto me: Thou hast beheld that the book proceeded forth from the mouth of a Jew; and when it proceeded forth from the mouth of a Jew it contained the plainness of the gospel of the Lord, of whom the twelve apostles bear record; and they bear record according to the truth which is in the Lamb of God.

Wherefore, these things go forth from the Jews in purity unto the Gentiles, according to the truth which is in God.

And after they go forth by the hand of the twelve apostles of the Lamb, from the Jews unto the Gentiles, thou seest the foundation of a great and abominable church, which is most abominable above all other churches; for behold, they have taken away from the gospel of the Lamb many parts which are plain and most precious; and also many covenants of the Lord have they taken away.

And all this have they done that they might pervert the right ways of the Lord, that they might blind the eyes and harden the hearts of the children of men.

Wherefore, thou seest that after the book hath gone forth through the hands of the great and abominable church, that there are many plain and precious things taken away from the book, which is the book of the Lamb of God.

And after these plain and precious things were taken away it goeth forth unto all the nations of the Gentiles; and after it goeth forth unto all the nations of the Gentiles, yea, even across the many waters which thou hast seen with the Gentiles which have gone forth out of captivity, thou seest—because of the many plain and precious things which have been taken out of the book, which were plain unto the understanding of the children of men, according to the plainness which is in the Lamb of God—because of these things which are taken out of the gospel of the Lamb, an exceeding great many do stumble, yea, insomuch that Satan hath great power over them. (1 Nephi 13:21-29.)

Joseph Smith Revises and Translates the Bible

Soon after Joseph Smith completed the work of translating and publishing the Book of Mormon, the Lord instructed him to revise and translate the Bible. The extracts from the translation of the Bible, now called the book of Moses in the Pearl of Great Price, were received as early as June, 1830. One of the earliest mentions of this work of translating the Bible is in the Doctrine and Covenants 37:1: ". . . it is not expedient in me that ye should translate any more until ye shall go to the Ohio . . ." This revelation was received in December, 1830. Joseph had begun the work earlier and he was asked to stop until his move to Kirtland.

It appears that the work of Joseph Smith, in translating and revising the Bible, began as early as June, 1830, with the revelation of the book of

Moses and continued until the following March. In March of 1831 the Lord directed the Prophet to work on the New Testament. (See D&C 45:60-61.) He completed this phase of the project by February, 1833. About a month later the Lord spoke to the Prophet about finishing "the translation of the prophets," that is, the Old Testament (D&C 90:13), and also counseled him not to revise the Apocrypha (D&C 91). On July 2, 1833, Joseph Smith recorded: "We this day finished the translating of the Scriptures, for which we returned gratitude to our Heavenly Father" (*History of the Church*, 1:368).

The Church of Jesus Christ of Latter-day Saints has not adopted the Inspired Version as one of its standard works because the Prophet never considered the project really completed. "The manuscript shows that the Prophet went all the way through the Bible from Genesis to Revelation. But it also shows that he did not make all the necessary corrections in one effort." (Robert J. Matthews, "A Plainer Translation": *Joseph Smith's Translation of the Bible*, p. 215.)

The Holy Bible, published in 1979 by The Church of Jesus Christ of Latter-day Saints, has many footnotes which refer to the Joseph Smith Translation and has included, in the appendix, other excerpts too lengthy for inclusion in the footnotes.

Perhaps the reason the Church has not published the Joseph Smith Translation of the Bible is because the manuscript, after the death of the Prophet in 1844, was left in the hands of Emma, his widow. There it remained until the spring of 1866 when it was delivered to William Marks, I. L. Rogers, and William W. Blair, a committee appointed by the annual conference of the Reorganized Church in April of 1866, for publication. In 1867, the Reorganized Church of Jesus Christ of Latter Day Saints, now headquartered in Independence, Missouri, published the first edition of the Joseph Smith Translation, called "the inspired version." They have continued to be the publishers of this version of the Bible.

It is very evident that one of Joseph's continual and stimulating works was his attempt to restore many of the plain and precious truths that had been lost from the Bible. This work became the "springboard" for many of the revelations contained in the Doctrine and Covenants. It also gave rise to much of the book of Moses found in the Pearl of Great Price.

Chapter one, in Moses, of the Pearl of Great Price is a preliminary revelation to Genesis in the King James translation of the Bible. In the Inspired Version of the Bible, as published by the Reorganized Church, it is properly placed in that Bible before the book of Genesis.

Before the publication of either the Pearl of Great Price or the Inspired Version of the Bible, the revelations were written down in the journal of Joseph Smith and in early Church periodicals. In June of 1830, the Prophet received the revelation of Moses 1:1-42, then in December, 1830, he recorded extracts from the prophecy of Enoch. The prophecy and writings of Enoch also contained a revelation of the gospel given to our father Adam after he was driven out of the Garden of Eden. "Line upon line, precept upon precept, here a little and there a little" the revelations unfolded.

When chapter one of Moses was given in June, 1830, there were approximately thirty members of the Church, but by December, 1830, there were some 280 members (Deseret News Church Almanac, 1983, p. 214). The need arose to contact, instruct, and edify a rapidly growing church. Interestingly, the Lord provided people to fill the need. W. W. Phelps, an experienced newsman, joined the Church in June of 1831. Before he was even baptized, a revelation called him to assist Oliver Cowdery to do the work of printing for the Church and to go to Missouri to set up a printing press. (See D&C 55.) W. W. Phelps became the first printer of the first Church newspaper—*The Evening and Morning Star*—in Independence, Missouri. One of the purposes of the paper was to disseminate revelations and instructions to the Church. In this paper are found the earliest publications of the book of Moses.

How Our Present Pearl of Great Price Came to Be Published

Because of the great missionary work done in England by such men as Heber C. Kimball, Brigham Young, Wilford Woodruff and others, there were more members of the Church in England than there were in America, at least for a time. At a general conference of all the British Isle Saints held at Preston, England, on April 15, 1840, there were present, or represented, 1636 members in thirty-four branches, raised up since the opening of that mission in 1837.

At this conference it was decided to publish a hymn book and a monthly periodical, under the direction and superintendency of the Twelve, for the benefit and information of members of the Church. It was also decided, in a council meeting of the apostles, to publish a monthly periodical called the *Latter-Day Saints Millennial Star*. The first number of the *Millennial Star* was issued, in Manchester, in pamphlet form of twenty-four pages on Wednesday, May 27, 1840. Later the place of publication was transferred to Liverpool which became the headquarters for most of the publications of the Church until recently. (See Joseph Fielding Smith, *Essentials in Church History*, p. 281.)

Because of a paper shortage in Utah, during the 1850s, the Book of Mormon, Doctrine and Covenants, the hymn books, and the *Millennial Star* were all published in England. In 1851 Franklin D. Richards, who was serving as mission president in England, wanted to publish some of the revelations that were not readily accessible to Church members in England and the British Isles. That first edition of the Pearl of Great Price contains the following preface which explains how Brother Richards reached the decision to publish the Pearl of Great Price.

First Edition of the Pearl of Great Price, 1851

PREFACE

The following compilation has been induced by the repeated solicitations of several friends of the publisher, who are desirous to be put in possession of the very important articles contained therein. Most of the Revelations composing this work were published at early periods of the Church, when the circulation of its journals was so very limited as to render them comparatively unknown at present, except to a few who have treasured up the productions of the Church with great care from the beginning. A smaller portion of this work has never before appeared in print; and altogether it is presumed, that true believers in the Divine mission of the Prophet Joseph Smith, will appreciate this little collection of precious truths as a *Pearl of Great Price* that will increase their ability to maintain and to defend the holy faith by becoming possessors of it.

Although not adapted, nor designed, as a pioneer of the faith among unbelievers, still it will commend itself to all careful students of the scriptures, as detailing many important facts which are therein only alluded to, or entirely unmentioned, but consonant with the whole tenor of the revealed will of God; and, to the beginner in the Gospel, will add confirmatory evidence of the rectitude of his faith, by showing him that the doctrines and ordinances thereof are the same as were revealed to Adam for his salvation after his expulsion from the garden, and the same that he handed down and caused to be taught to his generations after him, as the only means appointed of God by which the generations of men may regain His presence.

Nor do we conceive it possible for any unprejudiced person to arise from a careful perusal of this work, without being deeply impressed with a sense of the Divine calling, and holy ordination, of the man by whom these revelations, translations, and narrations have been communicated to us. As impervious as the minds of men may be at present to these convictions, the day is not far distant when sinners, as well as Saints, will know that Joseph Smith was one of the greatest men that ever lived upon the earth, and that under God he was the Prophet and founder of the dispensation of the fulness of times, in which will be gathered together in one all things which are in Christ, both which are in heaven and which are on earth.

Franklin D. Richards

15, Wilton Street, Liverpool
July 11th, 1851.

Table of Contents of the First Edition of
Pearl of Great Price, 1851

The references given in parentheses are added to show where the material is located in our present Pearl of Great Price (1921 ed.), Doctrine and Covenants, and Hymn Book.

CONTENTS

Editions and History of the Publication of the
Pearl of Great Price Since 1851

The 1851 edition of the Pearl of Great Price, compiled and published by Franklin D. Richards, continued to be used by members of the Church in England and in America until 1878. In that year Elder John Taylor, acting president of the Church, called Orson Pratt of the Council of the Twelve to prepare the first American edition of the British mission pamphlet—The Pearl of Great Price. Elder Pratt made several changes in that pamphlet. He deleted the preface since it was no longer applicable. He added missing portions of chapters 4, 5, and 6 of the book of Moses and he deleted Doctrine and Covenants 107:27, 33, 93-100 combining, in chronological order, the first two entries in the 1851 contents. He made several textual refinements and he added the revelation of the eternal and plural marriage covenant and commandment.

In 1878 the Church was under heavy attack by federal officers who were in opposition to the practice of polygamy. It seems apparent that the brethren wanted the revelation on plural marriage to have as wide a circulation as possible; thus it was published in the Pearl of Great Price as well as in the Doctrine and Covenants.

The 50th Semiannual Conference of the Church, in October 1880, was very significant and historical. The prophet, Brigham Young, had died in 1877 and during the next three years Elder John Taylor, President of the Quorum of Twelve Apostles, was the acting President of the Church.

The leading quorums were seated in solemn assembly to enact three important items of business: (1) President John Taylor was sustained as the third President of the Church; (2) the conference accepted the addition of twenty-five new sections to the Doctrine and Covenants; and (3) the Pearl of Great Price was sustained as the fourth standard work of the Church. The business of canonizing the new scripture was conducted as follows:

President George Q. Cannon said: "I hold in my hand the Book of Doctrine and Covenants and also the Book The Pearl of Great Price, which books contain revelations of God. In Kirtland, the Doctrine and Covenants in its original form as first printed, was submitted to the officers of the Church to vote upon. As there have been additions made to it by the publishing of revelations which were not contained in the original edition, it has been deemed wise to submit these books with their contents to the conference, to see whether the Conference will vote to accept the books and their contents as from God, and binding upon us as a people and as a Church."

President Joseph F. Smith said: "I move that we receive and accept the revelations contained in these books as revelations from God to the Church of Jesus Christ of Latter-day Saints, and to all the world." The Motion was seconded and sustained by unanimous vote of the whole conference. (Conference Report, October 10, 1880, Journal History, Oct. 10th, 1880.)

1890 Conference

In the October semiannual conference of 1890, the Articles of Faith were read to the assembled Saints by Elder Franklin D. Richards, still a member of the Council of the Twelve after forty years of service. Following his reading they were presented for a sustaining vote. Apparently there had been some confusion as to their scriptural status following their acceptance in 1880 so that it was necessary to present them again. They were sustained, as scripture, in 1890.

Revisions of the Pearl of Great Price, 1890

In 1900 Elder James E. Talmage was asked by the First Presidency to make some major revisions in the Pearl of Great Price. He divided it into chapters and verses and added numerous cross-references to other scriptures. He also deleted duplication of Doctrine and Covenant revelations and the poem "Truth" which had been set to music. (This poem is now in the hymn book under the title "O Say, What Is Truth.") The new format for the Pearl of Great Price was unanimously sustained by the Church at the October semiannual conference of 1902.

In 1921 Elder Talmage arranged the Pearl of Great Price in conformity with the newly adopted scriptural format of double-column pages. He also added the index and made several refinements in the text.

Additions to the Pearl of Great Price, 1976

At the April conference of 1976, President Spencer W. Kimball authorized President Nathan Eldon Tanner, First Counselor in the First Presidency, to read the following statement:

> At a meeting of the Council of the First Presidency and the Quorum of the Twelve held in the Salt Lake Temple on March 26, 1976, approval was given to add to the Pearl of Great Price the following revelations:
>
> First, a vision of the celestial kingdom given to Joseph Smith the Prophet in Kirtland Temple, on January 21, 1836, which deals with the salvation of those who die without a knowledge of the Gospel; and second, a vision given to President Joseph F. Smith in Salt Lake City, Utah, on October 3, 1918, showing the visit of the Lord Jesus Christ in the spirit world, and setting forth the doctrine of the redemption of the dead.
>
> It is proposed that we sustain and approve this action and adopt these revelations as part of the standard works of the Church of Jesus Christ of Latter-day Saints.
>
> All those in favor manifest it. Those opposed, if any, by the same sign.
>
> Thank you. President Kimball, the voting seems to be unanimous in the affirmative. (Conference Report, April 1976, p. 29.)

Further Changes, Deletions in the Pearl of Great Price, 1981

The two revelations which were approved at the April conference in 1976 were at first added to the Pearl of Great Price. However, in the 1981 printings of the Doctrine and Covenants and the Pearl of Great Price, these two newly accepted revelations were to be deleted from the Pearl of Great Price and would appear as sections 137 and 138 in the Doctrine and Covenants. Announcement of this change appeared in the Church section of the *Deseret News*, June 2, 1979, as follows:

> Joseph Smith's Vision of the Celestial Kingdom and Joseph F. Smith's Vision of the Redemption of the Dead have been transferred from the Pearl of Great Price to become Sections 137 and 138, respectively, in the Doctrine and Covenants.
>
> The statement of the First Presidency telling of the revelation extending the Priesthood to "all worthy male members of the Church" released June 9, 1978, will also be added to the Doctrine and Covenants.
>
> The decision to place these revelations in the Doctrine and Covenants has been made by the First Presidency and Council of the Twelve.

In the 1981 printing of the Pearl of Great Price, there were minor corrections to be made such as in dates, etc.

Rephrasing of some headings were made for clarification. Introductory notes to chapters were included for the first time and the Joseph Smith History, Joseph Smith—Matthew, and the Articles of Faith were footnoted. Following are other changes that were made:

•The date of Alvin's death (Joseph Smith—History, v. 4)
•Moses Chapter 2, June-October 1830
•Joseph Smith 1 (1981 edition called Joseph Smith—Matthew)
•Joseph Smith 2 (1981 edition called Joseph Smith—History)
•The tenth article of faith (the "New Jerusalem" is added)

This is how the Pearl of Great Price of The Church of Jesus Christ of Latter-day Saints came to be published in its present form. The book of Moses, in the Pearl of Great Price, and Joseph Smith—Matthew, were, in large part, a result of the Prophet Joseph Smith's work on the "translation" of the Bible. The coming forth of the book of Abraham, and the fascinating saga of this record found in the mummies of Egypt until it came into the hands of Joseph Smith, we will leave for later chapters.

Let us prepare now to relive, with Moses, the background and the great experience he had in climbing "an exceedingly high mountain." We will carefully read his revelations on the beginning of this earth and the great purpose God has for it and for its people.

Summary of Chapter Two

1. Some of the plain and simple truths of the Bible were lost and needed to be restored.

2. Soon after Joseph Smith completed the Book of Mormon, the Lord instructed him to revise the Bible.

3. Several extracts from the Prophet's translation, or revision, of the Bible are now called the book of Moses in the Pearl of Great Price.

4. The Church has not published the Joseph Smith translation of the Bible probably because the manuscript, at the death of the Prophet, was left in the hands of Emma, his widow, and she would not give the manuscript to the Church. Later, she gave the manuscript to the Reorganized Church and they published it.

5. The Holy Bible, published by The Church of Jesus Christ of Latter-day Saints in 1979, has many footnotes to the Joseph Smith translation of the Bible and in the appendix are many excerpts too lengthy for inclusion in the footnotes.

6. Before the publication of either the Pearl of Great Price or Joseph Smith's translation of the Bible, some early revelations were written in the Prophet's journal, and some were published in early Church periodicals.

7. The earliest book of Moses was published in the *Evening and Morning Star* by W. W. Phelps, in Missouri.

8. Franklin D. Richards, mission president in England, published the first edition of the Pearl of Great Price, in 1851, as a type of missionary tract.

9. The October conference of the Church, in 1880, voted to cannonize the Pearl of Great Price as scripture for the Church.

10. In 1900 Elder James E. Talmage was asked by the First Presidency to make major revisions in the Pearl of Great Price. The new format was sustained by the Church in October conference of 1902.

11. There were two new additions to the Pearl of Great Price in 1976, but later these additions became sections 137 and 138 in 1981 in the Doctrine and Covenants by the decision of the First Presidency.

Chapter Three

Moses Climbs
"An Exceedingly High Mountain"

Early Life of Moses

Most people who are at all familiar with the Bible or the movie epic, "The Ten Commandments," know some of the early life of Moses. Remember how he was hid in the bulrushes in a small waterproof basket to avoid being killed by the decree of the king of Egypt, who was afraid the children of Israel were getting too numerous and ordered the male babies to be killed? Moses was found by the daughter of the Pharaoh and she had compassion on the baby. She had the baby's own Hebrew mother nurse and care for him—thus Moses became the adopted son of the Pharaoh.

> And it came to pass in those days, when Moses was grown, that he went out unto his brethren, and looked on their burdens; and he spied an Egyptian smiting a Hebrew, one of his brethren.
> And he looked this and that way, and when he saw that there was no man, he slew the Egyptian, and hid him in the sand.
> And when he went out the second day, behold, two men of the Hebrews strove together; and he said to him that did the wrong, Wherefore smitest thou thy fellow?
> And he said, Who made thee a prince and a judge over us? intendest thou to kill me, as thou killedst the Egyptian? And Moses feared, and said, Surely this thing is known.
> Now when Pharaoh heard this thing he sought to slay Moses. But Moses fled from the face of Pharaoh, and dwelt in the land of Midian." (JST, Exodus 2:11-15.)

Moses befriended the seven daughters of the Priest of Midian and he was invited to stay and work with him. "And Moses was content to dwell with the man: and he gave Moses Zipporah his daughter. And she bare him a son, and he called his name Gershom: for he said, I have been a stranger in a strange land." (Exodus 2:21-22.)

Call of Moses by the Lord—"The Burning Bush"

> Now Moses kept the flock of Jethro his father-in-law, the priest of Midian; and he led the flock to the back side of the desert, and came to the mountain of God even to Horeb.
>
> And again, the presence of the Lord appeared unto him, in a flame of fire in the midst of a bush; and he looked, and, behold, the bush burned with fire, and the bush was not consumed.
>
> And Moses said, I will now turn aside, and see this great sight, why the bush is not consumed.
>
> And when the Lord saw that he turned aside to see, God called unto him out of the midst of the bush, and said, Moses, Moses. And he said, Here am I.
>
> And he said, Draw not nigh hither; put off thy shoes from off thy feet; for the place whereon thou standest is holy ground.
>
> Moreover he said, I am the God of thy father, the God of Abraham, the God of Isaac, and the God of Jacob. And Moses hid his face; for he was afraid to look upon God. (JST, Exodus 3:1-6.)

This was the call of Moses by the Lord to lead the children of Israel out of bondage and out of Egypt . . . this was one of Moses' climbs up "an exceedingly high mountain." It began on the mountain on the deserts of Midian, but ended in the presence of the Lord. The mountain served as a holy temple for the Lord's presence. Moses was called up spiritually to see the Lord "face to face." He was given an opportunity to see things from God's view—to see from His perspective—"A God's Eye-View of This World."

Moses had an experience not unlike that of a later prophet named Paul, who said:

> I knew a man in Christ above fourteen years ago, (whether in the body, I cannot tell; or whether out of the body, I cannot tell; God knoweth;) such a one caught up to the third heaven.
>
> How that he was caught up into paradise, and heard unspeakable words. (JST, 2 Corinthians 12:2, 4.)

As Moses talked with God, as one man talks with another, he was concerned about his ability to fulfill his calling: "And Moses said unto God, Who am I, that I should go unto Pharaoh, and that I should bring forth the children of Israel out of Egypt?" (Exodus 3:11.)

Leading Children of Israel Out of Bondage

There is an analogy that ought not to be missed in this great story. In a sense every prophet in every dispensation of the gospel is given a charge to "lead the children of Israel out of bondage and out of Egypt." The children of Israel are all the people of the world whom God would lead out of the "Egypt" of sin, ignorance, and the bondage of the ways of the world. The analogy could even be applied to a home teacher in the Church because every home teacher is called to "lead the children of Israel out of Egypt"—

to help his families escape the ways of the world and the bondage of sin. The task, whether for a prophet or a home teacher, may seem to be overwhelming and so we who are called might also ask: "Who am I, that I should bring forth the children of Israel out of Egypt?"

We ought to listen carefully to the answers and encouragements the Lord gives Moses. Much of what He tells Moses is applicable to the help He also grants to us in our callings. Listen to the first answer the Lord gives to the question of Moses: "And he said, Certainly I will be with thee" (JST, Exodus 3:12). No one who is asked to do the work of the Lord does it alone—the Lord promises to be with us—"Certainly I will be with thee!"

The next questions of Moses were, "Who is asking me to do this work? What is his name? What shall I say unto them?"

> And God said unto Moses, I AM THAT I AM; and he said, Thus shalt thou say unto the children of Israel, I AM hath sent me unto you." (JST, (Exodus 3:14.)

I AM, in Hebrew, is Yahweh or Jehovah. Jehovah is Jesus Christ. Who is asking me to do this? None other than the Lord Jesus Christ. The Lord Jesus Christ was asking Moses to lead the children of Israel out of bondage.

The next time a bishop, stake president, or anyone in an official church capacity asks us to do something in the Church and we think "Who is asking me to do this work? What is his name?" it is the same—it is Jehovah—Jesus Christ. It is "I AM [that] hath sent me unto you." Who is asking me to be a home teacher? I AM! Who is asking me to be a Primary worker? I AM! Who is asking me to pay tithing? I AM! Who is asking me to go to the temple? I AM! Who is asking me to go on a mission? I AM! You see, "whether by mine own voice, or by the voice of my servants, it is the same" (D&C 1:38).

Moses Also to Lead Children of Israel Out of Spiritual Bondage

Moses was given not just the physical task of leading the children of Israel out of bondage. It was not just his task to get the Pharaoh to let the people go and to lead them physically across the desert to the promised land. He had to lead them spiritually out of bondage; he had to teach them where they came from before they came to earth; he had to teach them why they were here on the earth and where they were going after death. The real "promised land" is not Palestine, or Israel, but God's kingdom. Moses was given the task of trying to get the people to climb the "exceedingly high mountain" that he climbed. He was trying to get the people to "see God face to face" as he did and to help them see the perspective that the Lord had given to him.

Signs and Symbols with Symbolic Meaning

Many signs were used by Moses in trying to convince the Pharaoh to let the children of Israel go. A rod that became a serpent, a hand that was leprous and was healed, a river of blood (JST, Exodus 4:3, 6, 9), a plague of frogs, lice, and flies (Exodus 8), boils and hail (Exodus 9) locusts and darkness (Exodus 10), and finally the death of the firstborn in the land (Exodus 11, 12). It was the death of the firstborn that caused the Pharaoh to rise "up in the night, he, and all his servants, and all the Egyptians; . . . for there was not a house where there was not one dead (JST, Exodus 12:30).

> And he called for Moses and Aaron by night, and said, Rise up, and get you forth from among my people, both ye and the children of Israel; and go, serve the Lord, as ye have said." (Exodus 12:31.)

Perhaps all these signs given to the Pharaoh and the Egyptians have a symbolic meaning. For example could the rod of Moses somehow represent the cross of Jesus that overcomes the serpent, Satan? Could the hand that was leprous, and is healed, be symbolic of the power of Jesus Christ to heal the lepers? (See Luke 5:12, 13.) Could the river of blood serve to illustrate that all the blood in the world cannot be enough to get the people out of bondage—that only the blood of Jesus Christ, shed in the process of the atonement, can free the people from the bondage of sin? Could the plague of frogs, lice, flies, locusts, and darkness all be vivid symbols of our sins, and the evil, distasteful, perverted acts of mankind without the light of the gospel and the moral code of the Lord? Could the death of the firstborn in the land be a sign and symbol of the death of God's own firstborn—even Jesus the Christ—whose death is the only death of the firstborn that frees us from the bondage of the grave and the only firstborn's death that allows us all to "escape from Egypt"?

Symbolism in Death of Firstborn

There is great symbolism in the "firstborn." "And the Lord spake unto Moses, saying, Sanctify unto me all the firstborn, whatsoever openeth the womb among the children of Israel, both of man and of beast; it is mine." (JST, Exodus 13:1-2.) This symbolism the first man, Adam, learned. Adam was commanded to offer the firstlings of their flocks "for an offering unto the Lord," and then had the reason for the sacrifice of the firstborn revealed to him: "This thing is a similitude of the sacrifice of the Only Begotten of the Father, which is full of grace and truth (see Moses 5:7).

Moses was taught the gospel in its fullness. Then he was told to write it in scripture that others who had faith in the Lord might be touched by the word symbols, and share his experiences.

Visions of Moses—Summary of Moses Chapter One

We are now ready to begin our study of chapter one of the book of Moses. No Christian people except members of The Church of Jesus Christ of Latter-day Saints, and the Reorganized Church of Jesus Christ of Latter Day Saints, have this great introduction to the Bible. There is no scripture equivalent in the Bible.

This chapter clearly tells us that God did reveal himself to Moses "face to face" and that Moses was transfigured so that he could "endure His presence." This chapter tells of a vivid confrontation Moses had with Satan, of how he tried to get Moses to worship him. After dismissing Satan, in the name of Jesus Christ, Moses is again lifted up into the presence of God. He sees worlds without number. He learns that they all were created by the power of Jesus Christ. Then he learns the answer not only to his great question—but every person's deep question: "Why did God make the earth, and what is His great purpose for it?" The answer: God's work and His glory is to bring to pass the immortality and eternal life of man.

Glory of God Upon Moses

> The words of God, which he spake unto Moses at a time when Moses was caught up into an exceedingly high mountain,
> And he saw God face to face, and he talked with him, and the glory of God was upon Moses; therefore Moses could endure his presence. (Moses 1:1-2.)

God lives on another planet, ". . . on a globe like a sea of glass and fire" (D&C 130:7). He lives on a celestialized world near the great star called, in Egyptian, "Kolob" (see Abraham 3:3). It is a great Urim and Thummim where all things are manifest; past, present, and future, and are continually before the Lord (D&C 130:6-8). It is like the sun in its brilliance and glory (see 1 Corinthians 15:40-41). No spaceship could land on Kolob's surface any more than a spaceship could land on the surface of the sun.

Our God's body is celestialized, glorified, resurrected, and though of flesh and bones after whose image man was created, yet His body is of such brightness and of such glory as to destroy, annihilate, and melt, as with fire, any and all mortal men who are not prepared for His presence. The scripture says, "for our God is a consuming fire" (Hebrews 12:29). We put space suits on our astronauts and they can withstand the rigors of outer space and the lack of atmosphere on the moon. No outer-space suit has been invented, no asbestos is thick enough, to prevent a mortal body from being consumed in the presence of God. How, then, was Moses able to see God "face to face" and live?

The account in the Pearl of Great Price simply says: "The glory of God was upon Moses; therefore Moses could endure his presence" (Moses 1:2). God changes the inner man through the Holy Ghost so man can endure God's presence. Modern scripture plainly says: "For no man has seen God at any time in the flesh, except quickened by the Spirit of God. Neither can any natural man abide the presence of God, . . ." (D&C 67:11-12; see also John 5:37, Acts 7:55-56, D&C 136:37.)

God Is Endless, Man Is Also Endless

> And God spake unto Moses, saying: Behold, I am the Lord God Almighty, and Endless is my name; for I am without beginning of days or end of years; and is not this endless?
>
> And, behold, thou art my son; wherefore look, and I will show thee the workmanship of mine hands; but not all, for my works are without end, and also my words, for they never cease." (Moses 1:3-4.)

God is without beginning of days or end of years and is Endless, but Moses is His son. If Moses is His son, then so are we His sons and daughters. As Paul said: "The Spirit itself beareth witness with our spirit, that we are the children of God" (Romans 8:16). A fundamental truth of the gospel of Jesus Christ is that "I am a child of God." This fundamental was taught to Moses. Joseph Smith also had revealed to him that, "Man was also in the beginning with God. Intelligence, or the light of truth, was not created or made, neither indeed can be." (D&C 93:29.)

> Wherefore, no man can behold all my works, except he behold all my glory; and no man can behold all my glory, and afterwards remain in the flesh on the earth.
>
> And I have a work for thee, Moses, my son; and thou art in the similitude of mine Only Begotten; . . . (Moses 1:5-6.)

Man Cannot See All of God's Works

Although Moses was in God's presence and filled with the Spirit, he could not see all of God's works. It takes a God to see as a God, but God was showing Moses the grandeur of the heavens and the magnitude of His works and creations. God showed Moses His own work, then told Moses of his work. God seemed to want Moses to see the "job" he was being assigned in perspective. Moses was given a work to lead Israel out of Egyptian bondage and to help the people reach the promised land. This, to Moses, seemed an awesome task but, seen in relationship to God's work in the universe, perhaps it "shrinks" in size a bit.

Moses must have been told a great deal about the Savior, Jesus Christ, and about His mission on earth, and how faithfully Christ would fulfill this work, for when the Lord reminded Moses that he was in the "similitude of mine Only Begotten," Moses seemed never to forget this great concept. As the Savior does and will do his work, so Moses could also fulfill his assignment. God has a great work. He takes care of worlds without number; His Only Begotten also has a great work and takes care of worlds without number. Moses was given a great work and he fulfilled his assignment—oh, then, what of us?

Can we fulfill our assignments in the kingdom as God, His Only Begotten, and as Moses? We, too, are in the "similitude of the Only Begotten." This ought to be in our minds as a great, motivational thought. Paul told the Philippian saints: "Let this mind be in you, which was also in Christ Jesus; Who, being in the form of God, thought it not robbery to be equal with God." (Philippians 2:5-6.)

God Withdraws from Moses

After the Lord had shown Moses a view of the world, and the ends thereof, and all the children of men which are, and which were created "he greatly marveled and wondered":

> And the presence of God withdrew from Moses, that his glory was not upon Moses; and Moses was left unto himself. And as he was left unto himself, he fell unto the earth.
> And it came to pass that it was for the space of many hours before Moses did again receive his natural strength like unto man; and he said unto himself: Now for this cause I know that man is nothing, which thing I never had supposed. (Moses 1:9-10.)

Moses had a "splash-down in the Pacific"; that is, after having been "up there" higher than any astronaut—on an "exceedingly high mountain"— in the presence of God, he was rather abruptly allowed to "fall to the earth." Why? What did God do in lifting him so high into heaven, then letting him come down to earth? Why does a missionary who may be on a "spiritual high" in the mission field have to come home and face the real world of Botany, Algebra, Freshman English, and girls? Why do all of us have spiritual and emotional ups and downs in life? When steel is tempered and made strong it is because the iron is made hot and then cooled and then made hot again. Is it the same with men? Do men also need to be tempered?

Sometimes man's pride in himself and in his accomplishments needs to be tempered. Moses had been raised as an Egyptian prince in one of the greatest civilizations in the world. The mighty pyramids and temples of Egypt, the many magnificent buildings of Egypt that remain even today, tell us some of the grandeur of that ancient empire and the pride the builders must have had.

Moses may have even helped supervise some of the tremendous building programs of the ancient Pharaohs. He may have shared some of the pride in the structures and the power of that mighty empire. However, after seeing Egypt from God's perspective—from atop the "exceedingly high mountain"—Egypt and man's puny efforts must have shrunk to insignificance.

"To know how little one knows is to have genuine knowledge" (*Tao Teh King* by Lao Tzu, p. 62). "Knowledge is so proud because he knows so much, but wisdom is so humble because she knows so little." One of the first steps in a man's real growth is a degree of humility. Perhaps this is the great lesson God wanted Moses to learn in withdrawing from Moses and letting him "fall unto the earth."

This feeling, or awareness, that man is nothing can be carried too far, as churches of some denominations have done. That is, God is Great—I am small—God is Infinite—I am finite—God is Good—I am evil, etc. These thoughts can become self-degrading. If we really begin to think of ourselves as nothing we can begin to think self-destructive thoughts. We can become discouraged, feel we are no good; that our lives are so small and insignificant that we count for nothing. Feelings of rejection, despondency, and depression can all come from accepting the idea that "we are nothing"—or that "I am nothing."

Very often, when we are at our lowest, Satan tries to give us his perspective. In a sense, like Moses, we can begin to have "revelations from Satan" and see "the bitterness of hell"—or be covered with a thick cloud of "blackness which could threaten us with utter destruction" like the experience of Joseph Smith (Joseph Smith—History 1:15).

Moses' Direct Confrontation with Satan

Moses had a direct confrontation with Satan, not altogether unlike the confrontation Jesus had in mortality with Satan after his baptism by John upon the mount of temptation (see Matthew 4:1-11). One of the great strengthening concepts that remains with Moses during his encounter with the devil was "Behold, I am a son of God, in the similitude of his Only Begotten" (Moses 1:13). Perhaps the words of the simple song, "I Am a Child of God," and the awareness that we, too, are in the similitude of the Only Begotten could give us strength when Satan confronts us.

Moses Overcomes the Devil

Because Moses had great experiences with the Lord, because he had felt deeply the Spirit of the Lord, because he had experienced the light and glory of the Lord, and because he had a deep testimony inside him of the truthfulness of these experiences he was able to say to Satan:

> Blessed be the name of my God, for his Spirit hath not altogether withdrawn from me, or else where is thy glory, for it is darkness unto me? And I can judge between thee and God (Moses 1:15).

Once we have an experience with beauty, with light and truth, once we have a great spiritual experience and develop a testimony of the gospel, we, too, can judge between Satan and God, and even in the moments of our temptations with Lucifer, we can say: "Blessed be the name of my God, for his Spirit hath not altogether withdrawn from me."

As Moses had his direct confrontation with Satan and saw the bitterness of hell as Satan raged, he began to fear exceedingly. He called fervently upon the Lord and upon the name of Jesus Christ commanding Satan to depart. After the departure of Satan, Moses lifted up his eyes unto heaven. He was filled with the Holy Ghost and, calling upon the name of God, he beheld his glory again. (See Moses 1:19-25.) He received assurance that he was chosen, that he would be made strong enough to deliver the people. He was even told he would be stronger than many waters: "For they shall obey thy command as if thou wert God" (Moses 1:25), referring to the future miracle he would perform in parting the Red Sea.

Moses Again Has Eternal View of God's Creations

Moses was again "caught up into an exceedingly high mountain" and, once again, through the Spirit of the Lord, had another "God's-eye view of things." Moses again beheld the earth "and there was not a particle of it which he did not behold, discerning it by the spirit of God" (Moses 1:27). Moses was shown more than his first vision; he saw many lands, "and each land was called earth, and there were inhabitants on the face thereof" (Moses 1:29). This is not the first earth in the universe, nor the last. We are not that unique in the universe. The experience we are going through as mortals on this earth is not a "brand-new" experiment that God is "toying" with. We are not the first nor the last of His worlds. There is life on other worlds besides our own. (See Moses 1:29.)

Moses asked about all these other worlds: "Tell me, I pray thee, why these things are so, and by what thou madest them" (Moses 1:30)? He may have asked many other questions about the other worlds. How did they begin? How many are there like our earth? Are they made of the same material as our earth? Are all the other people on the other worlds in the "similitude of the Only Begotten"? Was there ever a "first one"? How many earths like ours does the Savior preside over? Is the Savior the Savior of all the other earths? Does God have a Father? Where was the beginning? Was there ever a beginning? Yes, Moses may have asked many, many similar questions, but the Lord wisely limits his answers, for Moses could not comprehend all of God's work and worlds. "No man can behold all my works, except he behold all my glory; and no man can behold all my glory, and afterwards remain in the flesh" (Moses 1:5).

Moses had a work to do on this earth. His mission was on this earth. He was asking questions about the other earths when he really didn't know the answers to the questions of his own earth. The Lord kindly withheld some of the answers to some of Moses' questions: "For mine own purpose have I made these things. Here is wisdom and it remaineth in me." (Moses 1:31.) Then Moses spake unto the Lord, saying:

> Be merciful unto thy servant, O God, and tell me concerning this earth, and the inhabitants thereof, and also the heavens, and then thy servant will be content. (Moses 1:36.)

Questions the Lord Answers About This Earth

First of all the Lord tells Moses that "by the word of my power, have I created them, which is mine Only Begotten Son, who is full of grace and truth" (Moses 1:32). Through the delegation of His power to His son, even Jesus Christ, the other worlds were made. Jesus Christ is the "heir of all things, by whom also he made the worlds," as the writer of Hebrews also revealed (Hebrews 1:2). We know that this power of the Lord to ask in his name is the priesthood. Through the power of the priesthood and its proper use by the Savior, the worlds were created. Concerning this earth, the Savior, Jesus Christ is the power by which it was made.

Then the Lord said: "And the first man of all men have I called Adam, which is many" (Moses 1:34). This seems to clearly indicate that the first man on other worlds was also called "Adam." Thus if we learn about the "Adam" on our own world, we may be learning about other "Adams" on other worlds. (Our major concern ought to be learning about the Adam on our earth.)

At this time in our development, as children of our Father in Heaven, we neither number nor comprehend the vastness of God's worlds and king-doms. The stars in the heavens are some of them. How many stars are there? Abraham said: "And I saw the stars, that they were very great, and that one of them was nearest unto the throne of God; and there were many great ones which were near unto it" (Abraham 3:2). The Savior said, "Let not your heart be troubled: ye believe in God, believe also in me. In my Father's house are many mansions . . . I go to prepare a place for you." (John 14:1-2.) These things must have been taught to Moses:

> The heavens, they are many, and they cannot be numbered unto man; but they are numbered unto me, for they are mine.
> And as one earth shall pass away, and the heavens thereof even so shall another come, and there is no end to my works, neither to my words." (Moses 1:37-38.)

Moses' Most Significant Question

Moses asked the Lord "Why are these things so?" Why did God make this earth? What is God's work, and what is His glory in this work? What is the Great Purpose for this world? In the most succinct words the Lord could give to Moses, he said:

> FOR BEHOLD, THIS IS MY WORK AND MY GLORY—TO BRING TO PASS THE IMMORTALITY AND ETERNAL LIFE OF MAN. (Moses 1:39, emphasis added.)

This was the ultimate purpose for Moses in leading the children of Israel out of Egyptian bondage. Moses tried to assist the Lord in teaching them about the significance of the Savior in overcoming death through the res-urrection. Their Immortality was a free gift of grace through the Atonement of Jesus Christ. They were to remember it through the vivid sacrifice of their own first-born bullocks and male lambs. It was "a similitude of the sacrifice of the Only Begotten of the Father." The saving of their lives in the eternal sense came not with the sprinkling of blood of a lamb over their lintels and door posts (see Exodus 12:22) but in looking forward to their Immortality through the atonement and resurrection of Jesus Christ. Their Eternal Life would come through obedience to the way of life of the Savior, their obedience to His words of life, His gospel. Moses' work was to assist the Lord in teaching the children of Israel about God's work of helping them to gain Immortality and Eternal Life. This should be our real work and purpose on earth also, to assist our Father in Heaven in bringing to pass the Immortality and Eternal Life of all we have the privilege of working with.

Chapter one of the book of Moses concludes with the Lord's commandment to Moses to write the things He would reveal to him about the creation of the earth. It also states that the revelations in what is now chapter one of Moses, and other words of the Bible, would be taken out—deleted from Moses' writings. This made it necessary for the Lord to raise up a prophet "like unto Moses" to restore these words. Joseph Smith was the prophet "like unto Moses" who did, indeed, bring these words to light in restoring these "Pearls of Great Price."

Summary of Chapter Three

1. Moses was raised in Egypt as an Egyptian prince drawn "out of the water."

2. Moses was led from Egypt to the deserts of Midian and became a shepherd.

3. Moses' climb up an "exceedingly high mountain" began on the mountain in the deserts of Midian but ended in the presence of the Lord.

4. Moses was given not just the physical task of leading the children of Israel bodily out of Egypt; he was also to lead them out of spiritual captivity.

5. Moses was taught, by the Lord on the top of the mountain, the fullness of the gospel, then he was told to write what was revealed to him.

6. Moses had great visions from the Lord before he began to write the book of Genesis.

7. The presence of God withdrew from Moses to enable him to further develop humility and dependence upon the Lord.

8. Moses had a direct confrontation with Satan but he overcame him by calling upon the name of the Lord Jesus Christ, and he commanded the devil to depart.

9. Moses saw worlds without number and saw that our earth was not the first, nor the last, earth that God had created—or would create—in the future.

10. The Lord's revealed purpose for this earth: "This is my work and my glory—to bring to pass the immortality and eternal life of man."

11. Moses was told that many of the words he would write would be deleted from the Bible, that it would be necessary to raise up a prophet "like unto Moses"—even Joseph Smith—who would restore his words and bring to light many "Pearls of Great Price."

Chapter Four

Pre-Earth Planning—Council in Heaven

Before Earth Life

Before we can properly begin Moses, chapter two, on the creation of this earth, we need to review some things that have been revealed about "pre-earth planning": the Council in Heaven and our pre-earthly existence. Abraham was shown this existence and declared in these words:

> Now the Lord had shown unto me, Abraham, the intelligences that were organized before the world was; and among all these there were many of the noble and great ones;
>
> And God saw these souls that they were good, and he stood in the midst of them, and he said: These I will make my rulers; for he stood among those that were spirits, and he saw that they were good; and he said unto me: Abraham, thou art one of them; thou wast chosen before thou wast born.
>
> And there stood one among them that was like unto God, and he said unto those who were with him: We will go down, for there is space there, and we will take of these materials, and we will make an earth whereon these may dwell;
>
> And we will prove them herewith, to see if they will do all things whatsoever the Lord their God shall command them;
>
> And they who keep their first estate shall be added upon; and they who keep not their first estate shall not have glory in the same kingdom with those who keep their first estate; and they who keep their second estate shall have glory added upon their heads for ever and ever.
>
> And the Lord said: Whom shall I send? And one answered like unto the Son of Man: Here am I, send me. And another answered and said: Here am I, send me. And the Lord said: I will send the first.
>
> And the second was angry, and kept not his first estate, and, at that day, many followed after him. (Abraham 3:22-28.)

The prophet Jeremiah, in the Bible, was told by the Lord:

> Before I formed thee in the belly I knew thee; and before thou camest forth out of the womb I sanctified thee, and I ordained thee a prophet unto the nations. (Jeremiah 1:5.)

We know by revelation of our prophets that we all lived in a pre-earth before this life. We were among those Abraham saw and we, too, were chosen before we were born. Perhaps we were more than "sidewalk super-intendents," mere observers of the creation; perhaps we assisted in some way in the creation of our own earth upon which we would later dwell as mortals. Jehovah and Michael (Adam) played the dominant role as our leaders, acting under the direction of God, the Father, but perhaps we each had a part. Certainly we were interested in the work.

A great Council in Heaven was called so that Father could explain more fully our future mission calls to the earth as well as the Plan of Salvation—a plan that would enable us to gain Immortality and Eternal Life—to have the glory and the joy that He and the other gods enjoy in their glorified, resurrected state. He wanted us to have His Joy, His Life, Eternal Life. He and other gods, worlds without number, had followed the path which led to their Exaltation and Godhood. The Plan was a tried and proven plan. It was an Eternal Plan; it was God's Plan!

But Satan stood up boldly and opposed the Plan of the Gods:

> And he came before me, saying—Behold, here am I, send me, and I will be thy son, and I will redeem all mankind, that one soul shall not be lost, and surely I will do it; wherefore give me thine honor. (Moses 4:1.)

Isaiah recorded the rebellion and the attitude of Satan in these words:

> I will ascend into heaven, I will exalt my throne above the stars of God: I will sit also upon the mount of the congregation, in the sides of the north:
> I will ascend above the heights of the clouds; I will be like the most High. (Isaiah 14:13-14.)

Satan was Lucifer, a "son of the morning"—a great and intelligent being, also a son of God and also our brother. He acted contrary to light and truth although he knew better.

In sharp contrast to the attitude and rebellion of Satan, the Savior, Jesus Christ, the Beloved Son said: "Father, thy will be done, and the glory be thine forever" (Moses 4:2). The Savior did not present another plan. He supported and upheld the Father's plan. He was in perfect harmony with light and truth. He also wanted to be "like the most High," but would go about it in a much different way than Satan. Paul would later say of him and challenge us:

> Let this mind be in you, which was also in Christ Jesus:
> Who, being in the form of God, thought it not robbery to be equal with God:
> But made himself of no reputation, and took upon him the form of a servant, and was made in the likeness of men:
> And being found in fashion as a man, he humbled himself, and became obedient unto death, even the death of the cross.
> Wherefore God also hath highly exalted him, and given him a name which is above every name:
> That at the name of Jesus every knee should bow, of things in heaven, and things in earth, and things under the earth;

And that every tongue should confess that Jesus Christ is Lord, to the glory of God the Father. (Philippians 2:5-11.)

Yes, both the Savior and Satan desired to "be like the most High"— yet one would use love, reason, persuasion, sincerity, humility, obedience, example, patience, longsuffering, and meekness; the other would use hatred, force, deceit, lies, self-agrandizement, disobedience, rebellion, self-will, impatience and dictatorship. One would honor and respect free agency and allow people to choose for themselves the path they would follow; the other would take away free agency and replace it with conformity to his (Satan's) way, and force people to follow it.

There are great principles of leadership that seem self-evident to thinking beings. "Intelligent control exerts influence without appearing to do so. Unintelligent control tries to influence by making a show of force" (Lao Tzu, *Tao Teh King*, p. 39) and this thought by Lao Tzu: "If you are required to govern others, ought you not be able to guide them by example, rather than by forcing your will upon them" (Ibid., p. 17)? Jesus Christ understood these principles; Satan rejected them.

The "War in Heaven" came about because of the contrast in these two pre-earthly leaders. The "weapons" the Savior used (and also used by those who followed him) were free agency, the proper use of testimony, faith, love, joy, peace, long-suffering, gentleness, goodness, meekness, temperance, diligence, boldness but not overbearance. "Not with railing accusation, that ye be not overcome, neither with boasting" (D&C 50:33). Not the spirit of contention, for "he that hath the spirit of contention is not of me, but is of the devil" (3 Nephi 11:29). All the qualities of those who serve the Savior's work here on earth were the "weapons" used by the Savior and his followers in the War in Heaven. Actually the war has merely changed battlefields—that which was started in heaven goes on here on earth. The "battle cry" of the Savior to persuade the children of God to follow the Father's plan is the same as the words given to Joseph Smith's father in the beginning of the restoration of the gospel in this last dispensation:

O ye that embark in the service of God, see that ye serve him with all your heart, might, mind and strength, that ye may stand blameless before God at the last day.

And faith, hope, charity and love, with an eye single to the glory of God, qualify him for the work.

Remember faith, virtue, knowledge, temperance, patience, brotherly kindness, godliness, charity, humility, diligence.

Ask, and ye shall receive; knock, and it shall be opened unto you. (D&C 4:2, 5-7.)

The War in Heaven is recorded in scripture by John, the Revelator:

And there was a war in heaven; Michael [the pre-earth name of Adam, e.g., see Mark E. Peterson's Adam, *Who Is He?*, p. 11, chapter 2] and his angels [we who had accepted the Father's plan and Jesus Christ] fought against the dragon [Satan, Lucifer]; and the dragon and his angels fought against Michael;

And the dragon prevailed not against Michael, neither the child [Jesus Christ], nor the woman which was the church of God, who had been delivered of her pains, and brought forth the kingdom of our God and his Christ.

Neither was there place found in heaven for the great dragon, who was cast out; that old serpent called the devil, and also called Satan, which deceiveth the whole world; he was cast out into the earth; and his angels were cast out with him . . . they have overcome him by the blood of the Lamb, and by the word of their testimony. (JST, Revelation 12:6-8, 11.)

The influence of Satan in that pre-earth struggle was great enough to win a third of the "stars of heaven" (Revelation 12:4). A third of the spirit children of our Father in Heaven openly rebelled and followed Satan. They came to earth without tangible bodies of flesh, blood, and bone. Satan and his hosts were here on earth as spirits before Adam and Eve began to "multiply and replenish" the earth with their children. The account in Revelation said the third were cast to earth. "And the dragon stood before the woman which was delivered, ready to devour her child after it was born" (JST, Revelation 12:4). In other words from the days of Adam and Eve, and throughout mortality, everyone has been (and will be) born into an environment in which Satan and his hosts are very numerous. Today there are influences of Satan both seen and unseen which are ready to influence us to do evil.

In spite of the dangers inherent in being born into mortality, the blessings and opportunities to become like Father and Mother, to have a life like theirs—even Eternal Life—far outweigh the risk. We, with Job, "sang together, and . . . shouted for joy" (Job 38:7) at the opportunity and blessing of coming to earth for our progress and growth.

We also made a covenant that, once the earth was created and we reached maturity, we would marry and "be one flesh" with our mates in the creation of mortal bodies for other spirits who desired to come to mortality. We were told that this was one of the primary reasons for the creation of the earth: "That the earth might answer the end of its creation; And that it might be filled with the measure of man, according to his creation before the world was made" (D&C 49:16-17). Indeed, our charge was to "see if they will do all things whatsoever the Lord their God shall command them" (Abraham 3:25).

Summary of Chapter Four

1. Before we can begin to read about the creation, we need to review some things about "pre-earth planning."

2. Abraham saw "the intelligences that were organized before the world was."

3. A great pre-earth council was called so that God could explain the future mission calls of his children to earth and the great Plan of Salvation for them.

4. The plan was a tried and proven plan, a perfect plan designed by gods for gods—an Eternal Plan—God's plan.

5. Satan opposed God's plan and proposed a different plan which would take away man's free agency. He also wanted the honor, praise, and glory of God to go to him.

6. The Savior said, "Thy will be done, and the glory be thine forever." The Christ would allow all mankind their own free agency.

7. There was a "War in Heaven" fought over these opposing ideological differences.

8. The "weapons" the Savior and his forces used against Satan and his hosts were free agency, testimony, faith, love, joy, peace, longsuffering, gentleness, goodness, meekness, temperance, diligence; not the spirit of contention, etc.

9. All of the qualities of those who serve the Savior here on earth were the "weapons" used there. The war in heaven has merely changed battlefields. That which was started in heaven continues here on earth.

10. Satan and his followers were cast down to earth and were "ready to devour her child after it was born." They desired to take over the bodies of the children of Adam and Eve.

11. In spite of inherent dangers of being born into mortality, we, with Job, "shouted for joy" at the opportunity to be born and to come to earth with its challenges and chances for progress and growth.

12. We made pre-earth covenants that, when we reached maturity, we would marry and provide bodies for other spirits to come and experience mortality. This was one of the primary reasons for its creation: "That the earth might answer the end of its creation; And that it might be filled with the measure of man, according to his creation before the world was made." (D&C 49:16-17.)

Chapter Five

The Creation of the Earth and Man *Before* the Fall

Two Scriptural Accounts of the Creation

We are now ready to review the two accounts in the Pearl of Great Price on the creation of the earth and the placement of life on it—including man and woman. We have only two scriptural accounts of the actual creation; the account in Moses 2 and 3 and the account of Abraham 4 and 5. The Genesis account is merely the remnant that remained after the Bible went "through the hands of the great and abominable church" (1 Nephi 13:28). Moroni had access to an account of the creation which was written on the twenty-four plates found by the people of Limhi (an abridgment of the Jaredite people) and alludes to the fact that the sealed portion of the plates, which he gave to Joseph Smith, had the full account of the creation (see Ether 1:3-4; Ether 4 & 5). Unfortunately we do not have these accounts.

Creation Accounts Are of the World *Before* the Fall

It is very important to keep in mind that events described in Moses 2 and 3, and in Abraham 4 and 5 are events that occurred before the earth became as we know it today. They are events of the earth *before the Fall.* The book of Abraham, as we have it today, does not contain the account of the Fall. The Fall is a most important event in gospel history and a most significant focal point in the story of the creation. Everything we study, everything we know about the earth from our observation and scientific experimentation is a study of the earth *after the Fall.* This chapter will be talking about events *before the Fall.*

All Things to the Lord Are Spiritual

It would be helpful to understand the use of the word "spiritual," as it may be used in the context of this writing, and as it is also used in various ways in the scriptures. For example it has been revealed that "The Father has a body of flesh and bones as tangible as man's" (D&C 130:22) yet His body is "spiritual." God's world is real, tangible, a great "Urim and

Thummim," "a globe like a sea of glass and fire" (D&C 130:7), yet His kingdom, His world, is "spiritual." In fact He said "all things unto me are spiritual" (D&C 29:34). In talking about the creation, he said:

> For by the power of my Spirit created I them; yea, all things both spiritual and temporal—
> First spiritual, secondly temporal, which is the beginning of my work; and again, first temporal, and secondly spiritual, which is the last of my work—
> Speaking unto you that you may naturally understand; but unto myself my works have no end, neither beginning; but it is given unto you that ye may understand. (D&C 29:31-33.)

For the Lord there really is no beginning but, in revealing it to our understanding, He says: "In the beginning. . . ." We shall discover that the tangible world which God created before the Fall can be properly called "first spiritual," then, after the Fall, it can be called "secondly temporal" (which is the beginning of His work of redemption of this earth). We are living in this second "temporal" phase of the Lord's plan. When the earth is redeemed from the Fall, and we are resurrected, both the earth and mankind will be tangible, but this is "secondly spiritual which is the last of my work." We start out spiritual, we become temporal, then again we become spiritual. We start as spiritual beings, take upon us flesh and bones and blood (become temporal and mortal), then die and resurrect a "spiritual" body of either a celestial, terrestrial, or telestial flesh. (See JST, 1 Corinthians 15:39.) "It is sown a natural body [temporal]; it is raised a spiritual body" (1 Corinthians 15:44). The "spiritual body" of our Lord, Jesus Christ, after his resurrection, was a body of flesh and bones: "Handle me, and see; for a spirit hath not flesh and bones, as ye see me have" (Luke 24:39).

We know that we existed untold ages before we were placed on this earth. We existed as "intelligences." Our intelligence was not created nor made by God. We were co-eternal with God (D&C 93:29). We did not come out of the "nowhere into the here." Joseph Smith said: "Intelligence is eternal and exists upon a self-existent principle. It is a spirit from age to age, and there is no creation about it." It is also comforting to know, as the prophet continues, "All the minds and spirits that God ever sent into the world are susceptible of enlargement" (*Teachings of the Prophet Joseph Smith*, p. 354). The exact substance of intelligence we do not know, but it has been defined as "light and truth" (D&C 93:29, 36). It is not "immaterial matter" for the prophet said: "There is no such thing as immaterial matter" (D&C 131:7).

Whether our intelligences were clothed in "spirit matter" we do not know. "The Spirit itself beareth witness with our spirit, that we are the children of God (Romans 8:16). Thus we teach that we are all children of heavenly parents, but how this was done has not been revealed. Joseph Fielding Smith said: "We have no account of the creation of man or other forms of life when they were created as spirits" (Joseph Fielding Smith, *Doctrines of Salvation*, 1:75-76). Therefore, in the paragraphs to follow, when we talk about the creation of the earth and the creation of man we are not talking about the creation of the earth or man with matter that is spirit and "is more fine or pure, and can only be discerned by purer eyes" (see D&C 131:7). We have no account of that creation. We are not talking about a "spirit creation" of the earth and men. But it is "spiritual" because, with God, all things are spiritual.

The Earth Before the Fall

The earth *before the Fall* was framed, created, organized, prepared, formed, fashioned, and shaped from existing eternal matter. The earth was formed out of materials that have always existed and will never be destroyed. (See *Teachings,* p. 350-352.) Joseph Smith and Brigham Young both clearly state that "when the earth was framed and brought into existence and man was placed upon it, it was near the throne of our Father in Heaven" (in *Journal of Discourses*, 17:143). Our earth was "a new earth patterned after the old."

The time schedule, "days of creation," were days of God's world—not the days of the earth after the Fall as we know them. The earth had not "fallen" to its present place in the universe; had not begun its time schedule and revolutions about the sun. The earth before the Fall was on celestial time—Kolob time. When the Lord explained this to Abraham he said "that Kolob was after the manner of the Lord, according to its times and seasons in the revolutions thereof; that one revolution was a day unto the Lord, after his manner of reckoning, it being one thousand years according to the time appointed unto that whereon thou standest." (Abraham 3:4; see also 2 Peter 3:8, D&C 77:12.)

Delineation of Events in the Creation

With this realization that we are talking about events before the Fall, we can start to unfold the events of the creation as given in Moses, chapter 2 and Abraham, chapter 4. Let us begin with the Abraham account:

> And then the Lord said: Let us go down. And they went down at the beginning, and they, that is the Gods, organized and formed the heavens and the earth. (Abraham 4:1.)

This account helps us to know that it was "they" (the gods) who did the work. There is a plurality of gods, although "I AM," or Jehovah, was the major power. By the power of the Only Begotten the world was made (see Moses 1:32-33). The Abraham account also uses the phrase "the second time," the "third time," etc., to tell of the time framework of various phases of the earth's creation (see Abraham 4:8, 13, 19, 23, 31). The words "the Gods *prepared* the waters" (Abraham 4:21; italics added), and "the Gods *prepared* the earth" (Abraham 4:24; italics added) seem to be significant. In the Moses account and the Genesis account the words "God"— "Good"—"God"—"Good" are significant. God is good. His purpose and his creation are good. If we got nothing else out of the creation account but these two words, "God"—"Good," it would be beneficial to us.

Once the earth was prepared for life it was transplanted from God's world. Nor was it necessarily the elemental life that evolutionists would have us believe was brought to this earth. Listen to Joseph Fielding Smith on this point:

> . . . does it not appear to you that it is a foolish and ridiculous notion that when God created this earth he had to begin with a speck of protoplasm, and then take millions of years, if not billions, to bring conditions to pass by which his sons and daughters might obtain bodies made in his image? Why not the shorter route and transplant them from another earth as we are taught in the scriptures. (Joseph Fielding Smith, *Man, His Origin and Destiny*, p. 276-277.)

Hear the almost poetic words of Parley P. Pratt say it another way:

> A Royal Planter now decends from yonder world of older date, and bearing in his hands the choice seeds of the older paradise, He plants them in the virgin soil of our new-born earth. They grow and flourish there, and bearing seed, replant themselves, and thus clothe the naked earth with scenes of beauty, and the air with fragrant incense, ripening fruits and herbs at length abound, When Lo! From yonder world is transferred every species of animal life. Male and female, they come, with blessings on their head; and a voice is heard again, "Be fruitful and multiply."
>
> Earth—its mineral, vegetable and animal wealth—its paradise prepared, down comes from yonder world on high, a son of God, with his beloved spouse. And thus a colony from heaven, it may be from the sun, is transplanted to our soil . . .
>
> Darkness veiled the past and future from the heathen mind; man neither knew himself, from whence he came, nor whither he was bound. At length a Moses came, who knew his God and would fain have led mankind to know Him too, and see Him face to face. But they could not receive His heavenly laws, or bide His presence. Thus the holy man was forced again to veil the past in mystery, and in the beginning of his history, assign to man an earthly origin.
>
> Man, moulded from the earth, as a brick!
>
> A woman, manufactured from a rib!
>
> Thus, parents would fain conceal from budding manhood the mysteries of procreation, or the sources of life's ever-flowing river, by relating some childish tale of new-born life . . . O, man! When wilt thou cease to be a child in knowledge?
>
> Man, as we have said, is the offspring of Diety. The entire mystery of the past and future, with regard to his existence, is not yet solved by mortals. (Parley P. Pratt, *Key to the Science of Theology*, 5th ed., 1883, p. 54-55.)

By analogy, suppose modern men of science today decided to put life on the moon. We have already discovered the surface of the moon to be devoid of all life. The astronauts, after they came down from the moon, were put in an isolation chamber for a time, for examination, lest they bring some strange virus or germ from the moon to earth. None were found. As far as we can tell there is no life on the moon. Would it make much sense for us to just leave a petri dish with amoeba living in it and come back billions of years later to see if the life happened to evolve into something? Wouldn't we at least take some plant life from our earth; would we not build some kind of terrarium to sustain the plants? And after plants, trees, and water were established, would we not take animal life from our earth to put on the moon instead of waiting for them to "evolve" from some primordial soup? If we were going to colonize the moon with people, wouldn't it be simple to take a man and woman from the earth and instruct them to "multiply and replenish" themselves and take care of the "garden" we had planted for them?

The Creation, or Birth of Adam and Eve

After the earth was capable of sustaining life, and the gods declared "that all these things were good," Moses wrote this account:

> And I, God, said unto mine Only Begotten, which was with me from the beginning: Let us make man in our image, after our likeness; and it was so. And I, God, said: Let them have dominion over the fishes of the sea, and over the fowl of the air, and over the cattle, and over all the earth, and over every creeping thing that creepeth upon the earth.
>
> And I, God, created man in mine own image, in the image of mine Only Begotten created I him; male and female created I them.
>
> And I, God, blessed them, and said unto them: Be fruitful, and multiply, and replenish the earth, and subdue it, and have dominion over the fish of the sea, and over the fowl of the air, and over every living thing that moveth upon the earth. (Moses 2:26-28.)

Exactly how God made man is as mysterious as birth—and who of us, as parents, has not stood in awe and reverence looking at the miracle of the new life we have helped bring into the world? Surely it is a miracle that a microscopic cell, with the appearance of a tiny tadpole, can penetrate another small cell from the mother—the cell no larger than a piece of chalk dust. The miracle is in the uniting of the sperm and the ovum, the fertilization of the egg, the interlocking of the chromosomes, the development of two identical cells, then four, then eight, then sixteen. Then, miraculously, in the period of nine months, millions of cells form a child in the image of the parents. Yes, it is miraculous, that cells "evolve" into a human being. It is God's creative processes at work in our own birthing.

Speaking of Adam and Eve's creation as our first parents, Brigham Young said that God created man "as we create our children; for there is no other process of creation in heaven, on th earth, or under the earth, or in all the eternities, that is, that were, or ever will be . . ." (in *Journal of Discourses*, 11:122). He said:

> Our first parents were, indeed, created out of the dust of the earth, but in no sense differently from the way we ourselves are created out of it; save that it was perhaps the dust of some other earth! (in *Journal of Discourses*, 3:319.)

Joseph F. Smith said:

> Things upon the earth, so far as they have not been perverted by wickedness, are typical of things in heaven. Heaven was the prototype of this beautiful creation when it came from the hand of the creator and was pronounced "Good." (Joseph F. Smith, *Gospel Doctrine*, p. 21.)

And Elder B. H. Roberts stated:

> Man has descended from God; in fact, he is the same race as the Gods. His descent has not been from a lower form of life, but from the Highest Form of Life: in other words, man is, in the most literal sense, a child of God. This is not only true of the spirit but of his body also. (Course of Study for Priests, 1910, p. 35; also quoted in the course manual, CDFR 60, p. 4.)

This concept of having Adam and Eve being literal children of our heavenly parents does not take away from Jesus Christ being the "Only Begotten in the flesh" in mortality on the earth *after the Fall*. Jesus is the firstborn of the spirit children of our Heavenly Father, the Only Begotten of the Father in the flesh (of mortality after the Fall), and the first to rise from the dead in the resurrection. All of this is true, but we are talking about the creation (or birth) of Adam and Eve on God's world and their subsequent placement on the *new earth before the Fall.*

People sometimes ask why we make such a point of this, but it is such an ennobling concept. In a world where evolution and the ascent of man from the lower forms of life are so prevalently taught, this simple, yet profound, concept lifts one's horizons. We might use the words of Joseph Smith when we think on these things: "This is good doctrine. It tastes good. I can taste the principles of eternal life, and so can you." (*Teachings*, p. 335.)

Conditions on Our World Before the Fall

Conditions on our world before the Fall were very different from the conditions of our world after the Fall. All life in the sea, the air, on the earth before the Fall was without death. President Smith said: "Things were not changing as we find them changing in this mortal existence, for mortality had not come. Today we are living in a world of change because we are living under a very different condition from those which prevailed in the beginning and before the Fall of man." (*Doctrines of Salvation*, 1:108.)

The prophet Lehi, speaking of the time before the Fall, said:

> And all things which were created must have remained in the same state in
> which they were after they were created; and they must have remained forever,
> and had no end (2 Nephi 2:22).

Lehi also said that Adam and Eve would have had no children, that they
would have remained in a state of innocence but having no joy, nor doing
any good in this state before the Fall (2 Nephi 2:23).

The earth *before the Fall*, though it was pronounced "good" by the
gods, was not a celestial world. Our world lived on the "reflected light" of
God's world. In this state it was an inert world, a non-progressing world, a
non-changing world. In a homely example—if the world of God were
butter—our world was margarine. It was a paradise—yet it wasn't. It was
a world in "limbo," to use a Catholic term. It was a world without "flavor,"
without opposition, without contrasts; an unproved world. It was a potential celestial world, but there is so much difference between potential and
being. Had it remained forever in that state, if it had remained as one body
without contrasts or opposition, "it must needs remain as dead, having no
life neither death, nor corruption nor incorruption, happiness nor misery,
neither sense nor insensibility. Wherefore, it must needs have been created
for a thing of naught; wherefore there would have been no purpose in the
end of its creation." (2 Nephi 2:11-12.)

Such was the state of the earth *before the Fall*.

Summary of Chapter Five

1. We have only two scriptural accounts of the creation—the account
in Moses 2 and 3, and the account of Abraham 4 and 5.

2. The scriptural accounts are of the world *before* the Fall of Adam
and Eve.

3. All things to the Lord are spiritual—therefore the physical, or
tangible creation is also called "spiritual."

4. The earth was formed out of materials that have always existed and
will never be destroyed entirely. Matter is eternal.

5. The "days of creation" were days of God's world—not the days of
the earth after the Fall as we know 24-hour days.

6. The gods (plural) organized and formed the heavens and the earth.

7. Once the earth was prepared for life it was transplanted from God's
world.

8. Adam and Eve were created as we create our children. Man is, in the
most literal sense, a child of God.

9. All life in the sea, the air, and on the earth before the Fall was without death.

10. Our world before the Fall was an inert, non-progressing, non-
changing, "as dead" world.

Chapter Six

The Significance of "The Fall"

The most common usage of the word "fall" is for the season when leaves fall from trees, when school begins for our youth, when harvest is completed, football stadiums roar, and sweaters feel good on cool mornings. In Webster's dictionary fully half a page of definitions exist for the word "fall"—words like lagging, declining, dropping to a lower state, to subside, to abate, and many more.

In the gospel of Jesus Christ "The *Fall*" represents one of the most significant events in the whole of the plan of salvation. "Creation," "Fall," and "Atonement" are three of the deepest, the most important words in the gospel. This chapter will attempt to review the significance of the "Fall"—a "Great Season" in our quest for Eternal Life.

When Adam and Eve were in the pre-earthly existence they stood in the presence of God and understood the plan of salvation. However when Adam and Eve were placed on their new world, "patterned after the old," a veil of forgetfulness was drawn over their minds so that they remembered nothing of their former existence. This was necessary for Adam and Eve to express their own free agency in this new world. They had great intelligence and "free will"—that is, inherent *ability* to make choices which is the essence of intelligence but they did not, at first, have "free agency." Free agency is the *opportunity* to choose—the opportunity to express "free will."

It is the Lord who set the stage in the new world, and provided the opportunity for Adam and Eve to express their "free will." God gave Adam and Eve their "free agency," he did not give them their "free will." God gave Adam and Eve the opportunity to make choices. The opportunity to make choices is the essence of free agency.

Adam and Eve Given Their Free Agency

The Pearl of Great Price scriptural narrative tells us, briefly, of this setting in the Garden of Eden where Adam and Eve were given the first choices they had to make:

> And I, the Lord God, took the man, and put him into the Garden of Eden, to dress it, and to keep it.
>
> And I, the Lord God, commanded the man, saying: Of every tree of the garden thou mayest freely eat,
>
> But of the tree of the knowledge of good and evil, thou shalt not eat of it, nevertheless, *thou mayest choose for thyself*, for it is given unto thee; but, remember that I forbid it, for in the day thou eatest thereof thou shalt surely die. (Moses 3:15-17; italics added.)

Abraham has the same account, but adds this sentence to clarify the meaning of "the time that thou eatest thereof, thou shalt surely die":

> Now I, Abraham, saw that it was after the Lord's time, which was after the time of Kolob, for as yet the Gods had not appointed unto Adam his reckoning. (Abraham 5:13.)

In other words, Adam and Eve would die within the Lord's day or time. They would die within a thousand years from the time they partook of the forbidden fruit.

Both the Moses account and the Abraham account describe Eve's creation from Adam's rib (see Moses 3:21-23, Abraham 5:15-17). However, Eve was created in no way differently from Adam—or the way we are created. The description of her being made from one of Adam's ribs is purely figurative (see Bruce R. McConkie, *Mormon Doctrine*, p. 242). Although the scriptural narrative could be read that Adam, singly, was taught not to partake of the tree of knowledge of good and evil, they were both taught not to partake of the tree. Chapter three concludes with "And they were both naked, the man and his wife, and were not ashamed" (Moses 3:25).

Moses Chapter Four—Temptation of the Devil

Perhaps father Lehi's summary of the preliminary events of the Fall could be used at this point: "Wherefore, the Lord God gave unto man that he should act for himself. Wherefore, man could not act for himself save it should be that he was enticed by the one or the other." (2 Nephi 2:16.) Then Lehi tells of the role the devil played in bringing about the fall (see 2 Nephi 2:17). Let us go to the account in Moses:

> And Satan put it into the heart of the serpent, (for he had drawn away many after him,) and he sought also to beguile Eve, for he knew not the mind of God, wherefore he sought to destroy the world.
>
> And he said unto the woman: Yea, hath God said—Ye shall not eat of every tree of the garden? (And he spake by the mouth of the serpent.)
>
> And the woman said unto the serpent: We may eat of the fruit of the trees of the garden;
>
> But of the fruit of the tree which thou beholdest in the midst of the garden, God hath said—Ye shall not eat of it, neither shall ye touch it, lest ye die.
>
> And the serpent said unto the woman: Ye shall not surely die;

> For God doth know that in the day ye eat thereof, then your eyes shall be opened, and ye shall be as the gods, knowing good and evil.
>
> And when the woman saw that the tree was good for food, and that it became pleasant to the eyes, and a tree to be desired to make her wise, she took of the fruit thereof, and did eat, and also gave unto her husband with her, and he did eat.
>
> And the eyes of them both were opened, and they knew that they had been naked. And they sewed fig-leaves together and made themselves aprons. (Moses 4:6-13.)

Then the Lord confronted Adam and Eve in the garden and they both confessed that they had broken the commandment not to eat of the tree of the knowledge of good and evil. Satan also was confronted by the Lord and he confessed, reluctantly and defiantly, his role.

Satan is unrepentant. We know he desires to take over the world, to thwart God's plan for man if he can. His nature is to rule the world by force and to rule with blood and horror. His desire is to take over the bodies of the children of Adam and Eve, to have the spirits who followed him, to take over the bodies of the children of Adam and Eve. John the Revelator saw the nature of Satan and said it in these descriptive words: "And the dragon stood before the woman which was ready to be delivered, for to devour her child as soon as it was born" (Revelation 12:4).

But to this threat the Lord said:

> I will put enmity between thee and the woman, between thy seed and her seed; and he shall bruise thy head, and thou shalt bruise his heel (Moses 4:21).

Enmity Between Satan and Christ

Enmity means hatred or deep-seated dislike. Because Eve recognized Satan, and that she had been deceived, an enmity began at that time between Eve and the devil. Eve was a righteous woman and scripture never again records her having anything to do with Satan. The scripture also says there would be an enmity "between thy seed and her seed." There is a hatred between the "seed" or followers of Satan, and the "seed" of Eve—that is, her children. Satan and his followers have an enmity against all mortals. Little children have a natural enmity against Satan—they are not born evil. The Lord said, "little children are redeemed from the foundation of the world through mine Only Begotten; Wherefore, they cannot sin, for power is not given unto Satan to tempt little children, until they begin to become accountable before me" (D&C 29:46-47). The age of accountability is eight years of age (see D&C 68:25-27).

The years between birth and eight years of age have been called the formative years by several child development experts. These are the years when basic attitudes are formed. It is during these years that the Lord has challenged, and commanded, parents to teach their little ones the gospel:

And again, inasmuch as parents have children in Zion, or in any of her stakes which are organized, that teach them not to understand the doctrine of repentance, faith in Christ the Son of the living God, and of baptism and the gift of the Holy Ghost by the laying on of the hands, when eight years old, the sin be upon the heads of the parents . . . And they shall also teach their children to pray, and to walk uprightly before the Lord. (D&C 68:25, 28.)

These are the years in which there is an enmity between little children and Satan. These are the years when a love for Heavenly Father and His way of life can more easily be taught. These are the years when mothers and fathers will have their greatest influence on their children. These are the years the Proverbs refer to when they say: "Train up a child in the way he should go; and when he is old, he will not depart from it" (Proverbs 22:6). These are the years when mother needs to be in the home—not working, not having day-care centers training her children. These are the years when family home evening, where the gospel is taught in love by the father, can have a lasting effect on the children. These are the years when the Primary can assist with the teaching of little children, when sensitive, loving teachers can have such a lasting influence on children.

The enmity between Satan and his hosts and children helps "buy a little time." What we do with this precious time with our children is very important.

There is more to be understood in this scriptural "pearl," more that needs commentary. The greatest enmity between the seed of the woman and Satan is the distance between Jesus Christ and the devil. Jesus disliked evil. Satan loved evil. Thus there is a great enmity between Satan and Christ. Where the scripture says: ". . . and thou shalt bruise his heel" (Moses 4:21) the Lord is saying that Lucifer would have power to hurt the Savior. Satan helped "inspire" the men who were responsible for the beating, rejection, and crucifixion of Jesus Christ. In this way he (Satan) "bruised his heel." Satan did hurt our Lord and Savior, Jesus Christ, but he was not overcome. He endured the pain, the torment, the anguish. He died and was resurrected. He overcame death. He overcame Satan, and He "was caught up unto God, and to his throne" (Revelation 12:5). He will eventually rule triumphant over his Saints (see D&C 76:107-108). Jesus Christ comes through the posterity, or seed, of Eve through Mary, His mortal mother. Thus the "seed of Eve," Jesus Christ, "shall bruise thy (that is, Satan's) head." Although the Savior and his followers may be "bruised" by Satan and his hosts, Satan will not triumph over all—"his head will be bruised." Christ will overcome Satan.

John the Revelator said:

And she brought forth a man child, who was to rule all nations with a rod of iron: and her child was caught up unto God, and to his throne (Revelation 12:5).

Plainly stated, this means Mary brought forth a "man child," even Jesus Christ, who will rule all nations with the word of God, "the iron rod" (see 1 Nephi 11:25), and he was "caught up unto God" even as the writer of the book of Acts declares (see Acts 1:9-11).

Eve's Sorrow and Blessing

Because Eve was the first to partake of the forbidden fruit and then got Adam to partake, the Lord said:

> I will greatly multiply thy sorrow and thy conception. In sorrow thou shalt bring forth children, and thy desire shall be to thy husband, and he shall rule over thee (Moses 4:22).

Eve, and all women, will have some pain, or "sorrow," in childbearing. There is pain in the physical process of birth. Perhaps this scripture may also mean that there is some sorrow also in child rearing. Perhaps Eve was being warned, personally, that she would have great sorrow because some of her children would reject the gospel. One of her sons was to be a murderer; he would kill his own brother. Certainly Eve would have great sorrow over this calamity. Some grief, some pain, some sorrow over children is the lot of most mothers (and fathers) before they get through life. Having and rearing children is not a painless process but many would agree that the greatest joy of life is in bearing and rearing children. As the Psalmist said: "Children are an heritage of the Lord. . . . Happy is the man that hath his quiver full of them." (Psalms 127:3, 5.) And Paul said that Adam and Eve ". . . shall be saved in childbearing, if they continue in faith and charity and holiness with sobriety" (JST, 1 Timothy 2:15). As with Adam and Eve, so it shall be with us.

"Thy desire shall be to thy husband, and he shall rule over thee" (Moses 4:22) was not meant to make the woman a servant of the man—nor to make this a form of punishment for Eve. Adam was to be the priesthood holder and to represent the Lord in the home. Eve was to follow him as he was to follow the Lord; she was to follow him in righteousness. Adam was to govern his wife and his family by the power of the priesthood, but this power is "by persuasion, by long-suffering, by gentleness and meekness, and by love unfeigned; By kindness, and pure knowledge, which shall greatly enlarge the soul without hypocrisy, and without guile. (D&C 121: 41-42.)

What woman would not desire such a man and want such a man to preside over her?

Adam's Blessing of Work

And unto Adam the Lord said:

> Because thou hast hearkened unto the voice of thy wife, and hast eaten of the fruit of the tree of which I commanded thee, saying—Thou shalt not eat of

it, cursed shall be the ground for thy sake; in sorrow shalt thou eat of it all the days of thy life.

Thorns also, and thistles shall it bring forth to thee, and thou shalt eat the herb of the field.

By the sweat of thy face shalt thou eat bread, until thou shalt return unto the ground. (Moses 4:23-25.)

Adam would shortly be driven out of the Garden of Eden where he would work to earn his sustenance. Opposition in the soil such as thorns, thistles, and weeds, would need to be worked out of the ground in order for it to produce the "herb of the field." But this "curse" of the ground would be for his sake because, in overcoming the challenges of nature and the difficulty of raising his food, he would also experience the joy of accomplishment as the ground, after much work, did produce. This is the feeling of joy that the farmer, or the florist, the nursery man, or the gardener feels when, after much work and cultivation, the ground produces.

"By the sweat of thy face shalt thou eat bread" was the challenge of Adam to work for what he received. There is no real satisfaction in life without putting forth effort—without earning one's daily bread—no satisfaction without work. Work is not really a curse for man, it is his salvation— it is for "his sake." A man's attitude toward his work often makes all the difference in the world. Two men might be doing identical work—say cutting stones—but ask one man what he is doing and he might say: "Cutting stones for $8 per hour!" Ask another, and he might say: "Building a temple to God!"

In the apocryphal book of Jasher there is an interesting reference to "garments of skin which God made for Adam and his wife, when they went out of the garden" (see *The Book of Jasher*, VII:24). The Pearl of Great Price says clearly:

Unto Adam, and also unto his wife, did I, the Lord God, make coats of skins, and clothed them (Moses 4:27).

These clothes were to cover their nakedness, to keep them warm, to protect them from the elements. From this point on Adam and Eve would also work to clothe themselves and their children and thus it is with all of us to this day.

Adam and Eve Kept from the Tree of Life

And I, the Lord God, said unto mine Only Begotten: Behold, the man is become as one of us to know good and evil; and now lest he put forth his hand and partake also of the tree of life, and eat and live forever,

Therefore I, the Lord God, will send him forth from the Garden of Eden, to till the ground from whence he was taken;

For as I, the Lord God, liveth, even so my words cannot return void, for as they go forth out of my mouth they must be fulfilled.

So I drove out the man, and I placed at the east of the Garden of Eden, cherubim and a flaming sword, which turned every way to keep the way of the tree of life. (Moses 4:28-31.)

This concludes chapter four of Moses in the Pearl of Great Price. This is Moses' account of the Fall. The book of Abraham comes to an abrupt end before telling of the events of the Fall.

When Man Fell, the Earth Fell into Space

There is much more to ponder and understand about the Fall than we get from information found in the Pearl of Great Price. Before we begin Moses, chapter five, on the initial pioneering efforts of our first earthly parents, we need to review what some of the prophets have said concerning this most significant event in the earth's history.

First it might be well to ponder the great "inter-galactic" phenomena brought about by the Fall of Adam and Eve. Joseph Smith once observed that when this earth is redeemed from its fallen state, and made a celestial sphere in the resurrection, it "will be rolled back into the presence of God" (*Teachings*, p. 181). If the earth is to be "rolled back" into the presence of God we can assume that it was in His presence at the time it was created and later moved from that place. Brigham Young explained this in this way:

> When the earth was framed and brought into existence and man was placed upon it, it was near the throne of our Father in heaven. And when man fell . . . the earth fell into space and took up its abode in this planetary system, and the sun became our light . . . This is the glory the earth came from, and when it is glorified it will return again into the presence of the Father, and it will dwell there, and these intelligent beings that I am looking at, if they live worthy of it, will dwell upon this earth. . . . (in *Journal of Discourses,* 17:143.)

> This earthly ball, this little opake [sic] substance thrown off into space, is only a speck in the great universe; and when it is celestialized it will go back into the presence of God, where it was first framed. All belongs to God, and those who keep his celestial law will return to him. (in *Journal of Discourses,* 9:317.)

Father Lehi Talks About the Fall

When Lehi was an old man, and soon to die, he called each of his sons unto him to give them counsel and a blessing. His son, Jacob, was born during some of the most trying days of Lehi's life when the family was starving in the desert wilderness of Arabia. Jacob had also suffered afflictions and sorrow because of the rudeness of his inconsiderate brothers, Laman and Lemuel. Yet Lehi told his son Jacob, "Thou knowest the greatness of God; and he shall consecrate thine afflictions for thy gain" (2 Nephi 2:2). Then old father Lehi told his son some of the great gospel themes that went back to principles taught to Adam and Eve, and to events leading up to the Fall. He also taught the great meaning of the Fall.

. . . And the way is prepared from the fall of man, and salvation is free. And men are instructed sufficiently that they know good from evil. And the law is given unto men. And by the law no flesh is justified; or, by the law men are cut off. Yea, by the temporal law they were cut off; and also, by the spiritual law they perish from that which is good, and become miserable forever. (2 Nephi 2:4-5.)

Lehi is talking about the fundamentals taught to Adam and Eve. Adam and Eve are "instructed sufficiently to know good and evil," and the "law" is given to them. What law? God's law, part of which, in its basic words to Adam and Eve, was: "Be fruitful, and multiply, and replenish the earth, and subdue it" (Moses 2:28). There was also the law which said: ". . . of the tree of the knowledge of good and evil, thou shalt not eat of it, nevertheless, thou mayest choose for thyself" (Moses 3:17).

The tree of knowledge of good and evil was placed so that Adam and Eve could act for themselves—could express their intelligence, their free will. Lehi said: "Wherefore, the Lord God gave unto man that he should act for himself" (2 Nephi 2:16). The Doctrine and Covenants states:

Behold, here is the agency of man, and here is the condemnation of man; because that which was from the beginning is plainly manifest unto them, and they receive not the light (D&C 93:31).

Free agency is a two-edged sword—there is no freedom from the consequences of our choices. In the case of Adam, the consequence of his choice was death—"for in the day thou eatest thereof thou shalt surely die (Moses 3:17). Paul said: "The wages of sin is death" (Romans 6:23). Lehi said: "By the law no flesh is justified; or, by the law men are cut off" (2 Nephi 2:5). But the tree of knowledge of good and evil and the "law" regarding not partaking of its fruit were absolutely necessary in the newly created world of Adam and Eve. It was the opposition in Adam's world.

Lehi went on to explain:

For it must needs be, that there is an opposition in all things. If not so, my first-born in the wilderness, righteousness could not be brought to pass, neither wickedness, neither holiness nor misery, neither good nor bad. Wherefore, all things must needs be a compound in one; wherefore, if it should be one body [i.e., if there had been no tree of the "knowledge of good and evil"—no negative law] it must needs remain as dead, having no life neither death, nor corruption nor incorruption, happiness nor misery, neither sense nor insensibility.

Wherefore, it must needs have been created for a thing of naught; wherefore there would have been no purpose in the end of its creation. Wherefore, this thing must needs destroy the wisdom of God and his eternal purposes, and also the power, and the mercy, and the justice of God.

And if ye shall say there is no law, ye shall also say there is no sin. If ye shall say there is no sin, ye shall also say there is no righteousness. And if there be no righteousness there be no happiness. And if there be no righteousness nor happiness there be no punishment nor misery. And if these things are not there is no God. And if there is no God we are not, neither the earth; for there could have been no creation of things, neither to act nor to be acted upon; wherefore, all things must have vanished away.

And now, my sons, I speak unto you these things for your profit and learning; for there is a God, and he hath created all things, both the heavens and the earth, and all things that in them are, both things to act and things to be acted upon.

And to bring about his eternal purposes in the end of man, after he had created our first parents, and the beasts of the field and the fowls of the air, and in fine, all things which are created, it must needs be that there was an opposition; even the forbidden fruit in opposition to the tree of life; the one being sweet and the other bitter.

Wherefore, the Lord God gave unto man that he should act for himself. Wherefore, man could not act for himself save it should be that he was enticed by the one or the other. (2 Nephi 2:11-16.)

Lehi goes on to explain that Satan enticed them to make the choice. They made the choice, partook of the "forbidden fruit," and were driven out of the Garden of Eden. But the Lord knew they would do this. Lehi said: "But behold, all things have been done in the wisdom of him who knoweth all things. Adam fell that men might be; and men are, that they might have joy." (2 Nephi 2:24-25.)

The "Forbidden Fruit"

Just what was this "forbidden fruit"? In the minds of carnally minded people, the very words "forbidden fruit" conjure up thoughts of sexual indiscretion—some "X" or "R-rated" sin. Listen carefully to an Apostle of the Lord, Elder James E. Talmage, comment on this:

Here let me say that therein consisted the fall—the eating of things unfit, the taking into the body of the things that made of that body a thing of earth; and I take this occasion to raise my voice against the false interpretation of scripture, which has been adopted by certain people, and is current in their minds, and is referred to in hushed and half-secret ways, that the fall of man consisted in some offense against the laws of chastity and virtue. Such a doctrine is an abomination. What right have we to declare that God meant not what He said? The fall was a natural process, resulting through the incorporation into the bodies of our first parents of the things that came from food unfit. Don't go around whispering that the fall consisted in the mother of the race losing her chastity and her virtue. It is not true; the human race was not born of fornication. These bodies that are given to us are given in the way that God has provided. Let it not be said that the patriarch of the race, who stood with the gods before he came here upon the earth, and his equally royal consort, were guilty of any such foul offense. The adoption of that belief has led many to excuse departures from the path of chastity and the path of virtue, by saying that it is the sin of the race, that it is as old as Adam. It was not introduced by Adam. It was not committed by Eve. It was the introduction of the Devil and came in order that he might sow the seeds of early death in the bodies of men and women, that the race should degenerate as it has degenerated whenever the laws of virtue and of chastity have been transgressed.

Our first parents were pure and noble, and when we pass behind the veil we shall perhaps learn something of their high estate, more than we know now. But be it known that they were pure; they were noble. It is true that they disobeyed the law of God, in eating things they were told not to eat; but who amongst you can rise up and condemn? (James E. Talmage, *Jesus the Christ*, pp. 30-31.)

Adam did transgress God's law; in a sense he broke a "word of wisdom." He took into his body a food that made his body change. The results of the partaking of this food unfit brought about his death. The tree of the knowledge of good and evil may even be a tree of this telestial world—a food familiar to us but, under decree of God, a kind of poison to Adam. It was not a fast poison, for Adam was to live almost 1,000 years before the effects of this food caused his death (Genesis 5:5).

We have often heard the phrase: "We are what we eat." Perhaps telestial, or mortal, beings are what they are because of the food they eat. Adam partook of such a food. Such a poison, or defective, food could be offset by partaking of the antidote—the "Tree of Life"—but the Lord apparently wanted Adam and Eve to experience death.

. . . And now lest he put forth his hand and partake also of the tree of life, and eat and live forever,

Therefore I, the Lord God, will send him forth from the Garden of Eden, to till the ground from whence he was taken;

For as I, the Lord God, liveth, even so my words cannot return void, for as they go forth out of my mouth they must be fulfilled.

So I drove out the man, and I placed at the east of the Garden of Eden, cherubim and a flaming sword, which turned every way to keep the way of the tree of life. (Moses 4:28-31.)

Why Did the Lord Keep Adam and Eve from the Tree of Life?

Alma explained the answer to Antionah in the book of Mormon. First Antiohah's question:

What does the scripture mean, which saith that God placed cherubim and a flaming sword on the east of the garden of Eden, lest our first parents should enter and partake of the fruit of the tree of life, and live forever? And thus we see that there was no possible chance that they should live forever.

Now Alma said unto him: This is the thing which I was about to explain. Now we see that Adam did fall by the partaking of the forbidden fruit, according to the word of God; and thus we see, that by his fall, all mankind became a lost and fallen people.

And now behold, I say unto you that if it had been possible for Adam to have partaken of the fruit of the tree of life at that time, there would have been no death, and the word would have been void, making God a liar, for he said: If thou eat thou shalt surely die.

And we see that death comes upon mankind, yea, the death which has been spoken of by Amulek, which is the temporal death; nevertheless there was a space granted unto man in which he might repent; therefore this life became a probationary state; a time to prepare to meet God; a time to prepare for that endless state which has been spoken of by us which is after the resurrection of the dead.

Now, if it had not been for the plan of redemption, which was laid from the foundation of the world, there could have been no resurrection of the dead; but there was a plan of redemption laid, which shall bring to pass the resurrection of the dead, of which has been spoken.

And now behold, if it were possible that our first parents could have gone forth and partaken of the tree of life they would have been forever miserable, having no preparatory state; and thus the plan of redemption would have been frustrated, and the word of God would have been void, taking none effect. (Alma 12:21-26; also the rest of chapter 12.)

Adam and Eve, and all of us, need this "space"—this earth life—for the cleansing, redemption and education of our spirit. Paradise, the spirit world after this life, is also a place for repentance and for teaching the spirits there the gospel (see D&C 138:30). To experience death is a necessary step in our Eternal Progress. In a very real sense we are born to die. Then our resurrection, where spirit and body become inseparably connected, can enable us to have a "fulness of joy (D&C 93:33-34).

The Tree of Life

In the book of Revelation we find this interesting scripture concerning the tree of life: ". . . To him that overcometh will I give to eat of the tree of life, which is in the midst of the paradise of God" (Revelation 2:7). Later, in describing the paradise of God, John says:

In the midst of the street of it, and on either side of the river, was there the tree of life, which bare twelve manner of fruits, and yielded her fruit every month: and the leaves of the tree were for the healing of the nations (Revelation 22:2).

Lehi also saw a vision of the tree of life:

And it came to pass that I beheld a tree, whose fruit was desirable to make one happy.

And it came to pass that I did go forth and partake of the fruit thereof; and I beheld that it was most sweet, above all that I ever before tasted. Yea, and I beheld that the fruit thereof was white, to exceed all the whiteness that I had ever seen.

And as I partook of the fruit thereof it filled my soul with exceedingly great joy. (1 Nephi 8:10-12.)

Both of these prophets, Nephi and John the Revelator, saw the tree of life. The meaning of the visions has extremely important symbolic and figurative meanings. Elder Bruce R. McConkie, in commenting on the tree of life and on the experiences of both Nephi and John, said it was a figurative expression of the tree from which the faithful pick the fruit of eternal life. "To eat thereof is to inherit eternal life in the kingdom of God" (Bruce R. McConkie, *Doctrinal New Testament Commentary*, 3:447).

Is it possible that, in addition to the figurative and symbolic meaning of the tree of life, the "tree of life" (or "trees of life") could be real trees? Could there be trees in the celestial world the literal fruit of which perpetuates life? Is it possible that there is literal food, perfect food in the celestial world that can provide such energy and revitalization that the body completely sustains itself and does not degenerate or grow old? Is it possible that the symbolic experiences of both Lehi and John could also have been real experiences? In the celestial kingdom will all trees be "trees of life" with celestial food with which we shall sustain ourselves and which will assist us in our immortality?

Effects of the Fall

The effect of the Fall had extreme and eternal consequences for Adam and Eve, and for all mankind. Let us first go through what seem to be negative aspects of the Fall, before we look at the positive aspects. In this way we may more fully appreciate the Atonement and Redemption from the Fall made for us by Jesus Christ. Lehi said that "by the law—the breaking of the law—we are cut off both temporally and spiritually (2 Nephi 2:5). What does this mean?

First of all the earth itself was literally moved from the presence of God; our earth is "marooned" in space. When our astronauts viewed the earth from the perspective of outer space, one of them said something like this: "To see the earth as it truly is—in that bright blue loveliness in the eternal cold—is to see ourselves as riders on the earth—riders who know now that they are brothers" ("We Saw the World From the Edge of Space," Cmdr. M. D. Ross, USNR, Nov. 1961, National Geographic). We are, to all appearances, a long way from any other life in the universe. We appear to be a long way from "home"—from God's World. We are literally and temporally "cut off" (2 Nephi 2:5).

There is another way we are temporally cut off. Can't you hear the clicking and grating of the shovels? Someone said "We are a world of grave-diggers at work." Death is a most vivid reality of this world. No matter how hard we work—no matter how hard we try—no matter what we do, we grow older and we will die. By this "temporal law" we are "cut off."

The greatest men, the proudest men, the most humble men—the Ceasars, the Napoleons—the most evil men, the Stalins, the Hitlers— magnificent presidents such as Washington and Lincoln—the prophets, Joseph Smith, Brigham Young, President McKay, President Lee, President Smith and—yes—even our beloved Elder LeGrand Richards—all die, and so shall we. No change of hair color (only her hairdresser knows), no extensive jogging and exercising, no health foods, no medicine; artificial heart, lungs, liver, kidneys—none of these can forever forestall death. We are all under this effect of the Fall—we are all born to die.

Lehi so vividly taught his son, Jacob, about these things that Jacob, too, portrays graphically the meaning of being temporally cut off:

> And the fall came by reason of transgression; and because man became fallen they were cut off from the presence of the Lord.
>
> Wherefore, the first judgment which came upon man must needs have remained to an endless duration. And if so, this flesh must have laid down to rot and to crumble to its mother earth, to rise no more. (2 Nephi 9:6-7.)

Thus to be "cut off temporally" meant that Adam and all of his posterity would be subject to death—physical death—the separation of the spirit from the body, and the body would be "laid down to rot and to crumble to its mother earth, to rise no more." Not a very pleasant thought. We certainly need to be "saved" from this fate.

We may say, "Well, I still have my spirit. Even though my body dies my spirit still lives." But Lehi said: ". . . by the spiritual law they (i.e., Adam, and Eve, and all of us) perish from that which is good, and become miserable forever" (2 Nephi 2:5). Jacob understood his father on this point and vividly portrayed our "spiritual death" and what could happen to our spirits at the time of our death:

> For behold, if the flesh should rise no more our spirits must become subject to that angel who fell from before the presence of the Eternal God, and became the devil, to rise no more.
>
> And our spirits must have become like unto him, and we become devils, angels to a devil, to be shut out from the presence of our God, and to remain with the father of lies, in misery, like unto himself. (2 Nephi 9:8-9.)

In other words, at death our physical bodies would be put into the grave to rot and disintegrate into dust, to rise no more, and our spirits would not have gone back to God, but we would have gone through the veil to be greeted in the spirit world by Satan and his hosts. What a horrible thought! Just imagine the evil greeting of our rebellious brother and his wicked associates—nor would we, or they, have another place to go.

Sometimes we do not fully ponder and comprehend what the effect of the Fall would have meant to us without the gospel and the Atonement and the Resurrection. We truly would have been cut off temporally and spiritually. Let us pause to contemplate these things.

We often take the blessing of the gospel and the "good news" of the overcoming of these two deaths so much for granted that we do not deeply feel the gratitude that we ought to feel toward the Savior. At the conclusion of this chapter we will merely summarize the effects of the Fall and give this hint as to the contents of the next chapter:

> I, the Lord God, gave unto Adam and unto his seed, that they should not die as to the temporal death, until I, the Lord God, should send forth angels to declare unto them repentance and redemption, through faith on the name of mine Only Begotten Son (D&C 29:42).

Summary of Chapter Six

1. In the true gospel of Jesus Christ the "Fall" represents one of the most significant events in the whole plan of Salvation.

2. God gave Adam and Eve opportunity to make choices on this earth. He gave man free agency.

3. Satan's desire is to take over the world and thwart God's plan for man.

4. The enmity between Satan and Christ is the deep-seated hatred Satan and his followers have for Christ and his followers.

5. Little children have a natural enmity toward Satan—they are not born evil.

6. The enmity, between little children and Satan, "buys" us precious time to teach little children the gospel of Jesus Christ during their formative years.

7. Satan bruises Christ's "heel" but Christ will crush Satan's "head." Christ will triumph over Satan.

8. Eve, and all women who have children, will have some pain (or "sorrow") in childbearing (and rearing). Having and rearing children is not a painless process.

9. Adam's rule over Eve was to be in righteousness. She is to follow him as he follows the Lord.

10. Adam was "blessed" with work. There is no real satisfaction in life without putting forth effort—without work.

11. Adam and Eve were kept from the "Tree of Life." They, and all mankind, became subject to death, both temporal and spiritual.

12. When man fell the earth fell into space and took up "its abode in this planetary system."

13. Lehi and Jacob, in the Book of Mormon, gave profound commentaries and insights into the Fall of Adam.

14. The "Forbidden Fruit" was a literal fruit that made Adam and Eve's bodies mortal things of this earth.

15. The Lord kept Adam and Eve from the "Tree of Life" so that this mortal life could be a probationary state—a cleansing, redemptive, educational experience for the spirit.

16. The "Tree of Life" may be both figurative and real.

17. Results of the Fall:

   (a) Adam and Eve became mortal—subject to sickness, pain, aging, and death. All mankind have similar mortality and afflictions.

   (b) The basic human drives, or appetites, became activated—i.e., sleep, hunger, sex.

   (c) The "survival of the fittest" cycle of the plant and animal kingdom started after the Fall.

(d) The full activation of all the mortal senses came into being—taste, touch, smell, sight, sound—at least in a mortal sense.

(e) All the phenomena associated with our present geography of the earth came into being after the Fall.

(f) All the seasons with wind, rain, weather and the cycles of nature began after the Fall.

(g) All the pain and all the pleasures of the flesh of mortality came because of the Fall.

(h) Our opportunity to be born into mortality came because of the Fall.

"Adam fell that men might be; and men are, that they might have joy" (2 Nephi 2:25).

Chapter Seven

Adam and Eve Receive a "Fulness" of the Gospel

We have no scriptural account that describes the actual movement of the earth into its present place in our universe—nor whether Adam and Eve "rode" on the earth as it "fell" to its present state. Certainly there is a great symbolic meaning in the scripture which says: "So I drove out the man, and I placed at the east of the Garden of Eden, cherubim and a flaming sword, which turned every way to keep the way of the tree of life" (Moses 4:31). The account of Moses, chapter five, merely begins the pioneering adventure of Adam and Eve after the Fall with these words:

> And it came to pass that after I, the Lord God, had driven them out, that Adam began to till the earth, and to have dominion over all the beasts of the field, and to eat his bread by the sweat of his brow, as I the Lord had commanded him. And Eve, also, his wife, did labor with him.
> And Adam knew his wife, and she bare unto him sons and daughters, and they began to multiply and to replenish the earth.
> And from that time forth, the sons and daughters of Adam began to divide two and two in the land, and to till the land, and to tend flocks, and they also begat sons and daughters. (Moses 5:1-3.)

The way the narrative is written there is no indication that Adam and Eve, nor their children of the first generation, had any knowledge or understanding of their real purpose on earth. All they seem to know is that they broke God's commandment and, as a result, they were on the earth.

A Story Analogy

A few years ago a Hollywood movie called "Sometimes a Great Notion" was produced. In it were such notable stars as Henry Fonda, Paul Newman, and JoAnn Woodward. It was a story about hard-working lumberjacks and their lives in the Northwest. One day JoAnn, who became tired of their life style, asked her husband: "Is that all there is to life—work and sex?" And her husband, Paul Newman, said "What else?" We can feel a pathos for those whose lives are only "work and sex." The other worldly elements of "recreation and play" do not make such lives any less pathetic.

It appears from reading Moses 5:1-3 that, for a long time, Adam and Eve just worked, survived, and "begat" children. They probably remembered the good feelings they had when they had walked and talked with the Father and His Son in the garden, but now they were "cut off" for a time from the association (see 2 Nephi 2:5). Adam and Eve went through an "earthly probation," a testing time, a searching time, a time to "hunger and thirst after the Lord,"—a time to ask: "Is this all there is to life?"

Lehi said:

> The days of the children of men were prolonged, according to the will of God, that they might repent while in the flesh; wherefore, their state became a state of probation, and their time was lengthened . . . he showed unto all men that they were lost, because of the transgression of their parents. (2 Nephi 2:21.)

With almost perfect bodies Adam and Eve, and their children, lived long lives. Adam, for example, was 130 years old when Seth was born and the days of Adam, after he had begotten Seth, were 800 years making him 930 years old when he died. (N. B. Lundwall, "Lectures on Faith," Second Lecture, p. 19; see also Genesis 5:4, 5.)

People in the first dispensation on earth lived to be very old. Lamech, the father of Noah, along with Methuselah, Enoch, Jared, Mahalaleel, Cainan, Enos, Seth, and Adam were all living at the same time. ("Lectures of Faith," p. 19.) Lehi seems to be saying that one of the reasons "the days of the children of men were prolonged" was "that they might repent while in the flesh" (2 Nephi 2:21). They could not repent until they knew the gospel, and there seems to have been a time when Adam and Eve did not have the gospel.

The Lord Was Watching Over Adam and Eve

The Lord was watching over Adam and Eve and He was also waiting for them to really "knock"—to really desire to know more about the great purposes of life and to call upon Him. He also watched over and preserved them from death during the years before they received the gospel, because the scripture says:

> I, the Lord God, gave unto Adam and unto his seed, that they should not die as to the temporal death, until I, the Lord God, should send forth angels to declare unto them repentance and redemption, through faith on the name of mine Only Begotten (D&C 29:42).

Notice that the scripture does not say he preserved them from "spiritual death" because spiritual death is being but off not only from the presence of the Father and the Son, but cut off from the knowledge of the gospel as well. Adam and Eve, for a time, suffered a "spiritual death" (see D&C 29:41).

Adam and Eve Call Upon the Name of the Lord

If the scripture in Moses 5:1-3, cited at the beginning of this chapter, is chronologically correct, then Adam and Eve were grandparents before they "called upon the name of the Lord" (Moses 5:4). Prayer is a preliminary principle of the gospel: "Knock and it shall be opened unto you: For every one that asketh receiveth" (Matthew 7:7-8)—But let him ask in faith nothing wavering" (James 1:6). The poignant words of Adam's first prayer are preserved even in the Adamic language in a very sacred place.

A desire to believe can initiate prayer. Prayer is fundamental in helping us receive the Spirit of the Lord—and the Spirit is essential in helping us receive and accept the gospel. Ask our missionaries what the first fundamental is that they have to teach their investigators: they will answer "prayer." "Please ask the Lord if the things we are telling you are true" is not just a cliche: the question is vital for any sincere person who would ask a sincere question and "call upon the name of the Lord."

Adam and Eve Learn the Principle of Obedience

In response to their fervent prayer:

> They heard the voice of the Lord from the way toward the Garden of Eden, speaking unto them, and they saw him not; for they were shut out from his presence.
> And he gave unto them commandments, that they should worship the Lord their God, and should offer the firstlings of their flocks, for an offering unto the Lord. And Adam was obedient unto the commandments of the Lord. (Moses 5:4-5.)

"The first principles and ordinances of the Gospel are: first, Faith in the Lord Jesus Christ; second, Repentance; third, Baptism by immersion for the remission of sins; fourth, Laying on of hands for the gift of the Holy Ghost." (See Fourth Article of Faith.) But preliminary principles—or perhaps correlative principles—to faith in the Lord Jesus Christ are the principles of obedience and sacrifice. The fourth verse of the hymn "Praise to the Man" begins: "Sacrifice brings forth the blessings of heaven. . . ."

Missionaries know that the investigator of the Church is serious and sincere when the cup of tea or coffee is sacrificed; when the cigarettes are thrown away; when liquor is no longer used; when a person can sacrifice a tenth of his income for tithing. When people can sacrifice their time to go to sacrament meeting, priesthood meeting, or Relief Society; when people will sacrifice their time to teach in Primary or Sunday School; when they will sacrifice time to home teach or do visiting teaching they manifest their faith in the Lord Jesus Christ.

Adam's sacrifice was the firstlings of his flocks for an offering unto the Lord. There is no portrayal in the Pearl of Great Price of how this was done. We can presume that the sacrifices of the Mosaic dispensation administered by the Aaronic Priesthood were the same, or very similar, to Adam's sacrifice. The Lord spoke to Moses and said:

> Let him offer a male without blemish . . . And he shall put his hand upon the head of the burnt offering; and it shall be accepted for him to make atonement for him.
> And he shall kill the bullock before the LORD: and the priests, Aaron's sons, shall bring the blood, and sprinkle 'he blood round about upon the altar that is by the door of the tabernacle of the congregation.
> And if his offering be of the flocks, namely, of the sheep, or of the goats, for a burnt sacrifice; he shall bring it a male without blemish.
> And he shall kill it on the side of the altar northward before the LORD: and the priests, Aaron's sons, shall sprinkle his blood round about upon the altar.
> And he shall but it into his pieces, with his head and his fat: and the priest shall lay them in order on the wood that is on the fire which is upon the altar:
> But he shall wash the inwards and the legs with water: and the priest shall bring it all, and burn it upon the altar: it is a burnt sacrifice, an offering made by fire, or a sweet savour unto the LORD. (Leviticus 1:3-13.)

Joseph Smith, commenting on the ancient sacrifices said:

> It is a very prevalent opinion that the sacrifices which were offered were entirely consumed. This was not the case; if you read Leviticus 2:2-3, you will observe that the priests took a part as a memorial and offered it up before the Lord, while the remainder was kept for the maintenance of the priests; so that the offering and sacrifices are not all consumed upon the altar—but the blood is sprinkled, and the fat and certain other portions are consumed. (Joseph Smith, *Teachings of the Prophet Joseph Smith*, pp. 172-173.)

He also said:

> It is generally supposed that sacrifice was entirely done away when the Great Sacrifice, (i.e.) the sacrifice of the Lord Jesus was offered up, and that there will be no necessity for the ordinance of sacrifice in the future; but those who assert this are certainly not acquainted with the duties, privileges and authority of the Priesthood, or with the prophets.
> The offering of sacrifice has ever been connected and forms a part of the duties of the Priesthood. It began with the Priesthood, and will be continued until after the coming of Christ from generation to generation.
> It is not to be understood that the law of Moses will be established again with all its rites and variety of ceremonies; this has never been spoken of by the prophets; but those things which existed prior to Moses' day, namely, sacrifice, will be continued. (*Teachings,*, pp. 172-173.)

Commenting on this, Joseph Fielding Smith said:

> Sacrifice by the shedding of blood was instituted in the days of Adam and of necessity will have to be restored.
> The sacrifice of animals will be done to complete the restoration when the temple spoken of is built; at the beginning of the millennium or in the restoration, blood sacrifices will be performed long enough to complete the fulness of

the restoration in this dispensation. Afterwards sacrifice will be of some other character. (Joseph Fielding Smith, *Doctrines of Salvation*, 3:94.)

The law of sacrifice was practiced from the days of Adam until Christ's crucifixion. At the sacrament of the Lord's Supper the Savior "took bread," and when He had given thanks, He brake it and said,

> Take, eat: this is my body, which is broken for you: this do in remembrance of me.
> After the same manner also he took the cup, when he had supped, saying, This cup is the new testament in my blood: this do ye, as oft as ye drink it, in remembrance of me. (1 Corinthians 11:24-25; see also 1 Corinthians 10:16; Matthew 26:26-28.)

The sacrament is taken today in remembrance of His sacrifice, and animal sacrifice has been stopped by the Lord until the time spoken of by the prophets as quoted. Today we know the meaning of the original sacrifice offered by Adam, and down through the dispensations to the time of Christ, but when Adam first offered sacrifice he did not know the meaning. He simply was obedient.

Yes, Adam and Eve and their children and their children's children were tested by the law of obedience and sacrifice. We do not know how many days, or weeks, or months—or even years—this sacrifice was practiced before Adam received an explanation. The scripture merely states:

> And after many days an angel of the Lord appeared unto Adam, saying: Why dost thou offer sacrifices unto the Lord? And Adam said unto him: I know not, save the Lord commanded me. (Moses 5:6.)

We might wonder how many times this question had been put to Adam by his own wife or family before the angel asked him the same question. Adam was a man of great faith and a very patient man. Patience is also an aspect of the gospel and essential to a person's growth toward becoming like our Heavenly Father.

Adam Learns the Meaning of Blood Sacrifice

> And then the angel spake, saying: This thing is a similitude of the sacrifice of the Only Begotten of the Father, which is full of grace and truth.
> Wherefore, thou shalt do all that thou doest in the name of the Son, and thou shalt repent and call upon God in the name of the Son forevermore. (Moses 5:7-8.)

Adam was taught the gospel of Jesus Christ by an angel of the Lord. We are indebted to Enoch (seventh from Adam) who was able to personally know his great-grandfather seven times removed for more of what the Lord taught Adam. Enoch knew Adam. Adam was still living when Enoch was born.

Enoch was twenty-five years old when he was ordained under the hand of Adam; and he was sixty-five and Adam blessed him (D&C 107:48).

Enoch tells us more of what the Lord taught Adam about the gospel:

And he called upon our father Adam by his own voice, saying: I am God; I made the world, and men before they were in the flesh (Moses 6:51).

The scriptures are only a synopsis of what the Lord taught Adam. He would have told him about the pre-earth world—"men before they were in the flesh." Adam would have been taught about the role of the Savior, Jesus Christ, in the plan of salvation:

And he also said unto him: If thou wilt turn unto me, and hearken unto my voice, and believe, and repent of all thy transgressions, and be baptized, even in water, in the name of mine Only Begotten Son, who is full of grace and truth, which is Jesus Christ, the only name which shall be given under heaven, whereby salvation shall come unto the children of men, ye shall receive the gift of the Holy Ghost, asking all things in his name, and whatsoever ye shall ask, it shall be given you. (Moses 6:52.)

Some have thought that Adam received the gospel in the Garden of Eden as God walked and talked with him—but if he did receive the gospel he forgot it when he became mortal. Note the simple question of Adam on the fundamental question of baptism:

And our father Adam spake unto the Lord, and said: Why is it that men must repent and be baptized in water? And the Lord said unto Adam: Behold I have forgiven thee thy transgression in the Garden of Eden. (Moses 6:53.)

Adam would not have asked such a question if he had already been taught the gospel. The Pearl of Great Price clearly teaches that Adam received the gospel "line upon line, precept upon precept" when he came to earth and mortality after the Fall. The Lord's declaration that "I have forgiven thee thy transgression in the Garden of Eden" was "Good News" to Adam. For years Adam must have felt guilt for his transgression in the garden. When his children and his children's children asked him why they had to suffer pain, sickness, hardships of all kinds, why they had to work so hard to "subdue the earth," why all the weeds and thistles, why all the vicissitudes of life, all Adam and Eve could say was that it was their fault: they had transgressed God's commandment; they had "original guilt."

But with the revelation that, through the atonement of Christ, and then with the principles of repentance and baptism, the Lord had forgiven them of their transgression in the Garden of Eden. They were now free from this guilt. They were free from the conscience of guilt that had weighed upon them because of their transgression.

Enoch puts an interjection in his narrative to indicate how important this information was to Adam and Eve.

The Son of God Has Atoned for Original Guilt

> Hence came the saying abroad among the people, that the Son of God hath atoned for original guilt, wherein the sins of the parents cannot be answered upon the heads of the children, for they are whole from the foundation of the world (Moses 6:54).

Mormon's inspired epistle to Moroni on this subject is pertinent. The word of the Lord came to Mormon by the power of the Holy Ghost saying, ". . . little children are whole, for they are not capable of committing sin; wherefore the curse of Adam is taken from them in me, that it hath no power over them" (Moroni 8:8).

The Lord did tell Adam that children are born into an environment of sin in this world and that, as they grow up, they will be tempted and experience sin and its effects—that they will "taste the bitter, that they may know to prize the good. And it is given unto them to know good from evil." Moses 6:55-56.) Then the challenge is given to Adam (and to every parent) to teach the basic principles of the gospel to their children. Adam was told to teach these things freely to his children:

> That by reason of transgression cometh the fall, which fall bringeth death, and inasmuch as ye were born into the world by water, and blood, and the spirit, which I have made, and so became of dust a living soul, even so ye must be born again into the kingdom of heaven, of water, and of the Spirit, and be cleansed by blood, even the blood of mine Only Begotten; that ye might be sanctified from all sin, and enjoy the words of eternal life in this world, and eternal life in the world to come, even immortal glory (Moses 6:59).

A Vivid Analogy of Birth and Baptism

A vivid analogy comparing mortal birth with baptism was given to Adam. When Adam and Eve had their children there were no nice, white-sheeted hospitals with doctors and nurses, no antiseptically clean delivery rooms to help Eve and her daughters when their babies were born. Birth was (and still is) a vivid experience for those sensitive enough to witness and appreciate it.

Water surrounds and protects the baby in the mother's womb. When, after nine months, the "water breaks" birth is imminent. In the process of birth blood is shed. The placenta—the vascular organ in the womb with its thicket of blood vessels—is shed after the birth. Sometimes there is a tearing of the mother in the birth process: blood is literally shed. There is the anxious moment when the baby takes its first independent breath—when its spirit gives it independent life. The baby lives! Sometimes, if the umbilical cord is around the neck of the infant, or because of other problems, the baby is born dead—a "still born." How important the spirit is!

There is a miracle in every birth and three elements which are most essential: Water, Blood, and Spirit. Because he went through the birth experience of his children and grandchildren Adam had a vivid awareness of these essential elements. He was instructed to teach this great analogy to his children:

> And inasmuch as ye were born into the world by water, and blood, and the spirit, which I have made, and so became of dust a living soul, even so ye must be born again into the kingdom of heaven, of water, and of the Spirit, and be cleansed by blood, even the blood of mine Only Begotten; that ye might be sanctified from all sin, and enjoy the words of eternal life in this world, and eternal life in the world to come, even immortal glory (Moses 6:59).

In the analogy of birth with the "new birth into the kingdom of heaven" the waters of the baptismal font—or a river, or a lake—are symbolic of the water that surrounds and protects the baby in the mother's womb. The blood of Jesus Christ, which was shed in Gethsemane and upon the cross, is analogous to our mortal birth wherein our mother's blood was shed for us. Jesus shed his blood for us "as a mother" in helping us to be "born into the kingdom of heaven." The new spirit we must receive lest we be "stillborns" in the kingdom is the Holy Ghost. The Spirit is as essential to our new birth into the kingdom of heaven as our own spirit is to the life of our mortal bodies. Without this Spirit we are "dead" to the kingdom of heaven.

A "Pearl" of the Pearl of Great Price

Now comes a "pearl" of the Pearl of Great Price. No more succinct words than these, given to Adam to summarize the gospel, are presented in the scriptures:

> FOR BY THE WATER YE KEEP THE COMMANDMENT: BY THE SPIRIT YE ARE JUSTIFIED, AND BY THE BLOOD YE ARE SANCTIFIED (Moses 6:60).

When Adam and all mankind humble themselves, have faith in Jesus Christ and desire to do what he tells us to do, when we truly repent and follow after him and witness unto the Father that we will be obedient unto him in keeping his commandments, we will be baptized by someone having the proper authority to perform this essential ordinance—thus "by the water ye keep the commandment."

Sanctification or cleansing, purifying us, taking away our sins, making us holy, making us eligible, being our advocate, atoning for us, have all been done for us by the Savior—by His Blood. Thus "by the blood [of Jesus Christ] ye are sanctified."

How in the world can we be justified in having all this done for us? How can we be justified in having someone like the Savior atone for our sins?

> How great the wisdom and the love that filled the courts on high,
> And sent the Savior from above to suffer, bleed and die!

His precious blood he freely spilt; His life he freely gave,
A sinless sacrifice for guilt, a dying world to save.

By strict obedience Jesus won the prize with glory rife:
"Thy will, O God, not mine be done," Adorned his mortal life.

He marked the path and led the way, and every point defines
To light and life and endless day Where God's full presence shines.

("How Great the Wisdom and the Love," *Hymns*, p. 68.)

"Oh, it is wonderful that he should care for me, enough to die for me! Oh, it is wonderful, wonderful to me!" But how am I justified? What makes it right? What makes it fair or excusable for Him to do all of this for all of us?

I stand all amazed at the love Jesus offers me,
Confused at the grace that so fully he proffers me;
I tremble to know that for me he was crucified,
That for me, a sinner, he suffered, he bled and died.

I marvel that he would descend from his throne divine
To rescue a soul so rebellious and proud as mine;
That he should extend his great love unto such as I,
Sufficient to own, to redeem, and to justify.

("I Stand All Amazed," *Hymns*, p. 80.)

Again, how am I justified? The answer comes from the Pearl of Great Price: ". . . by the Spirit ye are justified." If I will receive and live to keep the Spirit, then I am justified. If I will offer unto the Savior a "broken heart and a contrite spirit" and receive the fire and the Holy Ghost (see 3 Nephi 9:20) deeply into my soul, then I am justified. It is this Spirit that enables me to have the "charity" that Paul talks about—"Now abideth faith, hope, charity, these three; but the greatest of these is charity" (1 Corinthians 13:13). No person can have this "charity," or pure love of Christ, without the Spirit—nor the Spirit without having this "charity." When I have these deep feelings of love and charity, then I am justified in having the Savior sanctify me through His Blood.

Great Synonyms of the Spirit

Therefore it [the Spirit] is given to abide in you; the record of heaven; the Comforter; the peaceable things of immortal glory; the truth of all things; that which quickeneth all things, which maketh alive all things; that which knoweth all things, and hath all power according to wisdom, mercy, truth, justice, and judgment (Moses 6:61).

The phrases are all great synonyms of the Spirit that were taught to Adam and are recorded for us to try to understand also.

This is the plan of salvation unto all men, through the blood of mine Only Begotten, who shall come in the meridian of time (Moses 6:62).

Through Adam's receiving of the true depth and significance of faith in Jesus Christ, repentance, baptism by immersion for the remission of his sins by someone having authority, and the laying on of hands for the gift of the Holy Ghost; and by living by that Spirit, Adam received the plan of salvation unto all men—the Fullness of the Gospel.

Adam Is Baptized

When the Lord had spoken with Adam, our father, "Adam cried unto the Lord" (Moses 6:64). This is a most poignant phrase. When a man "cries" it is the expression of his deepest emotions. When Adam "cried unto the Lord" his tears were of the Spirit and he was moved with gratitude to the Lord for the "Good News"—the gospel—that had been given to him. Tears of joy that express our heartfelt thanksgiving to the Lord for our blessings, for our understanding of the gospel, for feeling some of His love and mercy are some of the manifestations of the Spirit of the Lord in us.

> And he was caught away by the Spirit of the Lord, and was carried down into the water, and was laid under the water, and was brought forth out of the water.
> And thus he was baptized, and the Spirit of God descended upon him, and thus he was born of the Spirit, and became quickened in the inner man.
> And he heard a voice out of heaven, saying: Thou art baptized with fire, and with the Holy Ghost. This is the record of the Father, and the Son, from henceforth and forever. (Moses 6:64-66.)

Adam Is Ordained to the Higher Priesthood

After Adam was baptized and received the Holy Ghost, he was ordained to the priesthood. He was made a presiding high priest over the kingdom of God on earth. Joseph Smith said: "Christ is the Great High Priest; Adam next" (Joseph Smith, *Documentary History of the Church*, 3:387-388). Adam is the head and the keys were first given to him, and by him to others. He will have to give an account of his priesthood stewardship, and we to him. Adam is Michael the Archangel, spoken of in scriptures (*Documentary History of the Church*, p. 386; also Revelation 12:7). Joseph Smith further stated: "The priesthood is an everlasting principle, and existed with God from eternity, and will to eternity, without beginning of days or end of years. The keys have to be brought from heaven whenever the gospel is sent. When they are revealed from heaven, it is by Adam's authority." (*Documentary History of the Church*, 3:386.)

After Adam was ordained to the priesthood, the Lord said:

> And thou art after the order of him who was without beginning of days or end of years, from all eternity to all eternity.
> Behold, thou art one in me, a son of God; and thus may all become my sons. Amen. (Moses 6:67-68.)

Summary of Chapter Seven

1. Adam and Eve began their "pioneering" of this earth after the Fall without a full understanding of the gospel, or a true understanding of their purpose for being on earth.

2. The Lord watched over Adam and Eve and their children that they would not die temporally until the gospel was given to them.

3. Adam and Eve were apparently grandparents before they prayed significantly to the Lord and received an answer. "They heard the voice of the Lord from the way toward the Garden of Eden" (Moses 5:4).

4. Adam and Eve learned faith and obedience to the Lord.

5. Adam and Eve were told to offer sacrifice by the shedding of blood of the "firstlings of their flocks."

6. Adam and Eve learned that blood sacrifice was in similitude of the sacrifice of the Only Begotten of the Father.

7. Adam was taught the gospel of Jesus Christ by an angel of the Lord.

8. Adam learned about the plan of salvation from the angel.

9. Adam learned why men must repent and be baptized, and that the Son of God would atone for original guilt.

10. Baptism is a vivid analogy of birth if it is fully understood.

11. This "pearl" of the Pearl of Great Price was given to Adam: "By the water ye keep the commandment; by the Spirit ye are justified, and by the blood ye are sanctified (Moses 6:60).

12. Adam was baptized, received the Holy Ghost, and was ordained to the higher priesthood after the order of the Son of God.

13. Adam holds the keys of the higher priesthood for this earth under Christ's direction.

Chapter Eight

The First Great Apostasy—
Adam and Eve's Children
Reject the Gospel

Eve Receives and Believes the Gospel

After Adam received the gospel and was ordained to the priesthood, he was filled with the Spirit of the Lord:

> And in that day Adam blessed God and was filled, and began to prophesy concerning all the families of the earth, saying: Blessed be the name of God, for because of my transgression my eyes are opened, and in this life I shall have joy, and again in the flesh I shall see God (Moses 5:10).

In Enoch's account of Adam receiving the gospel (Moses 6:51-68), no mention is made of Eve being with Adam. The events of Moses 5:9-11 seem to have occurred after Enoch's account in Moses 6:51-68. Perhaps Eve was not there; however, the scripture is clear that she was present when "Adam was filled" with the Holy Ghost and prophesied and bore his fervent testimony of the gospel quoted above. She not only heard, but she accepted and understood the gospel.

It is every man's right, his duty, and his responsibility to teach his wife, in love and consideration, the gospel of Jesus Christ. In the order of heaven a righteous man, who honors his priesthood literally and figuratively, represents the Lord to his wife. The wife is to follow the husband as he follows and obeys the Lord. Eve was receptive and willing to accept the honest and fervent testimony of her husband borne through the Spirit:

> And Eve, his wife, heard all these things [Adam's testimony?] and was glad, saying: Were it not for our transgression we never should have had seed, and never should have known good and evil, and the joy of our redemption, and the eternal life which God giveth unto all the obedient (Moses 5:11).

It is a great principle of faith to learn to be receptive to a man who bears a fervent witness of God through the power of the Holy Ghost. Adam's wife and his descendants had to rely upon Adam's testimony of the gospel. Adam's children had to rely upon the testimony of their father for the proof of the existence of God. In the *Lectures on Faith*, as delivered at the School of the Prophets at Kirtland, Ohio, the Prophet Joseph said:

What testimony had the immediate descendents of Adam, in the proof of the existence of God? The testimony of their father. And after they were made acquainted with his existence, by the testimony of their father, they were dependent upon the exercise of their own faith, for a knowledge of his character, perfections, and attributes.

Had any other of the human family, besides Adam, a knowledge of the existence of God, in the first instance, by any other means then human testimony? They had not. For previous to the time that they could have power to obtain a manifestation for themselves, the all-important fact had been communicated to them by their common father; and so from father to child the knowledge was communicated as extensively as the knowledge of his existence was known; for it was by this means, in the first instance, that men had a knowledge of his existence. (*Lectures on Faith*, ii, 35, 36, p. 25.)

It began with Adam's testimony. His testimony converted his wife. Together "Adam and Eve blessed the name of God, and they made all things known unto their sons and their daughters" (Moses 5:12).

The First Children Reject the Gospel

How was the testimony of the first parents received by the sons and daughters? How would the testimony of a modern Adam and Eve be received today? How would the children, who were old enough to have children of their own, accept the testimony of their parents if they were not taught the gospel when they were young? What proof would the grown children have of their parent's testimonies? Only the testimony of the Spirit. What of children who have been taught the gospel in their youth by faithful parents? Is there any guarantee that they will accept and retain the gospel when they get older? No one can "inherit the gospel." We can be born under the covenant; we can be raised in the environment of the gospel—all of this helps, but we cannot live on "reflected light" forever. We cannot live on the testimony of our parents alone. Every child of every parent must hear the testimony and then know, by the power and witness of the Holy Ghost, whether that testimony is true.

Of the first dispensation, the Pearl of Great Price states: "And the Lord God called upon men by the Holy Ghost everywhere and commanded them that they should repent" (Moses 5:14). But in the days of Adam (and today):

Satan came among them, saying: I am also a son of God; and he commanded them, saying: Believe it not; and they believed it not, and they loved Satan more than God. And men began from that time forth to be carnal, sensual, and devilish. (Moses 5:13.)

Many of Adams and Eve's sons and daughters rejected their testimony of the gospel. This was the first great apostasy on earth. The apostasy has been going on ever since. Every time the testimony of a righteous man, or woman, filled with the Holy Ghost is rejected there is an apostasy of those who reject. With the rejection comes even more of the influence of Satan in their lives so that they become motivated by their own selfish, carnal, sensual, devilish desires when they love Satan more than they love God. Probably no greater heartache, no greater sorrow, can come to a righteous parent than to have a son or daughter reject the truth. But theirs is a God-like sorrow felt by such notables as Adam and Eve. Their sorrow is but an experience of God; how many of His children have caused him grief—and heartache?

Adam and Eve Pray for Another Child

Adam and Eve must have felt that, if they could just start earlier with their children, it would help them to accept and retain the gospel. "Train up a child in the way he should go: and when he is old, he will not depart from it" (Proverbs 22:6) was the early faith of Adam and Eve. Certainly this is a worthy desire—even commandment—for parents to teach their children before they are eight years of age (D&C 68:25).

A righteous environment can help. "Teach them, guide them, help them find the way"—this is important: to hold family home evening when they are young; to teach the little ones prayer as some of their first words; to lead them to church where they hear the little stories of the nursery about Jesus and about love; to send them to Primary, Sunday School, seminary, institute, priesthood meetings, Relief Society, Young Womens programs, Young Mens programs—all of these can and do help. We don't want to lose one of our children, do we? A beautiful little baby direct from Heavenly Father has so much potential for good—or for evil.

> And Adam and Eve, his wife, ceased not to call upon God. And Adam knew Eve his wife, and she conceived and bare Cain, and said: I have gotten a man from the Lord; wherefore he may not reject his words. (Moses 5:16.)

How exciting it must have been for Adam and Eve to have a beautiful baby boy to whom they could teach the gospel right from the cradle. Born under the covenant—what a blessing—born to goodly parents with all the advantages of the gospel from "day one" of their lives. Many of those born today could identify with the environment of Cain. Eve exclaims: "I have gotten a man from the Lord; wherefore he may not reject his words." But . . . . . .

Cain Hearkened Not

> But behold, Cain hearkened not, saying: Who is the Lord that I should know him (Moses 5:16)?

There is more to any person than heredity and environment. There is the free agency of man and his own uncreated intelligence, his own free will.

A man can pick a path far different than the path desired by parents—or by God. Although he was born innocent, as Cain began to grow up, "sin conceived in his heart."

Adam and Eve had another son whom they called Abel. "Abel hearkened unto the voice of the Lord" (Moses 5:17). "And Cain loved Satan more than God" (Moses 5:18). The stage is set for a conflict because of the enmity between the followers of Satan and the followers of the Lord:

> And in the process of time it came to pass that Cain brought of the fruit of the ground an offering unto the Lord.
> And Abel he also brought of the firstlings of his flock, and of the fat thereof. And the Lord had respect unto Abel, and to his offering;
> But unto Cain, and to his offering, he had not respect. Now Satan knew this, and it pleased him. And Cain was very wroth, and his countenance fell.
> And the Lord said unto Cain: Why art thou wroth? Why is thy countenance fallen?
> If thou doest well, thou shalt be accepted. And if thou doest not well, sin lieth at the door, and Satan desireth to have thee; and except thou shalt hearken unto my commandments, I will deliver thee up, and it shall be unto thee according to his desire. And thou shalt rule over him;
> For from this time forth thou shalt be the father of his lies; thou shalt be called Perdition; for thou wast also before the world. (Moses 5:19-24.)

Why Was Cain's Offering Rejected?

In the first place Satan had commanded Cain to make the offering—and it was a deliberate distortion of the sacrifice the Lord had taught Adam and his sons to offer. Instead of a blood sacrifice, which was symbolic of the sacrifice of the blood of Jesus Christ, Satan told Cain to use a substitute—"the fruit of the ground." Cain knew he was not offering the sacrifice correctly. Cain was in open defiance of God, of the sacredness of the sacrifice and of all it represented. (See *Teachings of the Prophet Joseph Smith*, p. 58.)

"Cain was very wroth, and his countenance fell." Who made Cain angry? Who made Cain "mad." Who makes you "mad"? Who makes you and me angry? Listen to Dr. Gene Emmet Clark, a modern writer and psychologist, speak in our language and in our day to this subject: "You Make You Mad."

> Do you believe this statement that follows? Your Attitude toward other people is not what they make it, but what you make it.
> Before you say, "No, and it's a lot of nonsense," reserve judgment at least until you have finished these two pages. When we close our minds, we're always shutting out more than we're shutting in.
> The simple truth is, you can make your attitude about anything whatever you want it to be.
> In the first place, you can think about anything you want to, if you want to think about London right now, you can do it. And you choose how you will

think about it. If you want to think of it as a dirty city where violent crimes are committed in the fog and where "everybody hates Americans", you can do so. If you prefer to think of London as the home of the beautiful Houses of Parliament buildings, where a great painting of the Pilgrims and the Mayflower hangs on the wall, honoring America's founding fathers, you can do that.

You make the choice of what you want to think about anything or anyone.

But I can hear you say, "You don't know that brother-in-law of mine—he makes me so mad!"

No, he doesn't. You make you mad. Who else could? No one but you has the power to make you angry. How can anyone else choose your feeling for you?

You say, "But that neighbor of mine next door—he makes me sick!" No, you make you sick. Only you can decide what feelings you are going to entertain.

Things happen around you and things are said, that's true—but they aren't what upset you. It's your reaction to them that upsets you, if it's a reaction of anger or resentment or fear.

In any situation, you always have a choice of reactions. And the choice you make determines how the situation will affect you.

If there is criticism around you, or unfriendliness, or jealousy, it has no power whatever to affect you—even if it's directed at you—unless you choose to take it into your own consciousness. You have to let it in and react to it. Then it does its damage. But not until then. Until then it belongs to the other fellow and has nothing to do with you at all.

Did you really think that anyone but you can choose your feelings and attitudes? (Reprinted from *Let's Talk About You!* 2936 Neb. Ave., Santa Monica, Calif. 90404, p. 6-7.)

So who made Cain angry? Cain made Cain angry. The Lord told Cain: "If thou doest well, thou shalt be accepted. And if thou doest not well, sin lieth at the door." (Moses 5:23.) Cain allowed the seeds of hate, animosity, and jealousy against his brother Abel to take root in his heart. Cain allowed Satan to tempt him so that he coveted his brother's flocks and even his brother's life. He entered into a "secret combination" (see Ether 8:18) with Satan and plotted the diabolical, premeditated murder of his brother. Nor was Cain alone in his wickedness: he took one of his other brother's daughters to wife, "and they loved Satan more than God" (Moses 5:28). One day, according to plan, Cain rose up against Abel and slew him and then "gloried in that which he had done" (Moses 5:33).

> And the Lord said unto Cain: Where is Abel, thy brother? And he said: I know not. Am I my brother's keeper?
>
> And the Lord said: What hast thou done? The voice of thy brother's blood cries unto me from the ground.
>
> And now thou shalt be cursed from the earth which hath opened her mouth to receive thy brother's blood from thy hand. (Moses 5:34-36.)

Cain did not take the responsibility for his sin. He blamed it on Satan. He blamed it on his brother's flocks. He even blamed God "for his offering thou didst accept and not mine" (Moses 5:38). When the Lord confronted him and told him he would be a fugitive and a vagabond, Cain was concerned only about one thing—his own "skin." No remorse, no concern about the feelings of his parents nor of the feelings of Abel's other brothers and sisters; Cain was concerned only about himself.

Punishment Given to Cain

This is the first murder recorded in the scriptures. Later the Lord would give this law: "Whoso sheddeth man's blood, by man shall his blood be shed: for in the image of God made he man" (Genesis 9:6). Yet, on this occasion, the Lord said:

> Whosoever slayeth thee, vengeance shall be taken on him sevenfold. And I the Lord set a mark upon Cain, lest any finding him should kill him.
> And Cain was shut out from the presence of the Lord, and with his wife and many of his brethren dwelt in the land of Nod, on the east of Eden. (Moses 5:40-41.)

As a punishment the Lord consigned the wicked Cain to be a fugitive and a vagabond, and a mark was placed upon him which would reveal his identity. Brigham Young said this mark ". . . is the flat nose and black skin" (*Journal of Discourses*, 7:290).

On the sad character Cain, an interesting story comes to us from Lycurgus A. Wilson's book on the life of David W. Patten. Here is an extract from a letter by Abraham O. Smoot giving his recollection of David Patten's account of meeting "a very remarkable person who had represented himself as being Cain."

> As I was riding along the road on my mule I suddenly noticed a very strange personage walking beside me . . . His head was about even with my shoulders as I sat in my saddle. He wore no clothing, but was covered with hair. His skin was very dark. I asked him where he dwelt and he replied that he had no home, that he was a wanderer in the earth and traveled to and fro. He said he was a very miserable creature, that he had earnestly sought death during his sojourn upon the earth, but that he could not die, and his mission was to destroy the souls of men. About the time he expressed himself thus, I rebuked him in the name of the Lord Jesus Christ and by virtue of the Holy Priesthood, and commanded him to go hence, and he immediately departed out of my sight. . . . (Quoted from Spencer W. Kimball, *The Miracle of Forgiveness*, p. 127-128.)

This is, indeed, a strange story. It is possible that Cain is "alive" today only in that the secrets of murder and destruction are still with us today. (See Ether 8:20.) In other words, Cain "lives" today because there are still followers of Satan who are as blood thirsty and as evil as Cain. There is no scriptural indication that Cain survived the flood at the time of Noah. One of his descendants, Egyptus, the wife of Ham, did survive the flood (see Abraham 1:22-24) and "thus the blood of the Canaanites was preserved in the land." (More will be said about this later.)

Enoch, the seventh from Adam, was shown a great panoramic vision of the world and "beheld the residue of the people which were the sons of Adam; and they were a mixture of all the seed of Adam save it was the seed of Cain, for *the seed of Cain were black*, and had not place among them" (Moses 7:22; italics added).

Book of Mormon Explanation for Dark Skin

Although about a different people, at a different time, and under different circumstances, the Book of Mormon gives an explanation for the dark skin which came upon the Lamanites. This may also give an explanation as to why Cain and his posterity were given a dark skin:

> And the skins of the Lamanites were dark, according to the mark which was set upon their fathers, which was a curse upon them because of their transgression and their rebellion against their brethren, who consisted of Nephi, Jacob, and Joseph, and Sam, who were just and holy men.
>
> And their brethren sought to destroy them, therefore they were cursed; and the Lord God set a mark upon them, yea, upon Laman and Lemuel, and also the sons of Ishmael, and Ishmaelitish women.
>
> And this was done that their seed might be distinguished from the seed of their brethren, that thereby the Lord God might preserve his people, *that they might not mix and believe in incorrect traditions* which would prove their destruction.
>
> And it came to pass that whosoever did mingle his seed with that of the Lamanites did bring the same curse upon his seed. (Alma 3:6-9; italics added.)

Because Cain and his followers set up evil "secret combinations," the Lord may well have marked them with a dark skin so that Adam and Eve's other children might not intermarry and "believe in incorrect traditions which would prove their destruction."

Song of Solomon Explanation for Dark Skin

The chiding of the black Ethiopian lover of Solomon comes to mind:

> I am black, but comely, O ye daughters of Jerusalem, [black] as the tents of Kedar, as the curtains of Solomon.
>
> Look not upon me, because I am black, because the sun hath looked upon me. (Song of Solomon 1:5-6.)

This black woman was trying to say she was black because "the sun hath looked upon me." There are many today who hold to this view—that because of the environmental influence of the sun's rays on the bodies of the people of Africa (or other peoples near the equator) over the thousands of years, the pigmentation of the skin has changed—hence, a blackness.

The only observable difference between white skin and black skin is the increased amounts of melanin, or black, pigmentation. There has been no scientific explanation to prove that exposure to the sun's rays causes such changes in the pigmentation. Science has no real explanation as to why there are different races. We will stay with the scriptural explanation that God spoke and it was done.

On June 8, 1978, the Lord, through a prophet, lifted the curse from Cain's posterity. (See Official Declaration 2, D&C.) We might paraphrase the second article of faith and say anew: "We believe that men will be punished for their own sins and *not for Cain's transgression.*"

Genealogy of Cain

After Cain killed Abel, and after the Lord pronounced the curse and the mark upon him, the Pearl of Great Price continues:

> And Cain was shut out from the presence of the Lord, and with his wife and many of his brethren dwelt in the land of Nod, on the east of Eden.
> . . . And he also begat many sons and daughters. (Moses 5:41-42.)

Six generations of the genealogy of Cain are given. The names of the sons of Cain who were, apparently, the eldest are given in a patriarchal order (see Moses 5:43):

Cain
|
Enoch
|
Irad
|
Mahujael
|
Methusael
|
Lamech

Lamech was a follower of Cain and also of Satan. He entered into a covenant with Satan after the manner of Cain. He became "Master Mahan" (see Moses 5:49), master of the great and evil secrets which were given to Cain by the devil. These were called "secret combinations" (Moses 5:51; Ether 8:18) and their works were in the dark. They included murder, intrigue, lying, stealing, carnal and sensual sex perversions, and all manner of wickedness and whoredoms.

Lamech was not the only one to accept the secret combinations. Many of Adam's other white-skinned sons and daughters also entered into the secret combinations and "thus the works of darkness began to prevail among all the sons of men" (Moses 5:55).

Secret Combinations

It has never been just the black descendants of Cain who have originated and perpetuated the secret combinations of Satan. Although they began with Cain, the secret combinations have been kept up by the power of the devil to administer the oaths and secrets unto all people—to help those who sought power to gain power, and to murder, and to plunder, and to lie, and to commit all manner of wickedness, and whoredoms, and abominations.

Moroni, the last Book of Mormon prophet, said such combinations were very prevalent among the great, white Jaredite civilization and also among the white Nephite nation. He said:

> And now, I, Moroni, do not write the manner of their oaths and combinations, for it hath been made known unto me that they are had among all people, and they are had among the Lamanites.
>
> And they have caused the destruction of this people of whom I am now speaking [the Jaredites], and also the destruction of the people of Nephi.
>
> And whatsoever nation shall uphold such secret combinations, to get power and gain, until they shall spread over the nation, behold, they shall be destroyed. (Ether 8:20-22).

Conclusion

As we conclude this chapter we need to see that the real "darkness" in Cain, and in his followers, was not the black skin but the darkness that was in their minds because they did not accept the light of the gospel. We must also see that it was not just the black seed of Cain that rejected the gospel. Many of Adam and Eve's other children, in that first dispensation of the world, also rejected the truth. Black skin does not indicate evil. White skin does not indicate good.

Viktor Frankl, survivor of the German concentration camps, and the extreme racist ideas of Hitler and his sadistic followers, said:

> From all this we may learn that there are two races of men in this world, but only these two—the "race" of the decent man and the "race" of the indecent man. Both are found everywhere; they penetrate into all groups of society. No group consists entirely of decent or indecent people. In this sense, no group is of "pure race." (*Man's Search for Meaning*, p. 137.)

We should also conclude this chapter by saying that, although the works of darkness of evil men "began to prevail among all the sons of men," the gospel was preached from the beginning:

> Being declared by holy angels sent forth from the presence of God, and by his own voice, and by the gift of the Holy Ghost.
>
> And thus all things were confirmed unto Adam, by an holy ordinance, and the Gospel preached, and a decree sent forth, that it should be in the world, until the end thereof; and thus it was. Amen. (Moses 5:58-59.)

Summary of Chapter Eight

1. Adam taught Eve the gospel and she accepted it. It is every man's right, his duty, and his responsibility to teach his wife, in love and consideration as well as by example, the gospel of Jesus Christ.

2. Adam and Eve's first children rejected the gospel. This was the first great apostasy.

3. Adam and Eve prayed for another child in order to teach, earlier, the gospel principles and teachings. Cain was born.

4. Cain hearkened not to the Lord nor to Adam's teachings but followed after Satan.

5. Cain deliberately offered a distortion of the sacrifice the Lord had taught Adam to offer; thus Cain's offering was rejected.

6. The Book of Mormon explanation as to why a dark skin was placed on the Lamanites was "that they might not mix and believe in incorrect traditions" (Alma 3:8). Perhaps it is the same with black skin placed on the descendants of Cain.

7. White descendants of Adam as well as black descendants of Cain have both perpetuated "secret combinations" of Satan.

8. There are only two races in the world: The "race" of the decent man—and the "race" of the indecent man.

Chapter Nine

Deeper Roots of the Black Civilization

Chapter five in Moses contains interesting information on Cain's posterity. Five generations from Cain a man named Lamech is mentioned. Lamech had two wives; one was Adah, the other, Zillah. Adah had a son named Jabal; they were keepers of cattle and dwelt in tents. Jabal's brother was named Jubal, a musician, and "the father of all such as handle the harp and organ (Moses 5:45).

Lamech's other wife, Zillah, had a son named Tubal Cain ". . . an instructor of every artificer in brass and iron" (Moses 5:46). Thus these early descendants of Cain were not ignorant savages with no culture and no learning. Some were highly intelligent people capable of development in music, industry, and creativity in metal.

In a book called _The Harp of Ethiopia_, there are some poetic lines that tell us some things often overlooked in the early history of the blacks:

Awake, O harp, and ring out clear,
Thy mournful notes let all men hear;
Start from Creation's early morn,
Speak ye to nations yet unborn,
In blood and sorrow do thou trace
The tortuous journey of a race
From superstition's vile discord,
Unto the knowledge of our Lord.

Of its beginning do thou ring,
Of its past glory, proudly sing,
Sing of its kingdoms perished gone,
Sing of its arts first to us known,
Sing of its architectural skill,
How nature yielded to its will;
Tell how as conquering warriors grand,
Subdued they all adjacent land.

Tell how in pomp and splendor bright,
Its haughty rulers did delight,
To dazzle with their wealth and gold,
The world's important kingdoms old.
Tell how the art to read and write
Its dusky solons brought to light;
Of all its lofty grandeur tell,—
Just how it rose and why it fell.

Sing thou of past Egyptian lore,
The greatest in the days of yore . . .
(M. N. Corbett, *The Harp of Ethiopia*, p. 18-19.)

Black studies have, quite recently, brought to light evidence of a great cultural heritage in the black descendants of Cain. The poem quoted above is but a small excerpt to illustrate what is being written and told to the world about black culture and heritage. Evidence is surfacing to prove that there were black civilizations whose art and architecture were as great as that in European, or Oriental, or Early American civilizations.

These kingdoms of the black civilizations had farms and crops that were highly productive. These kingdoms of old were able to "dazzle with wealth and gold." Their ancient peoples could read and write. They were an industrious, highly developed people. One of the earliest and best-known of these past kingdoms was the mighty Egyptian civilization whose roots are black. Let us tell how the Pearl of Great Price verifies this black beginning of Egypt.

Egyptian Roots

We learn that the sister of Tubal Cain was called Naamah (Moses 5:46). Since this is all the record tells of her (and the scriptures are not prone to mention women without a significant reason) one wonders if Naamah could have been the "forbidden one" that Noah's son, Ham, married. (See Abraham 1:23-24.) There may not be enough generations between them for this but the possibility remains.

Book of Mormon prophets warned the Nephites not to marry the Lamanites and mix with their people, not to "believe in incorrect traditions which would prove their destruction" (Alma 3:8). Noah tried to teach his family the same principle. Although he was warned against marrying a descendant of Cain, Ham disobeyed his father. He married Egyptus "which in the Chaldean signifies Egypt, which signifies that which is forbidden" (Abraham 1:23).

Noah had accepted the fullness of the gospel and was ordained to the priesthood at the age of ten under the hand of Methuselah (D&C 107:52).

Noah ordained his sons Japeth, Shem, and Ham to the priesthood—thus they were called "the sons of God." All who are faithful, all who receive the gospel and are baptized who receive the Holy Ghost and are ordained to the priesthood, and who remain faithful are called "the sons of God." (see Moses 6:68; also D&C 84:33-35.) Those who did not accept the gospel, or who did not remain faithful, were called "the sons of men."

> And Noah and his sons hearkened unto the Lord, and gave heed; and they were called the sons of God.
> And when these men began to multiply on the face of the earth, and daughters were born unto them, the sons of men saw that their daughters were fair, and they took them wives even as they chose.
> And the Lord said unto Noah, the daughters of thy sons have sold themselves, for behold, mine anger is kindled against the sons of men, for they will not hearken to my voice. (JST, Genesis 8:1-3.)

Thus we see that Noah's granddaughters were beautiful girls who attracted non-member young men, non-priesthood holders—gentiles, non-believers, "sons of men." Ham, son of Noah, also was attracted to the "gentiles." He not only married out of the faith; he married a black descendant of Cain.

D&C 107:41-56 The Priesthood Patriarchal Order	Moses 5:42-46 Cain's Lineage
Adam ————————————	———————————— Cain
Seth	Enoch
Enos	Irad
Cainan	Mahujael
Mahalaleel	Mathusael
Jared	Lamech—two wives:
Methuselah	Adah Zillah
Lamech	Jabal Jubal
Noah	& Jubal Cain
Shem——Japeth——Ham	(sister) Naamah
(Genesis 10:21, 31; 11:10-26) marries ———→	"Egyptus"—Forbidden
	Abraham 1:21-25
	Egyptus (daughter)
	First Pharoah

Marriage Outside the Church

It is a serious step to marry outside the faith or outside the Church. Often church standards are compromised and attendance at meetings decreases. Generations are affected by such marriages. Spirits who might have received a great birthright are often deprived of this blessing because of strife between the member and non-member. Blessings of baptism, confirmation, priesthood, and other opportunities may not be available to these children.

President Joseph F. Smith said:

> I would rather take one of my children to the grave than I would see him turn away from this gospel. I would rather take my children to the cemetery and see them buried in innocence, than I would see them corrupted by the ways of the world. I would rather go myself to the grave than to be associated with a wife outside of the bonds of the new and everlasting covenant. Now, I hold it just so sacred; but some members of the Church do not so regard the matter. Some people feel that it does not make very much difference whether a girl marries a man in the Church, full of the faith of the gospel, or an unbeliever. Some of our young people have married outside of the Church; but very few of those who have done it have failed to come to grief. . . .
>
> There is nothing that I can think of, in a religious way, that would grieve me more intensely than to see one of my boys marry an unbelieving girl, or one of my girls marry an unbelieving man. (Joseph F. Smith, *Gospel Doctrine,* p. 279.)

Since the days of the ancient patriarchs, the "sons of God" have been told not to intermarry with other races because this usually meant marrying out of the faith. Esau grieved his parents by marrying Hittite women (Genesis 6:2-3). Abraham was very concerned that Isaac marry well and that he not marry any of the Canaanite daughters (Genesis 24:2-3). Abraham wanted Isaac to marry someone who would help Isaac keep the priesthood covenants. Rebekah feared lest Jacob marry one of the daughters of Heth, and so she sent him to her brother, Laban (Genesis 27:43-46). Isaac, too, although he was very old, knew the best thing for their son Jacob was not to take a wife of the daughters of Canaan (Genesis 28:1). Samson's father asked his son why he sought after those outside their own people (Judges 14:3).

It is not race prejudice, but keeping the races separate in their marriages, that seems to be the Lord's decree through the prophets. Joseph Smith said: "Had I anything to do with the Negro, I would confine them by strict law to their own species, and put them on a national equalization." (*Teachings of the Prophet Joseph Smith*, p. 270.)

Egyptian Civilization Descended from Ham and Egyptus

In spite of the Lord's decree through the prophets not to marry outside of their race, and especially out of their faith, Ham—son of Noah—

disobeyed and thus "from Ham, sprang the race which preserved the curse in the land" (Abraham 1:24). Perhaps Ham taught Egyptus (or Naamah) the gospel. She may have been baptized before the flood. The apostle Peter said (concerning the flood and those saved): ". . . wherein few, that is, eight souls were saved *by water*. The like figure whereunto even baptism doth *also* now save us." (1 Peter 3:20-21; italics added.) Note the scripture says "by" water, not "from" water. To be saved "by water," in the gospel sense, is to be baptized.

The influence of Ham's wife is to be especially noted. In the scriptures women are rarely mentioned, yet Egyptus is credited with having a daughter whose son is the first Pharaoh of Egypt—and he is a righteous Pharaoh. Here is the scriptural account as given by Abraham:

> . . . Which Pharaoh signifies king by royal blood.
> Now this king of Egypt was a descendant from the loins of Ham, and was a partaker of the blood of the Canaanites by birth.
> From this descent sprang all the Egyptians, and thus the blood of the Canaanites was preserved in the land.
> The land of Egypt being first discovered by a woman, who was the daughter of Ham, and the daughter of Egyptus, which in the Chaldean signifies Egypt, which signifies that which is forbidden.
> When this woman discovered the land it was under water, who afterward settled her sons in it; and thus, from Ham, sprang that race which preserved the curse in the land.
> Now the first government of Egypt was established by Pharaoh, the eldest son of Egyptus, the daughter of Ham, and it was after the manner of the government of Ham, which was patriarchal.
> Pharaoh, being a righteous man, established his kingdom and judged his people wisely and justly all his days, seeking earnestly to imitate that order established by the fathers in the first generations, in the days of the first patriarchal reign, even in the reign of Adam, and also of Noah, his father, who blessed him with the blessings of the earth, and with the blessings of wisdom, but cursed him as pertaining to the Priesthood. (Abraham 1:20-26.)

This is the scriptural account of the origin of the Egyptians. It is another of the "pearls of great price." It tells us of "the roots beyond roots" of the great black peoples. Since Ham intermarried with Egyptus there is no verification of a pure black race. Professor James R. Clark, of Brigham Young University, states "the Egyptians were not a pure strain, and there is nothing to indicate that racial factors as such were important in the development of their culture" (James Ratcliffe Clark, *Story of the Pearl of Great Price*, p. 126.)

According to Dr. Hugh Nibley, "Being of the Black race did not prevent one from becoming Pharaoh, neither was it a requirement. There simply was no prejudice in the matter." (Hugh Nibley, *Abraham in Egypt*, p. 219.) He further states:

In the ancient records the blood of Ham is a mixture, always containing
more white than black. While Ham is the ancestor of Pharaoh, the Pharaohs'
line also includes the Philistines, from whom Palestine gets its name. Recent
studies of the genealogy of Cain emphasize the claims of such desert tribes as
the Kenites and the families of Kenaz and Caleb to belong to the family. Though
the Hamites are as conspicuously Asiatic as African, the oldest African stocks
as well—Libyans, Tahannu, Berber—were not only white, but often referred
to as pale-skinned and redheaded. Karst detected an extension of the chain of
Hamite people: Kushites, Egyptoids, and Libyo-Hamites in enclaves all over
the Mediterranean and the islands clear to Spain. (Nibley, *Abraham in Egypt*,
p. 219.)

It has been assumed by many in the Church that the priesthood was
denied to the descendants of Cain and Ham on purely racial factors. Dr.
Nibley suggests that the priesthood was not denied on racial factors but
because Egyptus (this dominant woman of the Egyptian origins) was claiming the priesthood through matriarchal succession rather than patriarchal
succession—by claiming it through her lineage and not the man's. Hugh
Nibley said:

> There is no exclusive equation between Ham and Pharaoh, or between
> Ham and the Egyptians, or between Egyptians and the blacks, or between any
> of the above and any particular curse. What was denied was recognition of
> patriarchal right to the priesthood made by claim of matriarchal succession.
> (Nibley, *Abraham in Egypt*, p. 220.)

Egyptian Civilization Predominant

Later in this work we will discover that ten generations from the first
Pharaoh of Egypt—in the days of Abraham—that Egypt had become the
dominant civilization of the Middle East. We will discover that Abraham
was called on a mission to declare the gospel in its fullness to these people.
Abraham seemed not to have racial prejudices in the matter. He gives no
indication that he taught only "Caucasian" people or descendants of Shem.
God called him to this "strange land" and Abraham responded.

Statements of our prophets make it clear "that the Lord placed the
black skin on the descendants of Cain, and they came through the flood in
the family of Ham (see Joseph Fielding Smith, *Man: His Origin and Destiny*,
p. 419). "Enoch also beheld the residue of the people which were the sons
of Adam; and they were a mixture of all the seed of Adam save it was the
seed of Cain, for the seed of Cain were black" (Moses 7:22). The origin of
the Blacks is clear in the scriptures. They are descendants of Cain, but we
need to look beyond the infamous murderer in the black heritage. We need
to affirm that we believe that man will be punished for his own sins, and not
Cain's transgressions.

In blood and sorrow do thou trace
The tortuous journey of a race
From superstition's vile discord,
Unto the knowledge of our Lord. (*Ethiopia*, p. 97.)

Implications for Our Day

For believers in the Pearl of Great Price there can be no doubt as to the origin of the Blacks. For believers in the book of Abraham, in the Pearl of Great Price, there can be no doubt that Abraham taught the gospel in Egypt. Some of these Egyptians, no doubt, would have been black. What may be hard for some members of the Church today to accept is that Abraham may have given the Higher Priesthood and the Temple Endowment to the faithful converts—who may have been black.

In our day "revelation has confirmed that the long-promised day has come when every faithful, worthy man in the Church may receive the holy priesthood, . . . Accordingly, all worthy male members of the Church may be ordained to the priesthood without regard for race or color" (D&C, Official Declaration—2, June 8, 1978).

As children of Abraham, we must be ready to take the gospel to "Egypt" both literally and figuratively. We must prepare ourselves to take the fullness of the gospel to every nation, kindred, tongue and people—with no prejudices about race or creed. We, too, must go to "strange lands" and teach the descendants of Cain and all the remainder of Adam's seed. Perhaps, when we do this, we will be but walking in the footsteps of our great father Abraham.

Chapter Summary

1. Descendants of Cain were not ignorant savages with no learning and no culture.

2. Recent studies give evidence of a great cultural heritage of the blacks.

3. Roots of Egypt can be traced to Ham, son of Noah, who married a descendant of Cain.

4. The reason the Book of Mormon gives for no intermarrying with other races is that the people "might not . . . believe in incorrect traditions which would prove their destruction."

5. "Sons of God" were those who were faithful, received the gospel, were baptized, received the Holy Ghost, and were ordained to the priesthood.

6. "Sons of men" did not accept the gospel and "would not hearken to his voice."

7. Marriage outside the Church, or the faith, is a very serious step and contrary to prophets' counsel, both ancient and modern.

8. Ham may have baptized Egyptus since she and seven others were "saved by water" (1 Peter 3:20).

  • 9. The first Pharaoh of Egypt was a son of Egyptus, daughter of Ham.

  10. There is no pure black, no pure Egyptian blood.

  11. Noah may have denied the priesthood to Ham and his descendants not on racial factors but because of false claims by Egyptus through matriarchal succession.

  12. The Egyptian civilization was predominant in the Middle East in the days of Abraham—ten generations from the Flood.

  13. Abraham took the fullness of the gospel to Egypt in his day. Our challenge today is to do the same.

Chapter Ten

The Great Prophet Enoch—
His Panoramic Vision
of the World

Seth, an Express Likeness of His Father

Let us now follow the other lineage of Adam—the priesthood lineage
of Adam through Seth. Though many of Adam's sons apostatized from the
teachings of the gospel, Adam continued faithful and he "hearkened unto
the voice of God, and called upon his sons to repent:"

> And Adam knew his wife again, and she bare a son, and he called his name
> Seth. And Adam glorified the name of God; for he said: God hath appointed
> me another seed, instead of Abel, whom Cain slew.
> And God revealed himself unto Seth, and he rebelled not, but offered an
> acceptable sacrifice, like unto his brother Abel. (Moses 6:1-3.)

Adam and Eve must have been extremely happy and thankful to the
Lord for their son, Seth. The scriptures say he was "a perfect man, and his
likeness was the express likeness of his father, insomuch that he seemed to
be like unto his father in all things, and could be distinguished from him
only by his age" (D&C 107:43). The description of Seth's likeness to his
father, Adam, is not unlike the description of the likeness of Jesus Christ to
his Father. Paul said Jesus was "the brightness of his glory, and the express
image of his person" (Hebrews 1:3).

Book of Remembrance

Adam had a language that was pure and undefiled. He could read and
he could write. It was not by oral tradition alone that man's knowledge of
God, and the gospel, was taught from father to son. Adam, Seth, Enos, and
others wrote under the spirit of inspiration and the scriptures began—even
from the beginning. The books of Moses and Genesis were not the first
recorded scriptures. These early writings were kept in a "book of remembrance" begun by Adam (Moses 6:5).

Patriarchal Order of the Priesthood

The patriarchal order of the priesthood was instituted in the days of
Adam. The eldest righteous son was to have the rights of leadership and

fatherhood over the family. Seth was ordained by Adam at the age of sixty-nine years, Enos was ordained at the age of one hundred and thirty-four years and four months, also by the hand of Adam. Cainan, Mahalaleel, Jared, Enoch, and Methuselah were all ordained to the priesthood under the hand of Adam. (See D&C 107:41-50.)

Calling and Life of Enoch

Enoch was twenty-five-years-old when he was ordained under the hand of Adam. The King James Bible, with which most of the world is familiar, contains almost nothing about this great prophet. Here is the Biblical account:

> And Enoch lived sixty and five years, and begat Methuselah:
> And Enoch walked with God after he begat Methuselah three hundred years, and begat sons and daughters:
> And all the days of Enoch were three hundred sixty and five years:
> And Enoch walked with God: and he was not; for God took him. (Genesis 5:21-24.)

Something Enoch said is mentioned in the Bible but this, also, is very brief. It is in the book of Jude:

> And Enoch also, the seventh from Adam, prophesied of these, saying, Behold, the Lord cometh with ten thousands of his saints,
> To execute judgment upon all, and to convince all that are ungodly among them of all their ungodly deeds which they have ungodly committed, and of all their hard speeches which ungodly sinners have spoken against him. (Jude 14-15.)

How fortunate we are to have more on the life and deeds of Enoch. These "pearls" are part of the Pearl of Great Price. They are found in Moses, chapters 6 and 7. Let us go to this account and read more of his life and mission:

> And it came to pass that Enoch journeyed in the land, among the people; and as he journeyed, the Spirit of God descended out of heaven, and abode upon him.
> And he heard a voice from heaven, saying: Enoch, my son, prophesy unto this people, and say unto them—Repent, for thus saith the Lord: I am angry with this people, and my fierce anger is kindled against them; for their hearts have waxed hard, and their ears are dull of hearing, and their eyes cannot see afar off;
> And for these many generations, ever since the day that I created them, have they gone astray, and have denied me, and have sought their own counsels in the dark; and in their own abominations have they devised murder, and have not kept the commandments, which I gave unto their father, Adam. (Moses 6:26-28.)

Enoch was called to be a prophet of the Lord, to speak for the Lord, to call the people to repentance. What an awesome responsibility. Some day we will learn that all calls in the Church are to represent the Lord—to speak for the Lord—to act for the Lord. Missionary calls, Sunday School teacher calls, Primary calls, home teaching calls—there are no unimportant calls in the Church. All calls, all talks we give in church, everything we are called to do in the Church from prophet to deacon—all are done to represent the Lord. Many times we may not feel worthy or capable. Listen to Enoch's reaction to his call:

> Why is it that I have found favor in thy sight, and am but a lad, and all the people hate me; for I am slow of speech; wherefore am I thy servant (Moses 6:31)?

Humble people are aware of their shortcomings and imperfections when church calls come. They may wonder whether they can do the task. They may feel that people will not respond to them—may even "hate" them. If their assignment is in speaking or teaching they may, like Enoch, say: "I'm not a teacher," or "I can't speak in church" or "I can't give a prayer in public" or "I am slow of speech." But can we hear the Lord as he told Enoch:

> Go forth and do as I have commanded thee, and no man shall pierce thee. Open thy mouth, and it shall be filled, and I will give thee utterance, for all flesh is in my hands, and I will do as seemeth me good.
> Say unto this people: Choose ye this day, to serve the Lord God who made you.
> Behold my Spirit is upon you. (Moses 6:32-34.)

Paul understood how the Lord made calls to the humble and the meek, to the young and receptive—to those the world would call the foolish and weak:

> For ye see your calling, brethren, how that not many wise men after the flesh, not many mighty, not many noble, are called:
> But God hath chosen the foolish things of the world to confound the wise; and God hath chosen the weak things of the world to confound the things which are mighty;
> And base things of the world, and things which are despised, hath God chosen, yea, and things which are not, to bring to nought things that are:
> That no flesh should glory in his presence. (1 Corinthians 1:26-29.)

What an affinity Joseph Smith must have felt with Enoch as he learned of Enoch's call and his response. Joseph was but a lad, an obscure boy, only between fourteen and fifteen years old when the Lord called him. Oh, that we could respond to church calls as did Enoch and Joseph.

Enoch Taught Plan of Salvation

The Lord taught Enoch the plan of salvation. He showed him the pre-earth world, the spirits that God had created and "he beheld also things which were not visible to the natural eye; and from thenceforth came the

saying abroad in the land: A seer hath the Lord raised up unto his people"
(Moses 6:36).

As Enoch went forth preaching the gospel, calling the people to repentance and "testifying against their works," many people were offended
because of him. (Seldom does a prophet receive recognition among a people
who are living in wickedness.) The people taunted Enoch and derided him,
saying, in mockery:

> Tarry ye here and keep the tents, while we go yonder to behold the seer, for
> he prophesieth, and there is a strange thing in the land; a wild man hath come
> among us (Moses 6:38).

Enoch was challenged to tell who he was—by what right did he come
to them—what right did he have to say the things he was saying? And
Enoch, in plain testimony, told them "My father taught me in all the ways
of God" (Moses 6:41). Then he bore witness of his divine call from the
Lord. He told them that the things he said had been plainly taught by all
their righteous fathers and they knew them "and even the first of all we
know, even Adam" (Moses 6:45). He was but teaching them what Adam
had taught them, and he was still teaching them in his old age. Enoch reminded them that their scriptures—"the book of remembrance"—given in
their own language testified of the things he was saying (see Moses 6:46).
"And as Enoch spake forth the words of God, the people trembled, and
could not stand in his presence" (Moses 6:47).

Enoch told how the gospel in its fullness was given to Adam, and of
how Adam had been commanded to teach it freely to his children and his
children's children. (We went over these great teachings in Chapter Seven
and will not repeat them here.) Enoch continued his speech, saying:

> Behold, our father Adam taught these things, and many have believed and
> become the sons of God, and many have believed not, and have perished in
> their sins (Moses 7:1).

Then Enoch told of an experience not unlike that of Moses in climbing
"an exceedingly high mountain" (referred to in the opening chapters of
this book). (Moses 7:3; compare Moses 1:1.) Enoch said a voice out of
heaven told him:

> Turn ye, and get ye upon the mount Simeon.
> And it came to pass that I turned and went up on the mount; and as I stood
> upon the mount, I beheld the heavens open, and I was clothed upon with glory;
> And I saw the Lord; and he stood before my face, and he talked with me,
> even as a man talketh one with another, face to face; and he said unto me:
> Look, and I will show unto thee the world for the space of many generations.
> (Moses 7:2-4.)

A marvelous panoramic vision was opened to Enoch. He saw the world
from a "God's-eye" view—an unobstructed, complete view of all the world

and of all the people of the world. He saw and heard the Lord's challenge to go to the people, to call them to repentance, to baptize the believers who did repent in the name "of the Father, and of the Son, which is full of grace and truth, and of the Holy Ghost, which beareth record of the Father and the Son" (Moses 7:11).

Enoch saw himself calling upon all the people except the people of Canaan. So many of the people of Canaan were following Satan and the "secret combinations" with their works of evil and wickedness that apparently they were not given the gospel at that time. Enoch saw a great division between the people of God who followed him, and the enemies of God—largely the people of Canaan. The division appeared to be also along racial lines for "there was a blackness came upon all the children of Canaan, that they were despised among all people" (Moses 7:8). There were great wars and bloodshed between the two peoples. In some respects the great wars are similar to the wars between the Nephites and the Lamanites in the Book of Mormon recorded much later.

> And so great was the faith of Enoch, that he led the people of God, and their enemies came to battle against them; and he spake the word of the Lord, and the earth trembled, and the mountains fled, even according to his command; and the rivers of water were turned out of their course; and the roar of the lions was heard out of the wilderness; and all nations feared greatly, so powerful was the word of Enoch, and so great was the power of the language which God had given him (Moses 7:13).

Like a great Moroni, like a great Mormon, like a Moses, Enoch was a strong and successful leader, soldier, commander, and prophet. Enoch spoke with the power of God and more than the Red Sea was parted: mountains moved; there were earthquakes; the whole face of the land was changed.

> The fear of the Lord was upon all nations, so great was the glory of the Lord, which was upon his people. And the Lord blessed the land, and they were blessed upon the mountains, and upon the high places, and did flourish.
> And the Lord called his people ZION, because they were of one heart and one mind, and dwelt in righteousness; and there was no poor among them.
> And Enoch continued his preaching in righteousness unto the people of God. And it came to pass in his days, that he built a city that was called the City of Holiness, even ZION. (Moses 7:17-19.)

All of this was shown to Enoch in vision before it happened—a preview of what would happen and did happen—"history" before it occurred. (Prophecy *is* history before it occurs.) With the success of the great city of Zion before his eyes, Enoch talked with the Lord and assumed it was so great it would last forever: "Surely Zion shall dwell in safety forever" (Moses 7:20).

> But the Lord said unto Enoch: Zion have I blessed, but the residue of the people have I cursed.

> And it came to pass that the Lord showed unto Enoch all the inhabitants of the earth; and he beheld, and lo, Zion, in process of time, was taken up into heaven. And the Lord said unto Enoch: Behold mine abode forever. (Moses 7:20-21.)

Enoch saw more of the future. His panoramic vision continued. After he saw Zion taken up, "Enoch beheld, and lo, all the nations of the earth were before him; And there came generation upon generation; and Enoch was high and lifted up, even in the bosom of the Father, and of the Son of Man" (Moses 7:23-24). From the top of this "exceedingly high mountain" he saw, as it were, the great war in heaven continuing on the earth, for he beheld the power of Satan upon all the face of the earth, but he also saw angels descending out of heaven bearing testimony of the Father and of the Son. He also saw that "the Holy Ghost fell on many, and they were caught up by the powers of heaven into Zion" (Moses 7:27).

Enoch was in the presence of the Lord. He saw some of the same things Moses saw from God's perspective: worlds without number—"millions of earths like this" (Moses 7:30), and people without number. He saw the Lord God as a Celestial Being—an Eternal Being in a glorious Eternal World where "naught but peace, justice, and truth is the habitation of thy throne" (Moses 7:31). He saw God as Holy, and from all Eternity to all Eternity, surrounded by other noble beings who were also Holy and Celestial.

In crude and modern vernacular: "God has it made." Yet as Enoch looked upon God and as they looked down together upon the residue of the people of this earth, after the city of Zion was taken up from the earth, they saw that the majority of the earth's inhabitants were wicked; and Enoch saw the God of heaven weep. Enoch was moved by this poignant display of emotion of God:

> How is it that the heavens weep, and shed forth their tears as the rain upon the mountains?
> . . . How is it that thou canst weep, seeing thou art holy, and from all eternity to all eternity? (Moses 7:28-29.)

The shortest scripture in the Bible is related to the knowledge and understanding Enoch was soon to learn—and that we need to learn and to feel: "Jesus wept" (John 11:35). How well do we understand the compassion and love of the Father? How well do we understand the compassion and love of the Son? How is it they can weep seeing that they are "holy, and from all eternity to all eternity"?

The Lord explained it to Enoch in these words:

> Behold these thy brethren; they are the workmanship of mine own hands, and I gave unto them their knowledge, in the day I created them; and in the Garden of Eden, gave I unto man his agency;
> And unto thy brethren have I said, and also given commandment, that they should love one another, and that they should choose me, their Father; but

behold, they are without affection, and they hate their own blood. (Moses 7:32-33).

Wicked people are still acknowledged as the "workmanship of mine own hands"; the Lord still cares. He gave everyone their free agency and the simple commandment that they should love one another and follow their Father—even God. Many with this agency choose to rebel against Him and to "hate their own blood"—to hurt, to hate, and even to kill their own brothers and sisters. We are all brothers and sisters with one God. That is, we ought to be. At the time Enoch and the Lord were looking upon the people of the earth, the people were so wicked that the Lord said "Among all the workmanship of mine hands there has not been so great wickedness as among thy brethren" (Moses 7:36).

Enoch Sees Results of Sin and Vision of the Flood

The Lord showed Enoch the results of sin upon his children and the misery it causes them. He showed him that, as they reject the Lord, "Satan shall be their father, and misery shall be their doom" (Moses 7:37). The Lord showed Enoch how the wicked world would be drowned in the flood, and the suffering its spirits would have in the spirit prison. The Lord showed Enoch the torment they will go through until, and unless, they repent and accept the atonement of His Chosen, even Jesus Christ. (See Moses 7:38-39; also 1 Peter 3:18-20.)

Enoch began to see things the way the Lord saw them, "wherefore Enoch knew, and looked upon their wickedness, and their misery, and wept and stretched forth his arms, and his heart swelled wide as eternity; and his bowels yearned" (Moses 7:41). What a wonderful thing it is when a man can "feel" even a portion of what the Lord feels for people—when a man can feel the love that God feels for all his children, the wicked as well as the righteous.

Enoch saw the conditions of the world in the days of Noah. He saw how the ark saved Noah and his sons and families, but he also saw how the rest of the wicked were drowned in the flood. The Lord must have shown Enoch a "close-up" of the effect of the great flood—the horror and panic on the faces of the people who, when it was too late, scrambled, clawed, and scratched to climb aboard the closed ark.

Enoch must have seen the effect of the terrible storm of rain, wind, and the sea heaving beyond its bounds in a catastrophe the likes of which the world had never seen. Think of the tornadoes, the hurricanes, the destructive tidal waves we have seen in our own day. Multiply this storm to global proportions. Have winds, rains, and oceans come over the entire earth. "The fountains of the great deep broken up, and the windows of heaven were opened" (Genesis 7:11), hardly are enough words to describe this massive "baptism" of the earth. (See Joseph Fielding Smith, *Man: His Origin and Destiny*, pp. 432-433.)

> And the waters prevailed exceedingly upon the earth; and all the high hills, that were under the whole heaven, were covered.
> Fifteen cubits upward did the waters prevail; and the mountains were covered.
> And all flesh died that moved upon the earth, both of fowl, and of cattle, and of beast, and of every creeping thing that creepeth upon the earth, and every man. (Genesis 7:19-21.)

Yes, God showed Enoch a very vivid vision of the forthcoming flood and its destruction of life:

> And as Enoch saw this, he had bitterness of soul, and wept over his brethren, and said unto the heavens: I will refuse to be comforted (Moses 7:44).

Enoch Sees Conditions After the Flood

The vision to Enoch continued. He saw the storm abate and the winds and rains stop. He saw the waters become calm and sun literally come from behind the clouds. And the Lord said unto Enoch: "Lift up your heart, and be glad; and look" (Moses 7:44).

Enoch would have seen the ark finally come to rest upon the mountain. He would have seen Noah, and his family, and all the pairs of animals going forth upon the earth "that they may breed abundantly in the earth, and be fruitful, and multiply upon the earth" (Genesis 8:17). Enoch would have heard God bless Noah and his sons, and say unto them, "Be fruitful, and multiply, and replenish the earth" (Genesis 9:1). Then Enoch asked the Lord, in the name of Jesus Christ, to never again have the entire earth covered by floods. The Lord assured him that the world would never again be entirely destroyed by water. The Lord also told Enoch that a remnant of Noah's seed would always be found among all nations while the earth should stand (see Moses 7:50-52).

Sign and Covenant of the Rainbow

Many of us were taught, as children, that the Lord made a rainbow as a sign and a covenant between Noah and his posterity that the Lord would never again destroy the world by a flood (see Genesis 9:13-17). However, there is more to the symbolism of the rainbow than the King James translation of the Bible gives us. In the Joseph Smith Translation of the Bible, the Prophet tied this symbolism in beautifully with Enoch's experience and this translation gives a deeper meaning to the rainbow:

> And the bow shall be in the cloud; and I will look upon it, that I may remember the everlasting covenant, which I made unto thy father Enoch; that, when men should keep all my commandments, Zion should again come on the earth, the city of Enoch which I have caught up unto myself.

> And this is mine everlasting covenant, that when thy posterity shall embrace the truth, and look upward, then shall Zion look downward, and all the heavens shall shake with gladness, and the earth shall tremble with joy;
>
> And the general assembly of the church of the firstborn shall come down out of heaven, and possess the earth, and shall have place until the end come. And this is mine everlasting covenant, which I made with thy father Enoch. (JST, Genesis 9:21-23.)

How beautiful the rainbow is, formed when there has been, or is, a rain. The ethereal arc exhibits, in concentric bands, the colors of the spectrum formed opposite the sun by the refraction and reflection of the sun's rays in raindrops, spray, or mist. One of the arcs of color, going downward, symbolizes that when we, the posterity of Noah, embrace the truth and fullness of the gospel and look "up to God," then the other arc, that touches downward, symbolizes that the city of Enoch and the righteous people in heaven will look downward and that Zion will again be on earth. It is a symbol that almost echoes the words of the Lord's prayer: "Thy kingdom (the arc going upward) come, thy will be done, on earth as it is in heaven" (the arc touching downward to earth). The fable of the "pot of gold" at the end of the rainbow is paltry, indeed, compared to the promise of the return of the "Golden City of Zion" if we will but embrace the gospel of Jesus Christ and look to heaven for guidance.

Enoch Asks About the Day of the Coming of the Lord

Sometime during the great vision of the future that Enoch saw, and following the vision of the promise and covenant of the rainbow, Enoch asked:

> When shall the day of the Lord come? When shall the blood of the Righteous be shed, that all they that mourn may be sanctified and have eternal life?
>
> And the Lord said: It shall be in the meridian of time, in the days of wickedness and vengeance. (Moses 7:45-46.)

Enoch then saw, in vision, the coming of the Son of Man, even in the flesh. He would have seen the baby Jesus lying in a manger—the beauty and peace of that moment when God's own son touched the earth in far-off Bethelehem.

The words of Isaiah, a later prophet who also saw the coming of the Son of God, come to mind:

> For unto us a child is born, unto us a son is given: and the government shall be upon his shoulder: and his name shall be called Wonderful, Counseller, The mighty God, The everlasting Father, The Prince of Peace (Isaiah 9:6).

Enoch would have known the Plan of Salvation. He would have rejoiced knowing that the great mission of the Savior was to be slain, and to be resurrected, that all mankind could live again. His reaction, when he saw

the Savior lifted up, may have been one of joy for the fulfillment of the
great mission of the Lord:

> The Righteous is lifted up, and the Lamb is slain from the foundation of
> the world; and through faith I am in the bosom of the Father, and behold, Zion
> is with me (Moses 7:47).

However, once again, the Lord God gave Enoch a closer look at the
mission of the Savior. Enoch would have been shown the poignant scenes
of the trial of Jesus, his abuse, his scourging, and finally, the Lord said
unto Enoch:

> Look, and he looked and beheld the Son of Man lifted up on the cross,
> after the manner of men (Moses 7:55).

And would Enoch then have heard a loud voice (Moses 7:56) say these
words of the Savior on the cross?

> My God, my God, why hast thou forsaken me? why art thou so far from
> helping me, and from the words of my roaring?
> O my God, I cry in the daytime, but thou hearest not; and in the night
> season, and am not silent.
> I am a worm, and no man; a reproach of men, and despised of the people.
> All they that see me laugh me to scorn: they shoot out the lip, they shake
> the head, saying,
> He trusted on the Lord that he would deliver him: let him deliver him.
> I was cast upon thee from the womb: thou art my God from my mother's
> belly.
> Be not far from me; for trouble is near; for there is none to help.
> They gaped upon me with their mouths, as a ravening and a roaring lion.
> I am poured out like water, and all my bones are out of joint: my heart is
> like wax; it is melted in the midst of my bowels.
> My strength is dried up like a potsherd; and my tongue cleaveth to my jaws;
> and thou hast brought me into the dust of death.
> For dogs have compassed me: the assembly of the wicked have inclosed me:
> they pierced my hands and my feet.
> They part my garments among them, and cast lots upon my vesture. (Psalms
> 22:1-2, 6-8, 10-11, 13-16, 18.)

Then Enoch saw that "the heavens were veiled; and all the creations of
God mourned; and the earth groaned; and the rocks were rent" (Moses
7:56).

> And it came to pass that Enoch looked upon the earth; and he heard a
> voice from the bowels thereof, saying: Wo, wo is me, the mother of men; I am
> pained, I am weary, because of the wickedness of my children. When shall I
> rest, and be cleansed from the filthiness which is gone forth out of me? When
> will my Creator sanctify me, that I may rest, and righteousness for a season
> abide upon my face? (Moses 7:48.)

The very earth recognizes the pain and suffering of the Savior and
Creator. Enoch heard the earth mourn at the time of the Savior's agony in

Gethsemane when "his sweat was as it were great drops of blood falling down to the ground" (Luke 22:44) and he saw the culmination of his great sacrifice on the cross:

> He wept, and cried unto the Lord, saying: O Lord, wilt thou not have compassion upon the earth? Wilt thou not bless the children of Noah? (Moses 7:49.)

Enoch Sees Effect of Atonement

Enoch was shown the immediate effect of the atonement and the resurrection for he saw that "the saints arose, and were crowned at the right hand of the Son of Man, with crowns of glory;

> And as many of the spirits as were in prison came forth, and stood on the right hand of God; and the remainder were reserved in chains of darkness until the judgment of the great day. (Moses 7:56-57; see also Matthew 27:52-53.)

Enoch saw that Christ's earthly mission, and his atonement, helped all the living and the dead, yet he also saw that not all believed and followed Him neither on earth nor in the spirit prison. So again Enoch wept and cried unto the Lord, saying: "When shall the earth rest?" (Moses 7:58.) He had seen the ascension of the Savior into heaven, and he had asked, fervently: "Wilt thou not come again upon the earth?" (Moses 7:59.)

Enoch Saw Events Before Second Coming

The Lord told Enoch that He would again return, but that the conditions on the earth would be no better than they had been in the days of Noah before the flood:

> And the Lord said unto Enoch: As I live, even so will I come in the last days, in the days of wickedness and vengeance, to fulfil the oath which I have made unto you concerning the children of Noah;
> And the day shall come that the earth shall rest, but before that day the heavens shall be darkened, and a veil of darkness shall cover the earth; and the heavens shall shake, and also the earth; and great tribulations shall be among the children of men, but my people will I preserve. (Moses 7:60-61.)

Enoch was shown that there would be terrible calamities on the earth before Christ's second coming. He was shown that there would be a great apostasy—"the heavens shall be darkened," and "a veil of darkness shall cover the earth" (Moses 7:61):

> For the Lord hath poured out upon you the spirit of deep sleep, and hath closed your eyes: the prophets and your rulers, the seers hath he covered (Isaiah 29:10).

The Lord, knowing "the calamity which should come upon the inhabitants of the earth [before Christ's second coming], called upon my servant

Joseph Smith, Jun., and spake unto him from heaven, and gave him commandments'' (D&C 1:17). Enoch saw this restoration of the gospel:

> And righteousness will I send down out of heaven; and truth will I send forth out of the earth, to bear testimony of mine Only Begotten; his resurrection from the dead; yea, and also the resurrection of all men; and righteousness and truth will I cause to sweep the earth as with a flood, to gather out mine elect from the four quarters of the earth, unto a place which I shall prepare, an Holy City, that my people may gird up their loins, and be looking forth for the time of my coming; for there shall be my tabernacle, and it shall be called Zion, a New Jerusalem (Moses 7:62).

The righteousness sent down from heaven was the visit of the Father and the Son to Joseph Smith. The truth that He will send forth out of the earth was, and is, the Book of Mormon which came forth out of the Hill Cumorah—buried in the earth. The Book of Mormon, among other things, is to "bear testimony of mine Only Begotten; his resurrection from the dead; yea, and also the resurrection of all men.'' Righteousness and truth which the Lord will cause to "sweep the earth as with a flood'' is the mighty missionary work that is—and has been—going on since the restoration of the gospel in these last days. The gathering of "mine elect'' from the four quarters of the earth is to prepare "an Holy City''—and to build and prepare a Holy Temple as the center of the Holy City.

> And that the gathering together upon the land of Zion, and upon her stakes, may be for a defense, and for a refuge from the storm, and from wrath when it shall be poured out without mixture upon the whole earth.
> . . . I command you to build a house unto me, for the gathering together of my saints, that they may worship me. (D&C 115:6, 8.)

Holy City Like Unto City of Zion

The Lord told Enoch that there would be built, in the last days, another Holy City like unto the city of Zion which he helped build. He told him there would be a great reunion of the people who had built the Holy City on earth with his city which would come down to meet and mingle with them:

> Then shalt thou and all thy city meet them there [on earth], and we will receive them into our bosom, and they shall see us; and we will fall upon their necks, and they shall fall upon our necks, and we will kiss each other;
> And there shall be mine abode, and it shall be Zion, which shall come forth out of all the creations which I have made; and for the space of a thousand years the earth shall rest. (Moses 7:63-64.)

Thus Enoch's question as to when the earth would rest was given to him. It would be when the Second Coming of the Savior occurred in the last days, when the Son of Man came to dwell on the earth in righteousness for the space of a thousand years—the Great Millennium! The Lord showed Enoch a grand preview of all things "even unto the end of the world; and he saw the day of the righteous, the hour of their redemption; and received a fulness of joy" (Moses 7:67).

This sublime revelation, given to Enoch, helped him teach righteous people their destiny:

> And Enoch and all his people walked with God, and he dwelt in the midst of Zion; and it came to pass that Zion was not, for God received it up into his own bosom; and from thence went forth the saying, ZION IS FLED (Moses 7:69).

Summary of Chapter Ten

1. Seth was a righteous son of Adam.

2. Adam had a language that was pure and undefiled. He could read and write; he kept a scripture called a "book of remembrance."

3. The patriarchal order of the priesthood was instituted in the days of Adam. The eldest righteous son was to have rights of leadership and fatherhood over the family.

4. Enoch was ordained at the age of twenty-five by Adam and he was later called to be a prophet of the Lord.

5. The Lord taught Enoch the Plan of Salvation.

6. Enoch had a "panoramic" vision of the world from beginning to end.

7. Enoch saw God weep, he understood why and he began also to weep.

8. Enoch saw the result of sin on the earth and saw a vision of the flood before it occurred.

9. Enoch saw conditions of the world after the flood.

10. The sign and covenant of the rainbow was a sign to show that when men on earth live righteously "the general assembly of the church of the firstborn shall come down . . . and possess the earth."

11. Enoch asked for, and saw, the day of the birth of the Savior.

12. Enoch saw the crucifixion, the resurrection, the immediate effect of the atonement.

13. Enoch saw events before Christ's second coming.

14. Enoch saw a holy city like unto the city of Zion again built up on the earth.

15. Enoch saw the day when the earth "rested"—the millennium of the world.

Concluding the Book of Moses— From Noah to Abraham

Nine Righteous Men from Adam to Noah

After Enoch and his city of Zion were taken to heaven, there were still some righteous people who remained on earth. The last chapter in the book of Moses, in our present Pearl of Great Price, tells us that "Methuselah, the son of Enoch, was not taken, that the covenants of the Lord might be fulfilled, which he made to Enoch" (Moses 8:2). Part of this covenant was that Noah should be of the fruit of his loins, and that "a remnant of his seed should always be found among all nations, while the earth should stand" (Moses 7:52).

Joseph Smith reminds us that there were nine noted righteous men from Adam to Noah which included Abel who was slain by his brother, Cain. In review, their names were: Abel, Seth, Enos, Cainan, Mahalaleel, Jared, Enoch, Methuselah, and Lamech, the father of Noah. The time from Adam to Noah was approximately one thousand and fifty-six years. (See *Lectures on Faith*, p. 26.) Lamech, the father of Noah, Methuselah, Enoch, Jared, Mahalaleel, Cainan, Enos, Seth, and Adam, were all living at the same time and they were all preachers of righteousness (*Lectures*, p. 19). Lamech, the father of Noah, was fifty-six years old when Adam died; thus the great testimony of Adam would have been heard personally by every righteous man up to, and including, Noah's father.

Noah, the son of Lamech, was also a righteous man and had three sons mentioned in the scriptures—Japheth, Shem, and Ham. Noah and his wife, and the three sons and their wives, were the "eight souls saved by water" mentioned by Peter in the New Testament (1 Peter 3:20). These were apparently the only souls who accepted the gospel as preached by Noah—the only ones who were baptized by the proper authority of the Holy Priesthood held by Noah in the name of the Father, and of the Son, and of the Holy Ghost. They were the only souls who were saved, temporally, from the waters of the flood and, spiritually, from the "flood" of sin and corruption that filled the earth at that time.

Noah taught the people plainly:

> Believe and repent of your sins and be baptized in the name of Jesus Christ, the Son of God, even as our fathers, and ye shall receive the Holy Ghost, that ye may have all things made manifest; and if ye do not this, the floods will come in upon you; nevertheless they hearkened not (Moses 8:24).

Because the people were so wicked and "every man was lifted up in the imagination of the thoughts of his heart, being only evil continually . . . it repented Noah, and his heart was pained that the Lord had made man on the earth" (Moses 8:22, 25).

> The earth was corrupt before God, and it was filled with violence.
> And God looked upon the earth, and, behold, it was corrupt, for all flesh had corrupted its way upon the earth.
> And God said unto Noah: The end of all flesh is come before me, for the earth is filled with violence, and behold I will destroy all flesh from off the earth. (Moses 8:28-30.)

Events Following the Book of Moses

These verses conclude the book of Moses in our present Pearl of Great Price. The fulfillment of the great prophetic vision of Enoch wherein he saw the days of Noah, and the flood before it occurred, was carried out (see chapter ten). To follow the chronology of events which took place after Moses 8:30, we need to turn to the Joseph Smith Translation of the Bible, Genesis 8:19 (or the King James Version, Genesis 6:14) and read: "Make thee therefore, an ark of gopher wood . . ." then read details of the making of the ark, the loading of the animals "two of every kind . . . male and female" into the ark.

Then Genesis tells of the fulfillment of the prophecy of Enoch as "all the fountains of the great deep [were] broken up, and the windows of heaven were opened, and the rain was upon the earth forty days and forty nights" (JST, Genesis 8:36; Genesis 7:11-12). The events would be a repetition of all the things seen by Enoch in vision before they happened. As mentioned before, prophecy is history in reverse, a foreseeing of an event before it happens. (Because we went over many of the events of Noah and the flood in Enoch's prophecy in chapter ten, they will not be repeated here.)

In chapter nine of this book we saw that the seed of Cain was preserved from the flood by Ham's marriage to Egyptus, a descendant of Cain. We also learned that "from this descent sprang all the Egyptians" (Abraham 1:22). Abraham was born into a world in which Egyptian influence was predominant. It is the purpose of this chapter to make a smooth and logical transition from the life of Noah, following the flood, to the book of Abraham and the life of Abraham. The Pearl of Great Price does not contain this information.

Life of Noah Following the Flood

> And the sons of Noah that went forth of the ark, were Shem, and Ham, and Japheth; and Ham was the father of Canaan. These were the three sons of Noah, and of them was the whole earth overspread. (JST, Genesis 9:26.)

The true gospel of Jesus Christ believes the Bible and the fact that it was from this event in the world's history that mankind began anew to spread over the face of the earth following the flood. Latter-day revelation also reveals that civilization began by Adam down to Noah was more or less upon the Western Hemisphere. Joseph Fielding Smith said:

> Contrary to the general view in the world, Noah built his ark and commenced his voyage in the flood from that part of the earth which is now known as the United States of America. All the land surface of the earth at that time was in one place and it was not until some time after the flood that the land surface of the earth was divided. However, the journey from the western part of the world as we know it today to Armenia was a very great journey. The first and oldest civilization was destroyed and it was very largely occupying this western hemisphere. The peopling of the earth commenced anew through the family of Noah about 1600 years from the fall of Adam. (Joseph Fielding Smith, *Man: His Origin and Destiny*, p. 458.)

Thus the ark of Noah traveled from the Western Hemisphere to the Middle East, where civilization began anew. After the waters receded off the land Noah "began to till the earth, and he was an husbandman; and he planted a vineyard, and he drank of the wine, and was drunken; and he was uncovered within his tent" (JST, Genesis 9:27). Members of the Church today, with their knowledge of the teachings of the Word of Wisdom as taught by modern prophets against drinking alcoholic beverages, might find it hard to believe that Noah, a righteous man, got drunk on his own wine and lay naked in his tent.

Possible Explanation

A noted scholarly commentary on this incident suggests that this was probably the first time that wine had been cultivated; and it is just as probable that the strength, or intoxicating power of the wine, was not yet known to man. Noah, therefore, might have drunk the wine without the least blame if he knew not, till this trial, the effects it would produce. (See Adam Clarke, *Bible Commentary of Genesis-Esther*, p. 82.)

The Biblical account of what happened after Noah's sons found their father, Noah, drunken and uncovered, is interesting:

> And Ham, the father of Canaan, saw the nakedness of his father, and told his brethren without; and Shem and Japheth took a garment and laid upon both their shoulders, and went backward and covered the nakedness of their father, and they saw not their father's nakedness.

And Noah awoke from his wine, and knew what his youngest son had done unto him, and he said, Cursed be Canaan; a servant of servants shall he be unto his brethren.

And he said, Blessed be the Lord God of Shem; and Canaan shall be his servant, and a veil of darkness shall cover him, that he shall be known among all men.

God shall enlarge Japheth, and he shall dwell in the tents of Shem; and Canaan shall be his servant. (JST, Genesis 9:28-31.)

Why the Curse on Ham and His Seed?

Ham, and very probably his son Canaan, had treated their father, Noah, on this occasion with contempt or reprehensible levity. The conduct of Shem and Japheth, as affectionate sons, would seem to indicate that they were in the habit of treating their father with decency, and reverence, and obedient respect. The curse upon Ham and Canaan that Noah pronounced was more of a prophetic utterance than a curse of an incensed father. It was not the curse pronounced by Noah that later caused Ham and his posterity to become slaves; it was merely a prophetic utterance that this would occur. (Clarke, *Bible Commentary of Genesis-Esther*, p. 82.)

Garment that Covered Noah's Nakedness

Just a brief note about the garment with which Shem and Japheth covered their naked father. In Jewish literature there is a book called "The Book of Jasher." It is apocryphal in nature but it is dated later than the Apocrypha. Such books need to be read with the caution given to the Prophet Joseph: "There are many things contained therein that are not true, which are interpolations by the hands of men" (D&C 91:2).

The Book of Jasher states that the garments of skin which God made for Adam and his wife were passed on from Adam even to Noah:

> Ham stole those garments from Noah his father, and he took them and hid them from his brothers.
> And when Ham begat his first born Cush, he gave him the garments in secret, and they were with Cush many days. (*The Book of Jasher*, VII:27-28, p. 15.)

Those who have been to the temple of The Church of Jesus Christ of Latter-day Saints know the significance of the temple garment—its origin and its sacredness. The irreverence of Ham and the severity of Noah's rebuke of Ham could certainly be understood if, indeed, it was Ham who stole the sacred garment from his father, leaving him naked. This may also explain why Noah treated the Pharaoh—the eldest son of Egyptus, the daughter of Ham—as he did and blessed him "with the blessings of the earth, and with the blessings of wisdom, but cursed him as pertaining to the Priesthood" (Abraham 1:26). He would also have withheld from him the sacred priesthood garment although the Egyptians sought "earnestly to imitate that order established by the fathers in the first generations'' (Abraham 1:26). There is much evidence to conclude that the Egyptians did imitate the priesthood garment. (See for example Hugh Nibley, *Message of Joseph Smith Papyri*, p. 98.) More light will be shed on this in chapters that follow.

Death of Noah and Genealogy of His Posterity

The Bible concludes Noah's great life with this simple verse:

> And Noah lived after the flood, three hundred and fifty years. And all the days of Noah were nine hundred and fifty years; and he died. (JST, Genesis 9:32; Genesis 9:28-29.)

The Bible does not go, in lengthy detail, into the lives and events of the posterity of Noah. Chapter ten of Genesis gives the rudiments of the genealogy of his sons and their posterity. The mighty geological phenomenon which affected the whole earth, and which literally separated the continents of North and South America from the other land mass, is mentioned in only one verse:

> And Peleg was a mighty man, for in his days was the earth divided (JST, Genesis 10:16; Genesis 10:25).

Tower of Babel

Chapter eleven of Genesis tells very briefly that all the earth was of the same language and of how the people built the Tower of Babel to avoid the Lord's commandment to scatter abroad upon the face of the whole earth:

> And they said, Come, go to, let us build us a city, and a tower whose top will be high, nigh unto heaven; and let us make us a name, lest we be scattered abroad upon the face of the whole earth (JST, Genesis 11:3; Genesis 11:4).

More details of this cataclysmic event can be found in the introductory chapters of the book of Ether in the Book of Mormon. This record, abridged by Moroni, tells about the scattering of one body of people, under the direction of the brother of Jared, back to the Americas, back to the lands set apart and divided by the event in the days of Peleg, back unto the "land of promise, which was choice above all other lands, which the Lord God had preserved for a righteous people" (Ether 2:7). These people, whom we know as the Jaredites, were told to serve the God of this land, who is Jesus Christ, or they would be "swept off" as the people in the days of Noah were swept off by the flood (see Ether 2:7-12). Also in the Book of Mormon an interesting allegory can be found of the tame and wild olive tree which may have application to the various scatterings of the people "abroad on the face thereof" (see Jacob 5).

Genealogy of Abraham

The main purpose of chapter eleven in Genesis seems to be to lay the genealogical background of Abraham. The verses from 10 to 26 (JST, verses 7 to 15) show that Abraham was a descendant of Shem. In his *Lectures on Faith*, Joseph Smith asked:

> How many noted characters lived from Noah to Abraham? Ten. What are their names? Shem, Arphaxad, Salah, Eber, Peleg, Reu, Serug, Nahor, Terah, and Nahor. How many of these were contemporary with Noah? The whole. How many with Abraham? Eight. What were their names? Nahor, Terah, Serug, Reu, Eber, Salah, Arphaxad, and Shem. (*Lectures on Faith*, p. 31-32.)

One of the facts the Prophet seems to want to bring out is that Shem was still alive when Abraham was born. He said that Abraham was one hundred and fifty years old when Shem died (*Lectures on Faith*, p. 22).

We can now begin our study of the book of Abraham in the Pearl of Great Price. (Some of this book is contemporary with Genesis, chapters 12 and 13.)

Summary of Chapter Eleven

1. From Adam to Noah there were nine noted, righteous men.
2. After the flood, civilization began anew in the Middle East.
3. Noah's rebuke of Ham could have been because of Ham's attempt to steal the sacred garment and his disrespect for that and for the priesthood.
4. From Noah to Abraham there were ten noted characters.

Chapter Twelve

The Book of Abraham— His Mission to Egypt

> And Terah lived seventy years, and begat Abram, Nahor, and Haran.
> And Haran died before his father Terah, in the land of his nativity, in Ur
> of the Chaldees. (JST, Genesis 11:15, 17.)

Early Life of Abraham

There is no account, in the book of Genesis, of the early life of Abraham
up to his marriage to Sarai other than the mention of his birth. Nor does the
book of Abraham, in the Pearl of Great Price, give us more of the early life
of Abraham other than to verify that his residence, at the time of his record,
was in the land of the Chaldeans (see Abraham 1:1).

The apocryphal *Book of Jasher* tells us that Abraham's father, Terah,
was able to rise to some prominence in the wicked kingdom of Nimrod and
his son, Mardon: "And the king and princes loved him, and they elevated
him very high" (*The Book of Jasher*, VII:49). Terah called the name of his
son Abram "because the king had raised him in those days, and dignified
him above all his princes that were with him" (*Jasher*, VII:51).

The Book of Jasher says that, because of a strange phenomena in the
skies when Abram was born in which one large star "swallowed up the four
stars from the four sides of the heavens," the wise men and "conjurors"
interpreted this to mean that the child, Abram, would "grow up . . . become
powerful, and kill all the kings of the earth, and inherit all their lands, he
and his seed forever" (*Jasher*, VIII:1-11).

The same account says that an attempt was made to bribe Terah into
selling his son for silver and gold and that an attempt was made to slay the
child Abram, but he was preserved "as it was the will of Providence not to
suffer Abram's death."

> And Terah took Abram his son secretly, together with his mother and
> nurse, and he concealed them in a cave, and he brought them their provisions . . .
> And the Lord was with Abram in the cave and he grew up, and Abram was
> in the cave ten years, and the king and his princes, soothsayers and sages,
> thought that the king had killed Abram. (*Jasher*, VIII:34-36.)

The account states further that when Abram came out from the cave "he went to Noah and his son Shem, and he remained with them to learn the instruction of the Lord and his ways, and no man knew where Abram was, and Abram served Noah and Shem his son for a long time" (*Jasher*, IX:5). The record says that Abram was in Noah's house thirty-nine years, "and Abram knew the Lord from three years old, and he went in the ways of the Lord until the day of his death, as Noah and his son Shem had taught him" (*Jasher*, IX:6).

This would explain why Abram was a follower of righteousness while his own father, Terah, became an idolater and worshiped false gods (Abraham 1:5). Elder Mark E. Peterson said:

> Abraham must have been taught the true Gospel in his youth, even though his father and other members of the family later apostatized. When his home became an open invitation for him to adopt idolatry, he did not yield. He remained true and faithful to the Gospel teachings. (Mark E. Peterson, *Abraham, Friend of God*, p. 41.)

It would be interesting to know how Terah and his family came to be in the Ur of the Chaldees, but both history and scripture are silent. We know that Ur was one of the most important cities in southern Mesopotamia. According to archaeologists, Ur was a city of about a half million people in the time of Abraham—a city of beautiful buildings, good schools, and extensive business dealings by sea as well as on land. Immense temples were built and there were many closely packed dwellings; yet the city was given over to wickedness and idolatry. (Peterson, *Abraham*, p. 37.) We know that the great Egyptian civilization had tremendous influence on the whole of the Middle East in the time of Abraham. The religious influence of the Egyptians helped make the conditions as they were.

> For their hearts were set to do evil, and were wholly turned to the god of Elkenah, and the god of Libnah, and the god Mahmackrah, and the god of Korash, and the god of Pharaoh, king of Egypt (Abraham 1:6).

Abraham Tells of Egypt's Origin

Abraham said the first Pharaoh was the son of the daughter of Ham and Egyptus (Abraham 1:25). He said that the land of Egypt was under water from the flood when it was first discovered, but when the waters receded the descendants of Ham and Egyptus settled there. In fact, he said: "From this descent sprang all the Egyptians, and thus the blood of the Canaanites was preserved in the land" (Abraham 1:22).

Abraham said the first Pharaoh was a righteous man who

> established his kingdom and judged his people wisely and justly all his days, seeking earnestly to imitate that order established by the fathers in the first generations, in the days of the first patriarchal reign, even in the reign of Adam,

and also of Noah, his father, who blessed him with the blessings of the earth, and with the blessings of wisdom, but cursed him as pertaining to the Priesthood (Abraham 1:26).

Although the priesthood, and the priesthood garment, were withheld from the descendants of Ham and Egyptus by Noah, the Egyptians sought "earnestly to imitate that order" (the order of the higher priesthood). It does not seem consistent with his other actions for Noah to withhold teachings of the gospel from his son Ham and from Ham's posterity. From the record it would appear that the grandson of Noah, the first Pharaoh of Egypt, tried very hard to follow these teachings and to implement them in his rule.

By the time Abraham was born, nine or ten generations from the time of the first Pharaoh, Egyptian worship had degenerated to a very pagan level. The Egyptians were a wicked and idolatrous people. Abraham said they had turned from the true meaning of sacrifice to human sacrifice—even to infant sacrifice—"even the thank-offering of a child did the priest of Pharaoh offer upon the altar" (Abraham 1:10).

The people had retrogressed to a point where strange fertility rites were part of their worship. Abraham tells of three virgins, daughters of Onitah (one of the royal descent directly from the loins of Ham) who were offered as human sacrifices because they would not submit to the loss of their virtue through these fertility rites with the Egyptian apostate priests and their sensuous lusts (see Abraham 1:11).

Abraham's own father was caught up in this idolatry (Abraham 1:27) and false worship. When Abraham opposed these religious practices of the Egyptians that had spread to Ur of Chaldea, he was seized by the priests and was about to be sacrificed and murdered in the same cruel manner as were the three virgins of Onitah. This included the disemboweling of the victim after which the murderous priests would reach into the thoracic cavity and pull out the bleeding—and still beating—heart and hold it up before their moronic false gods. (See W. C. Skousen, *First 2,000 Years*, p. 245.) This was a most insidious and perverted distortion of the Lord's commandment to "offer up to Him a broken heart and a contrite spirit." These diabolically inspired priests were, literally, offering the "broken hearts" of their victims to their gods.

Abraham was delivered by an angel of the Lord and his bands unloosed. The altar was broken down and the images of false gods destroyed, and the priest who tried to kill Abraham was killed. "There was great mourning in Chaldea, and also in the court of the Pharaoh" over this (Abraham 1:20).

Abraham Called on Mission to Egypt

Abraham's life was spared and the Lord called him on a mission. He was called "into a strange land which thou knowest not of (Abraham 1:16). He was called to be a minister of His name—a missionary—a preacher of the gospel of Jesus Christ, even Jehovah. He was to go to the very courts of the Pharaoh of Egypt—to the leaders of this mighty but degenerating civilization—to the heart of the Egyptian Empire.

Before Abraham went on his mission, he was prepared through the Lord's own MTC (Missionary Training Center). Abraham first "sought for the blessings of the fathers" (Abraham 1:2), the righteous, contemporary priesthood brethren. (Perhaps he was referring to his spiritual fathers Noah, Shem and others.) Abraham desired more knowledge, much more than he had. He wanted to be even more righteous than he was; he wanted to live and raise a family, "to be a father of many nations, a prince of peace . . . to receive instructions, and to keep the commandments of God" (see Abraham 1:2).

It is significant that Abraham desired these blessings before they were given, and the Lord blessed Abraham with all of the blessings before his life was over. The first great blessing he sought, in preparation for his mission to Egypt, was that of being ordained to the priesthood. Having sought this great blessing, he received it, for he says: "I became a rightful heir, a High Priest, holding the right belonging to the fathers. It was conferred upon me from the fathers." (Abraham 1:2-3.) Abraham received the priesthood from Melchizedek who received it through the lineage of his fathers, "even till Noah" (D&C 84:14).

The Joseph Smith Translation of the Bible gives us these words on the ordination of Abraham by Melchizedek:

> And thus, having been approved of God, he was ordained an high priest after the order of the covenant which God made with Enoch,
>
> It being after the order of the Son of God; which order came, not by man, nor the will of man; neither by father nor mother; neither by beginning of days nor end of years; but of God;
>
> Melchizedek was a priest of this order; therefore he obtained peace in Salem, and was called the Prince of Peace. [Note Abraham also wanted to be such a prince of peace (see Abraham 1:2).]
>
> This Melchizedek, having thus established righteousness, was called the king of heaven by his people, or, in other words, the King of peace. (JST, Genesis 14:27-28, 33, 36.)

Although there is not general consensus among the brethren on the matter, John Taylor affirmed that Melchizedek and Shem were the same person. "And with superior knowledge of men like Noah, Shem (who was Melchizedek) and Abraham the father of the faithful, three contemporaries, holding the keys of the highest order of the priesthood" (*Times and Seasons*, Dec. 15, 1844, Vol. 5, p. 746; see also Lundwall's *Lectures on Faith*, p. 93).

Highest Order of the Priesthood

What is this "highest order of the priesthood"? Is not one aspect of it the new and everlasting covenant of marriage and the temple ordinances associated with it? (See D&C 131:1-4.) The Doctrine and Covenants states further: "Abraham received all things, whatsoever he received, by revelation and commandment, by my word, saith the Lord. . . . Abraham received promises concerning his seed, and of the fruit of his loins . . . both in the world and out of the world should they continue as innumerable as the stars." (D&C 132:29-30.) Does that not sound as if Abraham received a "fullness" of the highest order of the priesthood?

We bless our missionaries who go out into the mission field today with the endowment in the temple. Would Abraham's great mission preparation be less? Would not Abraham have received the endowment before his mission to Egypt?

In Nibley's book, *Abraham in Egypt,* he succinctly puts it:

> Abraham frankly wants peace and happiness for himself and to be a blessing to all mankind . . . he would go about it in God's way, learning first the law of obedience, carrying out first the law of obedience, carrying out specific instructions regarding the building of altars, the bringing of sacrifices, the paying of tithes, the carrying out of explicit ordinances (circumcision), the bestowal of blessings, the keeping of family records, the making of covenants, prayer and the intercession for all mankind, works on behalf of the dead, marrying for eternal posterity—in short, the works of Abraham center around the temple. (Hugh Nibley, *Abraham in Egypt,* p. 250.)

Abraham went into Egypt thoroughly prepared with the priesthood and the knowledge of the endowment and temple ordinances.

Charge and Blessing to Abraham

When Abraham first left Ur of the Chaldees, he did not know fully where the Lord intended for him to go. "Therefore I left the land of Ur, of the Chaldees, to go into the land of Canaan . . ." (Abraham 2:4), but the Lord said "for I have purposed to take thee away out of Haran, and to make of thee a minister to bear my name in a strange land which I will give unto thy seed after thee for an everlasting possession, when they hearken to my voice" (Abraham 2:6).

Then came a great mission charge and blessing to Abraham before he went into Egypt. This charge and blessing was given by the Lord; it reaches far beyond the days of Abraham to the total mission the Lord has for this world through Abraham's seed. Since we claim to be Abraham's seed, and since we have received of the fullness of the gospel, this charge is as applicable to us today as it was when the Lord gave it to Abraham:

> My name is Jehovah, and I know the end from the beginning; therefore my hand shall be over thee.
> And I will make of thee a great nation, and I will bless thee above measure, and make thy name great among all nations, and thou shalt be a blessing unto thy seed after thee, that in their hands they shall bear this ministry and Priesthood unto all nations;

And I will bless them through thy name; for as many as receive this Gospel shall be called after thy name, and shall be accounted thy seed, and shall rise up and bless thee, as their father;

And I will bless them that bless thee, and curse them that curse thee; and in thee (that is, in thy Priesthood) and in thy seed (that is, thy Priesthood), for I give unto thee a promise that this right shall continue in thee, and in thy seed after thee (that is to say, the literal seed, or the seed of the body) shall all the families of the earth be blessed, even with the blessings of the Gospel, which are the blessings of salvation, even of life eternal. (Abraham 2:8-11.)

Abraham Receives Egyptian Language Background

Another thing Abraham needed before he went into Egypt was Egyptian language training. He also needed more cultural and educational background of the Egyptians before he could effectively teach them. He may have had some of this background but he needed to know more. He needed to be aware of the major interests of the Egyptians and how to use these interests to lead them to hear, and accept, the gospel.

One of the important interests and skills of the Egyptians of Abraham's day was astronomy—and the organization of the heavens in relation to the earth. Abraham had an instrument with greater "seeing" capacity than any Egyptian observatory (or even our own modern observatories such as the Mt. Palomar Telescope). Abraham had a Urim and Thummim with which he could observe the heavens.

Latter-day Saints are familiar with the Urim and Thummim because of its use by the Prophet Joseph Smith in assisting with the translation of the plates of the Book of Mormon. Joseph Smith described the Urim and Thummim as two stones set in silver bows (JS—H 2:35). Through the Urim and Thummim Abraham beheld the stars and suns of the universe (Abraham 3:1-4). A parallel here is that the book of Abraham was at least partially translated by Joseph Smith with the aid of the Urim and Thummim (see *Millennial Star*, July, 1842, 3:46).

Not only did Abraham see the stars and suns, planets of the universe, but he was told the times and seasons of this earth in relation to the times and seasons of God's world (see Abraham 3:4, 5). These were things that those in the civilization of Egypt were already interested in knowing. Abraham's revelations on these facts were used as an approach to interest Egyptian leaders in other concepts of the gospel. Abraham needed to know the Egyptian terminology of the planets, suns, and stars. Words like "Shinehah," which is sun, "Kokob," which is star, "Olea," which is moon, "Kolob," meaning governing one, etc. "And the Lord said unto me: Abraham, I show these things unto thee before ye go into Egypt, that ye may declare all these words" (Abraham 3:15).

Abraham Teaches the Gospel

Abraham needed a "first discussion," an approach, a way to use simple logic to lead the Egyptians to understand the God of whom Abraham was to bear witness. Listen to the simple yet profound way God taught Abraham to teach the Egyptians:

> If two things exist, and there be one above the other, there shall be greater things above them; therefore Kolob is the greatest of all the Kokaubeam that thou hast seen, because it is nearest unto me.
>
> Now, if there be two things, one above the other, and the moon be above the earth, then it may be that a planet or a star may exist above it; and there is nothing that the Lord thy God shall take in his heart to do but what he will do it.
>
> Howbeit that he made the greater star; as, also, if there be two spirits, and one shall be more intelligent than the other, yet these two spirits, notwithstanding one is more intelligent than the other, have no beginning; they existed before, they shall have no end, they shall exist after, for they are gnolaum, or eternal.
>
> And the Lord said unto me: These two facts do exist, that there are two spirits, one being more intelligent than the other; there shall be another more intelligent than they; I am the Lord thy God, I am more intelligent than they all. (Abraham 3:16-19.)

Abraham learned and taught the first principles of the gospel. He knew, as the Prophet Joseph Smith was later to teach:

> It is the first principle of the Gospel to know for a certainty the Character of God, and to know that we may converse with him as one man converses with another, and that he was once a man like us, yea, that God himself, the Father of us all dwelt on an earth, the same as Jesus Christ himself did (Joseph Fielding Smith, *Teachings of the Prophet Joseph Smith*, p. 345).

Abraham taught the answers to life's most puzzling questions. Where did we come from before this life on earth? Why are we here? Where are we going after death? Note the clear, concise statements that Abraham both learned and taught:

Where did we come from?

> Now the Lord had shown unto me, Abraham, the intelligences that were organized before the world was; and among all these were many of the noble and great ones (Abraham 3:22).

Why are we here on earth?

> And we will prove them herewith, to see if they will do all things whatsoever the Lord their God shall command them (Abraham 3:25).

Where are we going?

> And they who keep their first estate shall be added upon; and they who keep not their first estate shall not have glory in the same kingdom with those who keep their first estate; and they who keep their second estate shall have glory added upon their heads for ever and ever (Abraham 3:26).

Abraham learned, and taught, that the first estate was our pre-earth life where we lived as intelligences and spirits. Those who kept their first estate, in the pre-earth life, would be added upon—would have flesh and bone added upon their spirits as well as opportunities to use their free agency in keeping God's commandments. They who kept not their first estate (the devil and his angels) would not have the same glory and would come to the earth as spirits without bodies of flesh and bones. They who come to earth, and keep their second estate and keep the commandments of God, will become like God—will have immortality and Eternal Life which God has promised to the obedient—will have "glory added upon their heads for ever and ever."

Abraham Taught About Earth's Creation

Abraham learned—and taught the Egyptians—about the creation of the earth by the Gods—how they went down at the beginning and they, "that is the Gods, organized and formed the heavens and the earth" (Abraham 4:1). Abraham taught the Egyptians how seven great time frames were used in the "preparation of the earth" for the life which was placed upon it. He taught how the Gods "took counsel among themselves and said: Let us go down and form man in our image, after our likeness; and we will give dominion over the fish of the sea, and over the fowl of the air, and over the cattle, and over all the earth. . . ." Then he taught how the Gods went down and organized man in their own image, male and female, and then asked them "to be fruitful and multiply, and replenish the earth, and subdue it." (Abraham 4:26-28.)

Then Abraham learned and taught how the Gods commanded the man Adam, saying:

> Of every tree of the garden thou mayest freely eat,
> But of the tree of knowledge of good and evil, thou shalt not eat of it; for in the time that thou eatest thereof, thou shalt surely die. Now I, Abraham, saw that it was after the Lord's time, which was after the time of Kolob; for as yet the Gods had not appointed unto Adam his reckoning." (Abraham 5:12-13.)

Final Line in Account of Abraham

The last line in our present account of Abraham in the Pearl of Great Price reads:

> And Adam gave names to all cattle, to the fowl of the air, to every beast of the field; and for Adam, there was found an help meet for him (Abraham 5:21).

Although this is the last published writing of the book of Abraham in our current Pearl of Great Price, there is evidence that Abraham both learned and taught much more than is in our present account. (Some of this evidence will be shown in later chapters in this book.)

Abraham's Preparation and Mission to Egypt

Abraham was well prepared before he went on his mission to Egypt. He had the priesthood, he had the great teachings of the gospel, and he had received the temple endowment. He also had the scriptures or "the records of the fathers, even the patriarchs" (Abraham 1:31).

The Lord gave Abraham a very practical reason for going into Egypt— a reason the Egyptians would understand and accept. They certainly would not have accepted him as a "minister of the Gospel come to preach the Gospel of Jesus Christ," but

> . . . there was a continuation of a famine in the land; and I, Abraham, con- cluded to go down into Egypt, to sojourn there, for the famine became very grievous (Abraham 2:21).

Here was the reason Egypt would accept Abraham into their land—a famine. Egypt was not usually touched with famine even when other parts of the Middle East were because the Nile River seldom dried up. They did not then, in Egypt (nor do they today) depend upon rain because they used the waters of the Nile to irrigate their crops and keep them alive.

The Lord also knew the sensuous heart of the Pharaoh who was ruling Egypt at the time of Abraham: he was a king who took for himself any beautiful woman who caught his eye and who killed any husband who objected. He was motivated by his own carnal desires and passions; there- fore, he would not be very prone to honor Abraham or to give him any recognition—not even grain for his needs. How, then, was Abraham to get an opportunity to teach the gospel to leaders of the country—to have any real influence on the people?

Abraham's wife was very beautiful—so beautiful that Abraham knew the Pharaoh would do anything—even to killing Abraham—to get this beautiful woman for himself. The Lord also knew this and with His fore- knowledge and insight into the Pharaoh's heart, He told Abraham:

> Behold, Sarai, thy wife, is a very fair woman to look upon;
> Therefore it shall come to pass, when the Egyptians shall see her, they will say—She is his wife; and they will kill you, but they will save her alive; therefore see that ye do on this wise:
> Let her say unto the Egyptians, she is thy sister, and thy soul shall live.
> And it came to pass that I, Abraham, told Sarai, my wife, all that the Lord had said unto me—Therefore say unto them, I pray thee, thou art my sister, that it may be well with me for thy sake, and my soul shall live because of thee. (Abraham 2:22-25.)

Thus with a courtship pattern and motives as old as the world—that Sarai was Abraham's sister and not his wife—the Pharaoh would try to win Abraham's favor. As any suitor knows who competes for the hand of a fair woman, to have a girl's brother speak well of you is to help win the approval of the woman. Why, Abraham might speak well of the Pharaoh to the girl's parents as well and an approved marriage arranged. Thus when news of the beautiful woman (who was thought to be Abraham's sister) reached the Pharaoh, Abraham was given the "red carpet" treatment in Egypt instead of death.

Abraham was invited to stay in Egypt: no need to get grain and return to lands still affected by the famine. Stay until the famine abates—(stay until the Pharaoh can woo and win Abraham's "sister"). Abraham may have been treated like royalty, might even have been given an opportunity to teach in the royal courts of Egypt. Of course we can only surmise, but it is probably safe to assume that the Pharaoh would usually be "conveniently" absent when Abraham spoke. He was probably cruising down the Nile with his harpists playing love songs, and with his servants providing sumptuous meals and all the amenities of a royal courtship of Sarai, who continued to coyly play her part. (How she kept the interest of the Pharaoh, and still kept him at a discreet distance, would make an interesting Egyptian romance story.)

While Sarai was being courted, Abraham could have been teaching the gospel. Not that she may not have been with "her brother" on some occasions, but the scripture is silent on her part in the missionary role of Abraham. Our present book of Abraham gives some evidence that Abraham taught in clear terms—in beauty and simplicity—the gospel of Jesus Christ to the Egyptians. The Lord said: "Abraham, I show these things unto thee before ye go into Egypt, that ye may declare all these words" (Abraham 3:15). The words of Abraham must have been sacred and meaningful to someone because the scrolls containing Abraham's account were preserved carefully and were eventually buried with Egyptian mummies.

Abraham Taught Deeper Gospel Aspects

That Abraham taught some of the deeper aspects of the gospel is also evidenced in the book of Abraham. Ten generations before Abraham, the first Pharaoh of Egypt sought earnestly to "imitate that order established by the fathers in the first generations" (Abraham 1:26). Could part of the imitation have been an attempt by the Egyptians to carry out aspects of the temple endowment which is part of the "highest order of the priesthood"? By the time of Abraham, fundamental errors and gross distortions had entered into Egyptian worship—and into their temples. To those who believed the gospel, and who accepted the fundamentals he taught them, could Abraham have shared with them some of the truths of the temple ceremony?

As Joseph Smith was translating the Egyptian papyri that came into his hands through Michael Chandler, he said of Facsimile No. 2, Fig. 8: "Contains writing that cannot be revealed unto the world; but is to be had in the Holy Temple of God." (See Pearl of Great Price, "Explanation of the

Foregoing Cut," p. 35.) There is some intimation that figures 9 through 20 in the same facsimile were also related to the temple endowment, for Joseph Smith wrote: "Ought not to be revealed at the present time" (Fig. 9). It seems evident that part of the scrolls from which the book of Abraham was translated also contained some very sacred information regarding Egyptian temple rites which, if they were not entirely correct, "were a very good imitation."

In another chapter in this book we will attempt to show just how good the "imitation" was that the Egyptians had in their temple worship. After many years of working on some of the papyri which came into the Church's hands in 1967, Brother Nibley concluded: "They were temple texts used in the performance of ordinances, 'an inventory of the holiest mysteries,' the saving ordinances, which were 'carried out or witnessed' by both the living and the dead" (Hugh Nibley, *The Message of the Joseph Smith Papyri*, p. 6).

Is it possible that Abraham gave the sacred temple endowment to some of the righteous Egyptians who accepted the gospel? How could he give the endowment without giving them the priesthood? How could he give them the priesthood if they were descendants of Cain, through Ham and Egyptus, and were black? Was Abraham talking only to the Egyptians who were Semitic in origin—the Hyksos rulers of Egypt? Is it possible that Abraham, under the direction of the Lord—and to only a few of the Egyptians—did not withhold the priesthood as his forefather Noah had done? Why would the Lord call Abraham to this strange land and prepare him so carefully to be a minister to them if he was to proclaim only part of the gospel?

Abraham's Stay in Egypt Halted

How long Abraham stayed in Egypt is not known: weeks, months, or even years. It seems, however, that his mission and sojourn was rather abruptly interrupted. Following is the Bible narrative:

> And it came to pass, that when Abram was come into Egypt, the Egyptians beheld the woman, that she was very fair.
>
> The princes also of Pharaoh saw her, and commanded her to be brought before Pharaoh; and the woman was taken into Pharaoh's house.
>
> And he entreated Abram well for her sake; and he had sheep, and oxen, and he asses, and menservants, and maidservants, and she asses, and camels.
>
> And the Lord plagued Pharaoh and his house with great plagues, because of Sarai, Abram's wife.
>
> And Pharaoh called Abram, and said, What hast thou done unto me in this thing? Why didst thou not tell me that she was thy wife? Why saidst thou, She is my sister? so I might have taken her unto me to wife; now therefore, behold I say unto thee, Take thy wife and go thy way.
>
> And Pharaoh commanded men concerning him; and they sent him away, and his wife, and all that he had.
>
> And Abram went up out of Egypt, he, and his wife, and all that he had, and Lot with him, unto the south. And Abram was very rich in cattle, in silver, and in gold. (JST, Genesis 12:10-15; 13:1.)

Such a brief Biblical narrative for so interesting and significant a mission. One has to smile at the way the Lord used the sensuous, murderous Pharaoh for his own purposes and to accomplish Abraham's great mission. The Pharaoh apparently gave Abraham great wealth and great status: "He entreated Abram well for her sake." The god-king Pharaoh was to know all things and never make mistakes or be "taken in," but he did not know all things and he was "taken in." Imagine this powerful Pharaoh trying desperately to win the love and favor of Sarai only to have his efforts frustrated time and time again. One wonders what kind of "plagues" Pharaoh was plagued with because of Abraham's wife. To have all wealth, status and power—to be able to woo and win, or to take any woman he so desired—but unable to win over Sarai must have, indeed, "plagued" the Pharaoh.

We can only guess at the scene when, perhaps in desperation to save herself from the advances of the frustrated Pharaoh, Sarai had to tell the whole truth—she was already married to Abraham. What a shock to a god-king who knows all things. Why, then, did not the Pharaoh, in anger, have Abraham killed for deception and for being made "the fool"? We can only surmise.

Perhaps Abraham was, by then, well-known and respected for his great wisdom and his teachings. The Pharaoh himself had given Abraham gold, silver—perhaps letters of recommendation—and opportunities to speak in the great courts of Egypt. When confronted by the Pharaoh about the "apparent lie," Abraham could have explained that Sarai's father was a brother to his own father, Terah, and that, when her father died, Terah raised her as a daughter—a "sister" to Abraham. It was not uncommon for a man to marry such a "sister" who was, in reality, a cousin. Egyptians often married close relatives to preserve royal blood lines.

Abraham could have told the Pharaoh how the gospel teaches us that everyone who is baptized in the Faith becomes one family—"brothers and sisters" in a spiritual sense. He may have borne his testimony with such power and spirit as to "almost" convince the Pharaoh. The Pharaoh may have admired and felt the integrity and spirit of this great man even though he, himself, was a wicked man. All the narrative in the scripture says is that the Pharaoh, to save face, said: "Take thy wife and go thy way." Abraham left, but he accomplished his mission of teaching the gospel to the "strange land" and he was given safe conduct out of the country.

The book of Abraham, in our current Pearl of Great Price, is one of the great legacies Abraham left in Egypt that the world does not have. The story of the saga of the papyri (from which Joseph Smith translated the book of Abraham) from ancient Egypt into the hands of the Church, then out, then in again is a most fascinating history. (Parts of this story will be reviewed in another chapter of this writing.)

Summary of Chapter Twelve

1. There is very little in either the Bible or the book of Abraham on the early life of Abraham.

2. The apocryphal Book of Jasher gives some of the early life of Abraham.

3. Abraham must have been taught the true gospel in his youth even though his father, and other members of the family, later apostatized.

4. Abraham told us of the origin of the Egyptians.

5. By the time of Abraham, Egyptian worship had degenerated to a very pagan level.

6. Abraham was delivered from being offered as a human sacrifice to the Egyptian gods by an angel of the Lord.

7. Abraham was called by the Lord to go on a mission into the heart of Egypt.

8. Before going on his mission, Abraham was given the Melchizedek Priesthood, and the higher ordinances of this priesthood—the temple endowment.

9. Before Abraham went into Egypt he was given some Egyptian language and cultural background.

10. Abraham learned from the Urim and Thummim the relationship of the planets and stars of our earth, both to teach and to interest the Egyptians.

11. Abraham learned where we came from before we were born, why we are here on earth, and where we go after this earth.

12. Abraham learned, and taught the Egyptians, about the earth's creation.

13. After Abraham's preparation he went on a mission to Egypt.

14. A famine was the practical reason for the Egyptians to have let him into their country.

15. Abraham's beautiful wife, Sarai, was introduced to the Pharaoh as his "sister" so Abraham could have time to teach the gospel while the Pharaoh courted Sarai.

16. Abraham taught some of the deeper aspects of the gospel to someone in Egypt—even the temple endowment.

17. Abraham's stay in Egypt came to a halt when the Pharaoh learned that Sarai was Abraham's wife.

18. The book of Abraham is part of the legacy Abraham left in Egypt which was finally to be buried with some mummies.

Chapter Thirteen

The Scroll of Joseph—
His Mission in Egypt

Joseph's Mission in Egypt

Within just three generations of Abraham (Abraham, Isaac, Jacob, Joseph), the Lord sent another prophet to Egypt, and Joseph's "mission call" to Egypt came in a most unusual way.

You will recall that Joseph's brothers hated their younger brother because they felt their father, Jacob (Israel), loved Joseph more than he loved Joseph's brethren (see JST, Genesis 37:4). Also, there were Joseph's troublesome dreams which indicated he was to be a ruler over them (Genesis 37:5). The coat of many colors, which Jacob gave to Joseph, capped their envy and hatred. As Joseph came to bring supplies to his brothers, who were tending flocks in Shechem, they plotted against him:

> When Joseph was come unto his brethren, . . . they stript Joseph out of his coat, his coat of many colours that was on him;
> And they took him, and cast him into a pit (Genesis 37:23-24).

Then the brothers decided that, rather than kill Joseph, they would sell him:

> Then there passed by Midianites merchantmen; and they drew and lifted up Joseph out of the pit, and sold Joseph to the Ishmeelites for twenty pieces of silver: and they brought Joseph into Egypt.
> And the Midianites sold him into Egypt unto Potiphar, an officer of Pharaoh's, and captain of the guard. (Genesis 37:28, 36.)
> And the Lord was with Joseph, and he was a prosperous man; and he was in the house of his master the Egyptian.
> And Joseph found grace in his sight, and he served him: and he made him overseer over his house, and all that he had he put into his hand. (Genesis 39:2, 4.)

When Potiphar's wife falsely accused Joseph of adultery after he had resisted her advances (Genesis 39), Potiphar caused Joseph to be thrown into prison, but

> The Lord was with Joseph, and showed him mercy, and gave him favor in the sight of the keeper of the prison.

And the keeper of the prison committed to Joseph's hand all the prisoners that were in the prison; and whatsoever they did there, he was the overseer of it. (JST, Genesis 39:21-22.)

While he was in prison Joseph was able to interpret, correctly, the dreams of both the butler of the King of Egypt, and the baker. These two men had offended their king and they were in prison with Joseph. Later, the butler was released and found favor with the Pharaoh king. One day, when the Pharaoh had a dream he could not interpret, the butler remembered Joseph, and he told the Pharaoh that Joseph could interpret his dream.

Joseph was called from prison and, with inspiration from the Lord, he was able to interpret the Pharaoh's dream. Because of the favorable impression Joseph made on the Pharaoh, he was made second in command over all Egypt. Joseph's leadership, and his insights from the Lord, saved Egypt from a terrible famine because Joseph's interpretation of the Pharaoh's dream led to storage of food for the lean years. (Genesis 41.)

Joseph as "Savior" of His Household

And all countries came into Egypt to Joseph for to buy corn; because that the famine was so sore in all lands.

Now when Jacob saw that there was corn in Egypt, Jacob said unto his sons, Why do ye look one upon another?

And he said, Behold, I have heard that there is corn in Egypt: get you down thither, and buy for us from thence; that we may live, and not die.

And Joseph's ten brethren went down to buy corn in Egypt. (Genesis 41:57; 42:1-3.)

Joseph became a type of "savior" of his own father's household. Temporally, he saved "Israel" from famine. To summarize the story, the brothers came into Egypt not knowing their younger brother, Joseph. They bowed before him. He accused them roughly, imprisoned Simeon, and sent them back for Benjamin, his youngest brother. (Genesis 42.) Jacob was reluctantly persuaded to send Benjamin to Egypt. Again Joseph's brethren make obeisance to him, and they ate and drank together. (Genesis 43.)

Joseph then arranged to stop the return of his brethren to Canaan. Judah offered himself in place of Benjamin for their father's sake. Joseph realized that his brethren had truly repented of their former offense against him. (Genesis 44.) Joseph made himself known to his brethren and they rejoiced together. Then the Pharaoh invited Jacob and his family to come and dwell in Egypt and to eat the fat of the land. (Genesis 45.) Jacob and his family of seventy souls came into Egypt and were greeted with great love from Joseph.

The Pharaoh spake unto Joseph, saying,

Thy father and thy brethren are come unto thee:

The land of Egypt is before thee; in the best of the land make thy father and brethren to dwell; in the land of Goshen let them dwell: and if thou knowest any men of activity among them, then make them rulers over my cattle. (Genesis 47:5-6.)

Symbolism in Joseph's Life to that of the Savior

One cannot help but see some symbolism in the whole life of Joseph as a parallel, and a prologue, of the coming of the Savior, Jesus Christ, to the world many years later. In the world-renowned Oberammergau Passion Play, performed every ten years in Germany, a distinctive analogy is drawn between those who sold Joseph into the hands of foreign traders and Jesus Christ, sold by Judas to the High Council of the Sanhedrin.

The prologue to Act V of the Passion Play says:

See the false disciple now joins the open enemies, and a few pieces of silver efface all love and loyalty from his impious heart.

Without a conscience he goes to make a shameful bargain; for him, the best of teachers can be sold for a traitor's reward.

The same spirit hardened the sons of Jacob, when they, without mercy, sold their own brother for a pitiful price into the hands of foreign traders.

Where the heart worships the idol of money, every more noble feeling is deadened; honour can be sold, and with it a man's word, love and friendship.

A grand still tableau then shows Jacob's sons selling their brother, Joseph, for twenty pieces of silver (Genesis 37:23-28). A contralto soloist sings:

What will you offer for this boy?
Said Joseph's brothers there:
How much will you give us?
Quickly they give away their brother's
Blood and life for a profit
Of twenty pieces of silver.
What will you give? What will be my reward?
Says Iscariot also, if I betray
The Master to you?
For thirty pieces of silver
He makes his blood bargain—and Jesus is
Sold to the High Council.
(The Oberammergau Passion Play 1980 English text: pp. 43, 44; revised and published by the Parish of Oberammergau.)

Joseph's father, Jacob—prophet and patriarch of Israel—recognized that Joseph was not only the temporal salvation of their family, but he saw him as their spiritual leader:

Therefore, O my son, he hath blessed me in raising thee up to be a servant unto me, in saving my house from death;

In delivering my people, thy brethren, from famine which was sore in the land; wherefore the God of thy fathers shall bless thee, and the fruit of thy loins, that they shall be blessed above thy brethren, and above thy father's house;

For thou has prevailed, and thy father's house hath bowed down unto thee, even as it was shown unto thee, before thou was sold into Egypt by the hands of thy brethren; wherefore thy brethren shall bow down unto thee, from generation to generation, unto the fruit of thy loins forever;

For thou shalt be a light unto my people, to deliver them in the days of their captivity, from bondage; and to bring salvation unto them, when they are altogether bowed down under sin. (JST, Genesis 48:8-11.)

Jacob Blesses Joseph's Sons

Two sons were born to Joseph while he was in Egypt: Manasseh and Ephraim. Jacob accepted these sons of Joseph as if they were his own. He said: "Wherefore they shall be called after my name. (Therefore they were called Israel.)" (JST, Genesis 48:5.) Jacob, the aged father of Joseph, called for the two sons so that he might give them a blessing:

Bring them, I pray thee, unto me, and I will bless them.

Now the eyes of Israel were dim for age, so that he could not see well. And he brought them near unto him; and he kissed them, and embraced them. (JST, Genesis 48:15-16.)

Jacob put his right hand on Ephraim and his left hand on Manasseh to bless them. Joseph tried to help his partially blind father by moving his right hand from Ephraim and putting it on Manasseh, for Manasseh was the first-born and Joseph thought he should have the greater blessing and be patriarchal leader but Jacob refused to have his hands moved. He said:

I know it, my son, I know it; he also shall become a people, and he also shall be great; but truly his younger brother shall be greater than he, and his seed shall become a multitude of nations.

. . . And he set Ephraim before Manasseh. (JST, Genesis 48:25-26.)

Jacob Prophesies and Blesses His Sons

Jacob then called together his sons. He wanted to tell them what would befall them in the last days. Each of Jacob's sons were then given a blessing—or a prophetic utterance—as to their future or character. (See Genesis 49:1-33.) Joseph's blessing is especially significant: the blessing covers a broad spectrum of the history of Israel through Joseph and his posterity. It speaks of sacred things which have been fulfilled by the restoration of the gospel in the latter days by one of Joseph's descendants, even Joseph Smith. (Joseph's blessing is a blessing which could be pronounced upon modern Latter-day Saints by their own fathers or by stake patriarchs.)

Blessing of Joseph

Joseph is a fruitful bough, even a fruitful bough by a well; whose branches run over the wall;

The archers have sorely grieved him, and shot at him, and hated him:

But his bow abode in strength, and the arms of his hands were made strong by the hands of the mighty God of Jacob; (from thence is the shepherd, the stone of Israel:)

Even by the God of thy father, who shall help thee; and by the Almighty, who shall bless thee with blessings of heaven above, blessings of the deep that lieth under, blessings of the breasts, and of the womb:

The blessings of thy father have prevailed above the blessings of my progenitors unto the utmost bound of the everlasting hills: they shall be on the head of Joseph, and on the crown of the head of him that was separate from his brethren. (Genesis 49:22-26.)

Joseph is a fruitful bough. Yes, Joseph has brought forth much posterity, good people have come from Joseph's loins, and they have brought forth good works; "by their fruits ye shall know them" (Matthew 7:20). Most members of The Church of Jesus Christ of Latter-day Saints lay claim to being of the lineage of Joseph through either Ephraim or Manasseh. The great Nephite peoples were descendants of Joseph (2 Nephi 3:4; 1 Nephi 6:2).

Even a fruitful bough by a well. Joseph's posterity will be by large bodies of water. The largest bodies of water in the world are the Pacific and Atlantic oceans. *Whose branches run over the wall.* The Nephites, Columbus, other scattered remnants of Joseph throughout Europe and even Asia, will not be stopped by the "wall" or barrier that the ocean at one time presented. (See 1 Nephi 13:12-13.) The "wall" was also the lack of knowledge of these vast American continents. Lehi said:

> It is wisdom that this land should be kept as yet from the knowledge of other nations; for behold, many nations would overrun the land, that there would be no place for an inheritance (2 Nephi 1:8).

There would have been no place for the posterity of Joseph to receive a great inheritance if these lands of America had not been preserved from other nations as long as they were.

The archers have sorely grieved him, and shot at him, and hated him. Joseph's own brothers plotted to kill him; Potiphar's wife tried to break him morally. He was put down time and time again only to arise stronger each time. Such was the character of Joseph.

Nephi, the seed of Joseph, would go through similar trials. So would other prophets of Joseph's seed. Joseph Smith, a descendant of Joseph (see 2 Nephi 3:6-9), was persecuted, reviled against, and had all manner of evil spoken against him (JS—H 1:33), and was finally not only "shot at" but martyred. The posterity of Joseph did not find peace and security in Kirtland, nor in Missouri, nor in Nauvoo. "The archers sorely grieved him, and shot at him, and hated him."

But his bow abode in strength, and the arms of his hands were made strong by the hands of the mighty God of Jacob; (from thence is the shepherd, the stone of Israel). The Lord, the God of Jacob, the Shepherd, the Stone, the Rock, Jesus Christ, Jehovah, the Lord strong and mighty, the King of Glory—this is the Lord who makes the hands of Joseph strong. As Joseph is tempted by Potiphar's wife he is made strong by saying, "How . . . can I do this great wickedness, and sin against God? (Genesis 39:9). Surely all of our strength lies in our testimony of the Lord. Modern Israel's strength, like Joseph's of old, comes from the Mighty God of Jacob.

And by the Almighty, who shall bless thee with blessings of heaven above. The God of Jesus Christ, the Almighty, our Father and His Father blessed Joseph Smith (and all the posterity of Joseph) with a personal visitation:

> I saw two Personages, whose brightness and glory defy all description, standing above me in the air. One of them spake unto me, calling me by name and said, pointing to the other—*This is My Beloved Son. Hear Him!* (JS—H 1:17.)

Through this testimony, if we believe, we, who are the posterity of Joseph of old, are "blessed with blessings of heaven above." What greater blessing from heaven above than the visit of God the Father and His Son, Jesus Christ.

Blessings of the deep that lieth under. This blessing of the deep that lieth under is the Book of Mormon. "It shall be as if the fruit of thy loins had cried unto them from the dust" (2 Nephi 3:19; Moroni 10:27). More precious than the minerals of the lands of America—the coal, the gas, the oil, the gold, the silver, the copper, the iron. More precious than the rich soil of the Americas are the "blessings of the deep that lieth under"—the plates of the Book of Mormon.

This is part of the great blessing of Joseph. This record contains the "fulness of the everlasting Gospel . . . as delivered by the Savior to the ancient inhabitants" of this land (JS—H 1:34).

Blessings of the breasts, and of the womb. These are the beautiful children born to those who are the posterity of Joseph and who keep the covenants and live the gospel. This posterity are those who have "clean hands and pure hearts" when they live the gospel. They are clean inside and out. Tobacco, liquor, drugs, and other harmful things are not taken by the seed of Joseph who honor their heritage. The attitude and spirit of parents who know their true purpose on earth see their children as "blessings of the breasts, and of the womb." Joseph's posterity who keep the commandments "multiply and replenish the earth" and fill the earth "with the measure of man" (D&C 49:17) and have joy and rejoicing in their children.

The blessings of thy father have prevailed above the blessings of my progenitors unto the utmost bound of the everlasting hills. Joseph's blessing was to be above Jacob's other progenitors. Part of this blessing is the land of America which is the inheritance of the posterity of Joseph. Father

Lehi said this land of America was "a land of promise, a land which is choice above all other lands; a land which the Lord God hath covenanted with me should be a land for the inheritance of my seed. Yea, the Lord hath covenanted this land unto me, and to my children forever, and also all those who should be led out of other countries by the hand of the Lord." (2 Nephi 1:5.)

> Wherefore, Joseph truly saw our day. And he obtained a promise of the Lord, that out of the fruit of his loins the Lord God would raise up a righteous branch unto the house of Israel; not the Messiah, but a branch which was to be brought down into captivity; if so, it shall be because of iniquity; for if iniquity shall abound cursed shall be the land for their sakes, but unto the righteous it shall be blessed forever. (2 Nephi 1:7.)

After the death of the prophet Joseph Smith, Brigham Young led the exodus of the Mormon pioneers (Joseph's posterity) from Nauvoo to the valleys of the mountains, to *the utmost bound of the everlasting hills*. The scriptures in Isaiah 2:2-3, and Micah 4:1-2, have often been cited in missionary work to verify the necessity of the transfer of the seed of Joseph to the mountains. Following is the quotation from Micah:

> In the last days it shall come to pass, that the mountain of the house of the Lord shall be established in the top of the mountains, and it shall be exalted above the hills; and people shall flow unto it.
> And many nations shall come, and say, Come, and let us go up to the mountain of the Lord, and to the house of the God of Jacob; and he will teach us of his ways, and we will walk in his paths: for the law shall go forth of Zion, and the word of the Lord from Jerusalem (Micah 4:1-2).

One of the most important factors in the gathering of the saints (the posterity of Joseph) has been "the mountain of the Lord, . . . the house of the God of Jacob": in other words, the temple and the blessings of the temple endowment. Through the restoration of the gospel has come the restoration of the sacred temple ordinances, thus the blessings of the posterity of Joseph have prevailed above the blessings of other posterity of Jacob. These blessings, however, can come to all who will accept and live the gospel of Jesus Christ in its fullness. The seed of Joseph are willing and anxious to share the great blessing which has been given to them.

Lehi saw his people as a partial fulfillment of the promise given to Joseph that the blessing would be *on the crown of the head of him that was separate from his brethren*. Since Lehi was led away to America, away from the main branch of Israel, he saw himself and his seed as a "branch which was broken off"—separated from his brethren:

> Wherefore, Joseph truly saw our day. And he obtained a promise of the Lord, that out of the fruit of his loins the Lord God would raise up a righteous branch unto the house of Israel; not the Messiah, but a branch which was to be

broken off, nevertheless, to be remembered in the covenants of the Lord that the Messiah should be made manifest unto them in the latter days, in the spirit of power, unto the bringing of them out of darkness unto light—yea, out of hidden darkness and out of captivity into freedom. (2 Nephi 3:5.)

Joseph Smith, who was also of the posterity of Joseph, and thus of the "fruit of his loins," who also "was separate from his brethren"—separated and called as a prophet to this dispensation—was to be a great blessing to the seed of Lehi in bringing them again to the knowledge of the gospel as well as to the other seed of Joseph:

> A choice seer will I raise up out of the fruit of thy loins; and he shall be esteemed highly among the fruit of thy loins. And unto him will I give commandment that he shall do a work for the fruit of thy loins, his brethren, which shall be of great worth unto them, even to the bringing of them to the knowledge of the covenants which I have made with thy fathers. (2 Nephi 3:7.)

Part of the work of Joseph Smith was to bring forth the Book of Mormon to help confound false doctrines and the laying down of contentions and to establish peace among all the fruit of Joseph's loins. This meant not only the Lamanites, who were the fruit of Joseph's loins, but all other peoples who would heed the teachings. Thus the magnificent blessing given to Joseph of old by his father, Jacob, finds some of its most remarkable fulfillment in these latter days.

Joseph Smith Like Joseph of Old

Joseph of old likened Joseph Smith unto himself in bringing salvation to his people. He said of Joseph Smith:

> And his name shall be called after me; and it shall be after the name of his father. And he shall be like unto me; for the thing, which the Lord shall bring forth by his hand, by the power of the Lord shall bring my people unto salvation. (2 Nephi 3:15.)

Joseph of old was one of the greatest of the prophets: he brought both temporal and spiritual salvation to Israel, his family. He also brought temporal salvation to the Egyptians in saving them from famine. There is evidence that he, like Abraham, shared with them the gospel—at least to those who believed. Joseph Smith also brought the means of temporal and spiritual salvation to Israel, and he, too, desired to share the gospel with "Egypt" (or the world).

Writings of Joseph of Old

Joseph of old, Joseph of Egypt, had many revelations given unto him and many prophecies. He wrote many of them down but the King James Version of the Bible does not have them. The brass plates that Lehi sent his sons back to Jerusalem to obtain, before they came across the ocean to

America, contained some of the writings of Joseph (see 2 Nephi 3, 4, 5). Nephi, speaking of the prophecies of his father concerning Joseph who was carried into Egypt, said:

> For behold, he [Joseph] truly prophesied concerning all his seed. And the prophecies which he wrote, there are not many greater. And he prophesied concerning us, and our future generations; and *they are written upon the plates of brass.* (2 Nephi 4:2; italics added.)

Lehi, of course, quoted from these writings of Joseph when he was speaking to his own last born son also named Joseph (see 2 Nephi 3). Not only were Joseph's words written upon the plates of brass but some of them must also have been written upon papyri in the Egyptian language. Some of the writings of Joseph of old were on the papyri which came into Joseph Smith's hands.

The entries in the *History of the Church* tell a fascinating story of the message—or perhaps the message behind the message—of the Egyptian papyri. The entry recorded after July 5, 1835, but before the next entry of July 9th, is most interesting because it clearly states that some of the papyrus rolls contained the writings of Joseph of Egypt:

> Soon after this, some of the Saints at Kirtland purchased the mummies and papyrus, a description of which will appear hereafter, and with W. W. Phelps and Oliver Cowdery as scribes, I commenced the translation of some of the characters or hieroglyphics, and much to our joy found that one of the rolls contained the writings of Abraham, *another writings of Joseph of Egypt*, etc., a more full account of which will appear in its place, as I proceed to examine or unfold them. Truly we can say, the Lord is beginning to reveal the abundance of peace and truth. (Jay Todd, *The Saga of the Book of Abraham*, pp. 171-172.)

In a letter, dated July 19 and 20, 1835, written by Elder William W. Phelps to his wife, Sally, he mentioned that the rolls of papyrus contained the sacred record kept of Joseph in Pharaoh's court in Egypt:

> Beloved Sally,
>
> Last evening we received our first letter after an absence of twelve weeks and twelve hours. Our tears of joy were the witness of its welcome reception . . .
>
> The last of June four Egyptian mummies were brought here; there were two papyrus rolls besides some other ancient Egyptian writings with them. As no one could translate these writings, they were presented to President Smith. He soon knew what they were and said they, the "rolls of papyrus," *contained the sacred record kept of Joseph in Pharaoh's Court in Egypt*, and the teachings of Father Abraham. God has so ordered it that these mummies and writings have been brought in the Church, and the sacred writing I had just locked up in Brother Joseph's house when your letter came, so I had two consolations of good things in one day. These records of old times, when we translate and print them in a book, will make a good witness for the Book of Mormon. There is nothing secret or hidden that shall not be revealed, and they come to the Saints. (See *Improvement Era*, Aug. 1942, p. 529.)

First Notice from the Church on Mummies and Papyri

An article was prepared for the Kirtland church newspaper, *The Latter-day Saint's Messenger and Advocate*, dated December 31, 1835, which was probably motivated by the Prophet Joseph Smith. The article dealt with the story of how the Church acquired the mummies, what the Saints knew of them, and so forth. The article is the first written notice by the Church concerning the mummies and papyri, and it appeared nearly six months after Michael Chandler went to Kirtland and brought the papyrus and the mummies to the Prophet's attention. The second part of the article contained a letter written by Oliver Cowdery which gives details on how the records came to be in Joseph's hands. He relates the saga of the papyrus from Egypt to Kirtland, gives a description of the papyrus and some explanation as to what they were about. Oliver Cowdery clearly stated that the Egyptian records were of Abraham and Joseph:

> Upon the subject of the Egyptian records, or rather the writings of Abraham and Joseph, I may say a few words. This record is beautifully written on papyrus with black, and a small part, red ink or paint, in perfect preservation. The characters are such as you find upon the coffins of mummies, hieroglyphics, etc. with many characters or letters exactly like the present, (though probably not quite so square,) form of the Hebrew without points.
>
> These records were obtained from one of the catacombs in Egypt, near the place where once stood the renowned city of Thebes, Egypt, by the celebrated French traveller Antonio Lebolo; in the year 1831. He procured license from Mehemet Ali, then Viceroy of Egypt, under the protection of Chevalier Drovetti, the French Consul, in the year 1828; employed 433 men four months and two days, (if I understand correctly, Egyptian or Turkish soldiers,) at from four to six cents per diem, each man; entered the catacomb June 7th, 1831, and obtained eleven Mummies. There were several hundred Mummies in the same catacomb; about one hundred embalmed after the first order, and deposited and placed in niches, and two or three hundred after the second and third order, and laid upon the floor or bottom of the grand cavity, the two last orders of embalmed were so decayed that they could not be moved, and only eleven of the first, found in the niches. On his way from Alexandria to Paris he put in at Trieste, and after ten days illness, expired. This was in the year 1832. Previous to his decease, he made a will of the whole to Mr. Michael H. Chandler, then in Philadelphia, Pa. his nephew, whom he supposed to have been in Ireland. Accordingly the whole were sent to Dublin, addressed according, and Mr. Chandler's friends ordered them sent to New York, where they were received at the custom house, in the winter or spring of 1833. In April of the same year Mr. Chandler paid the duties upon his Mummies, and took possession of the same. Up to this time they had not been taken out of the coffins nor the coffins opened. On opening the coffins he discovered that in connection with two of the bodies, were something rolled up with the same kind of linnen [sic], saturated with the same bitumen, which, when examined, proved to be two rolls of papyrus, previously mentioned. I may add that two or three other small pieces of papyrus, with astronomical calculations, epitaphs, &c. were found with others of the Mummies.

When Mr. Chandler discovered that there was something with the Mummies, he supposed, or hoped it might be some diamonds or other valuable metal, and was no little chagrined when he saw his disappointment. He was immediately told, while yet in the Custom House, that there was no man in that city, who could translate his roll; but was referred by the same gentleman, (a stranger,) to Mr. Joseph Smith, Jr. who, continued he, possessed some kind of power or gifts by which he had previously translated similar characters. Bro. Smith was then unknown to Mr. Chandler, neither did he know that such a book or work as the record of the Nephites had been brought before the public. From New York he took his collection to Philadelphia, where he exhibited them for a compensation. The following is a certificate put into my hands by Mr. Chandler, which he obtained while in Philadelphia and will show the opinion of the scientific of that city:

"Having examined with considerable attention and deep interest, a number of Mummies from the Catacombs, near Thebes, in Egypt, and now exhibiting in the Arcade, we beg leave to recommend them to the observation of the curious inquirer on subjects of a period so long elapsed; probably not less than three thousand years ago.—The features of some of these Mummies are in perfect expression. The papyrus, covered with black or red ink, or paint, in excellent preservation, are very interesting. The undersigned, unsolicited by any person connected by interest with this exhibition, have voluntarily set their names hereunto, for the simple purpose of calling the attention of the public, to an interesting collection, not sufficiently known in this city."

> John Redman Coxe, M.D.
> Richard Harlan, M.D.
> J. Pancoast, M.D.
> William P.C. Barton, M.D.
> E. F. Rivinus, M.D.
> Samuel G. Morgan, M.D.

While Mr. Chandler was in Philadelphia, he used every exertion to find some one who could give him the translation of his papyrus, but could not, satisfactorily, though from some few men of the first eminence, he obtained in a small degree, the translation of a few characters. Here he was referred to Bro. Smith. From Philadelphia he visited Harrisburgh, and other places east of the mountains, and was frequently referred to Bro. Smith for a translation of his Egyptian Relic.

It would be beyond my purpose to follow this gentleman in his different circuits to the time he visited this place the last of June, or the first of July, at which time he presented Bro. Smith with his papyrus. Till then neither myself nor Brother Smith knew of such relics being in America. Mr. Chandler was told that his writings could be deciphered, and very politely gave me a priviledge [sic] of copying some four or five different sentences or separate pieces, stating, at the same time, that unless he found some one who could give him a translation soon, he would carry them to London.

I am a little in advance of my narration; the morning Mr. Chandler first presented his papyrus to Bro. Smith, he was shown, by the latter, a number of characters like those upon the writings of Mr. C. which were previously copied from the plates, containing the history of the Nephites, or Book of Mormon.

Being solicited by Mr. Chandler to give an opinion concerning his antiquities, or a translation of some of the characters, Bro. S. gave him the interpretation of some few for his satisfaction. For your gratification I will here annex a certificate which I hold, from under the hand of Mr. Chandler, unsolicited, however, by any person in this place, which will show how far he believed Bro. Smith able to unfold from these long obscured rolls the wonders contained therein:

> "This is to make known to all who may be desirous, concerning the knowledge of Mr. Joseph Smith, Jr. in deciphering the ancient Egyptian hieroglyphic characters, in my possession, which I have, in many eminent cities, shown to the most learned: And, from the information that I could ever learn, or meet with, I find that of Mr. Joseph Smith, Jr. to correspond in the most minute matters."

> (signed)
> "Michael H. Chandler"
> Travelling with, and proprietor
> of Egyptian Mummies.

The foregoing is verbatim as given by Mr. C. excepting the addition of punctuation, and speaks sufficiently plain without requiring comment from me. It was given previous to the purchase of the antiquities, by any person here.

The language in which this record is written is very comprehensive, and many of the hieroglyphics exceedingly striking. The evidence is apparent upon the face, that they were written by persons acquainted with the history of the creation, the fall of man, and more or less of the correct ideas of notions of the Deity. The representation of the god-head—three, yet in one, is curiously drawn to give simply, though impressively, the writer's views of that exalted personage. The serpent, represented as walking, or formed in a manner to be able to walk, standing in front of, and near a female figure, is to me, one of the greatest representations I have ever seen upon paper, or a writing substance; and must go so far towards convincing the rational mind of the correctness and divine authority of the holy scriptures, and especially that part which has ever been assailed by the infidel community, as being a fiction, as to carry away, with one mighty sweep, the whole atheistical fabric without leaving a vestige sufficient for a foundation stone. Enoch's Pillar, as mentioned by Josephus, is upon the same roll. True, our present version of the Bible does not mention this fact, though it speaks of the righteousness of Abel and the holiness of Enoch,— one slain because his offering was accepted of the Lord, and the other taken to the regions of everlasting day without being confined to the narrow limits of the tomb, or tasting death; but Josephus says that the descendants of Seth were virtuous, and possessed a great knowledge of the heavenly bodies, and, that, in consequence of the prophecy of Adam, that the world should be destroyed once by water and again by fire, Enoch wrote a history or an account of the same, and put into two pillars one of brick and the other of stone; and that the same were in being at his (Josephus') day. The inner end of the same roll, *(Joseph's record)*, presents a representation of the judgment: At one view you behold the Savior seated upon his throne, crowned, and holding the scepters of righteousness and power, before whom also, are assembled the twelve tribes of Israel, the nations, languages and tongues of the earth, the kingdoms of the world over which satan is represented as reigning, Michael the archangel, holding the key of the bottomless pit, and at the same time the devil as being chained and shut up in the bottomless pit. But upon this last scene, I am able only to give you a shadow, to the real picture. I am certain it cannot be viewed without filling the mind with awe, unless the mind is far estranged from God: and I sincerely hope, that mine may never go so far astray, nor wander from those rational principles of the doctrine of our Savior, so much, as to become darkened in the least, and thereby fail to have that, to us, the greatest of all days, and the most sublime of all transactions, so impressively fixed upon the heart, that I become not like the beast, not knowing whither I am going, nor what shall be my final end!

I might continue my communication to a great length upon the different figures and characters represented upon the two rolls, But I have no doubt my subject has already become sufficiently prolix for your patience: I will therefore soon cease for the present—When the translation of these valuable documents will be completed, I am unable to say; neither can I give you a probable idea how large volumes they will make; but judging from their size, and the comprehensiveness of the language, one might reasonably expect to see a sufficient to develop much upon the mighty acts of the ancient men of God, and of his dealing with the children of men when they saw him face to face. Be there little or much, it must be an inestimable acquisition to our present scriptures, fulfilling, in a small degree, the word of the prophet: For the earth shall be full of the knowledge of the Lord as the waters cover the sea.

P.S. You will have understood from the foregoing, that eleven mummies were taken from the catacomb, at the time of which I have been speaking, and nothing definite having been said as to their disposal, I may, with propriety add a few words. Seven of the said eleven were purchased by gentlemen for private museums, previous to Mr. Chandler's visit to this place, with a small quantity of papyrus, similar, (as he says,) to the astronomical representation, contained with the present two rolls, of which I previously spoke, and the remaining four by gentlemen resident here.

Though the Mummies themselves are a curiosity, and an astonishment, well calculated to arouse the mind to a reflection of past ages, when men strove, as at this day, to immortalize their names, though in another manner, yet I do not consider them of much value compared with those records which were deposited with them.

If Providence permits, I will, ere long, write you again upon the propriety of looking for additions to our present scriptures, according to their own literal reading.

Believe me to be, sir, sincerely and truly, your brother in the bonds of the new and everlasting covenant.

Oliver Cowdery
To Wm. Frye, Esq. Gilead,
Calhoon Co., Ill.

More Extracts from Book of Abraham Promised

The book of Abraham, translated from the Egyptian papyri, was first published in the *Times and Seasons*, the newspaper of the Saints at Nauvoo, in two numbers: Vol. III, Nos. 9 and 10, March 1-4, and March 15-19, 1842, respectively. More extracts from the scroll of Abraham were promised.

In an article in the *Times and Seasons*, February 1843, eleven months after the printing of the book of Abraham, John Taylor, editor of the paper, in a notice to subscribers said:

> We would respectfully announce to those of our subscribers (and there are a good many of them), who commenced their subscription for the *Times and Seasons* at the time when Brother Joseph told the editorial department that the term for which they subscribed is nearly at a close; most of those commenced at the seventh and eighth numbers; at the time when the translations from the book of Abraham commenced. This is the sixth number, which leaves only four weeks until the time that they subscribed for, will be fullfilled.
>
> We have given this timely notice that our friends may prepare themselves. We would further state that we have the promise of Br. Joseph, to furnish us with further extracts from the Book of Abraham.

The promised extracts never came forth but anyone who is familiar with the life of Joseph Smith during his last two years will understand why he was not able to complete his promise to furnish further extracts from the book of Abraham. A year and four months from the above notice Joseph would lie dead—one of the most obvious reasons why the work of translation of the scrolls of Abraham and of Joseph of Egypt was not completed.

Other Possible Reasons Why Writings Have Not Come Forth

The reason that translation of the papyri was not completed was certainly not because they were thought to be unimportant. Nephi said about ancient Joseph's writings: "There are not many greater" (2 Nephi 4:2). Surely further extracts from the book of Abraham were as important as those which were revealed and translated. Why do we not have them? The explanation that Joseph Smith's death stopped the work is not sufficient. Why has no subsequent prophet been called to reveal these writings?

Perhaps the fault lies with members of the Church. Maybe we have not been curious enough, anxious enough, desirous enough, prayed enough. (When was the last time anyone prayed to receive more of the writings of Abraham and Joseph?) Maybe we have not "knocked" enough to have the Lord reveal these things to our living prophets.

As for additional material being translated from the ancient papyrus, the Prophet Joseph Smith's commentary on Facsimile No. 2 in the Pearl of Great Price may be significant:

> The above translation is given as far as we have any right to give at the present time." ("Explanation of the Foregoing Cut," Pearl of Great Price.)

And under Fig. 8, he said: "Contains writing that cannot be revealed unto the world; but is to be had in the Holy Temple of God" (see also 9, 11, and 12).

Is part of the reason we do not have further extracts from the book of Abraham—from the papyri of Abraham—because these were sacred writings meant only for the temple? Could part of the reason we do not have Joseph of Egypt's writings of the papyri be because they, too, may contain sacred things that "cannot be revealed unto the world; but is to be had in the Holy Temple of God"?

> "We believe all that God has revealed, all that He does now reveal, and we believe that He will yet reveal many great and important things pertaining to the Kingdom of God" (Ninth Article of Faith, The Church of Jesus Christ of Letter-day Saints, Pearl of Great Price; see History of the Church, Vol. 4, pp. 535-541.)

Summary of Chapter Thirteen

1. Three generations from Abraham, the Lord sent another prophet to Egypt—even Joseph.

2. Joseph was a type of "Savior" to the house of Israel.

3. Jacob's blessing of Joseph is a blessing to all who have been or are, or will be, descendants of this great prophet.

4. We, today, are recipients also of Joseph's great prophetic blessing.

5. Joseph Smith was like unto Joseph of old.

6. Joseph of old, Joseph of Egypt, had many revelations and many prophecies. He wrote them down but they are not in our Bible. A few of these writings are in the Book of Mormon because they were on the brass plates.

7. Some of the writings of Joseph of old were upon the papyri which fell into Joseph Smith's hands.

8. More extracts from the book of Abraham were promised by the editor of the *Times and Seasons*, but never came forth.

9. There are several possible reasons why the writings have not come forth:

•Joseph's death.

•We have not sought and desired them deeply enough as a church and as a people.

•Some of the material may be so sacred that it can only be known in the temple.

Chapter Fourteen

The Current Discovery of the Book of Breathings— An Egyptian Endowment

What Happened to the Mummies and Papyri After Joseph Smith's Death?

Even though some of the Saints at Kirtland had purchased the mummies and papyri originally from Mr. Chandler, and had made a gift of them to the Prophet, it is very likely that the Prophet's own mother, Lucy Mack Smith, helped purchase them. Thus, after the Prophet's death, it was understood that the mummies and papyri belonged to her. Lucy Mack Smith, for a time, exhibited the mummies and artifacts to visitors for a few cents and thus helped sustain herself. (*Saga*, pp. 160-161, 266.) Because of age and poor health, Lucy Mack Smith remained in Nauvoo with the Prophet's widow, Emma, and did not go west with the main body of the Church.

The Church Historian's Office has a list entitled "Inventory of Church Property Del'd N. K. Whitney, March 17, '47," which includes "a small parchment roll of hieroglyphics." This small fragment was part of the Church property brought to Utah along with an "Egyptian Grammar" book the Prophet was using and working on. However, the mummies and most of the scrolls remained in Nauvoo. (*Saga*, pp. 283-284, 286.)

Almon W. Babbitt, who had been left behind at Nauvoo as Trustee-in-Trust for the Church, wrote this interesting comment about the mummies to Brigham Young:

> President Brigham Young
>
> Dear Brother
>
> . . . William Smith has got the mummies from Mother Smith and refuses to give them up. . . . (*Saga*, p. 284; also *Journal History of the Church*, Jan. 31, 1847.)

William Smith, brother of the Prophet and former member of the Council of the Twelve, had been excommunicated October 12, 1845. William may have convinced his mother that he had a right to the mummies, or that he could make better financial use of them for their mutual benefit; however, how much William had to do with the mummies and papyri is not clear. (*Saga*, 285.)

When Lucy Mack Smith died in May, 1855, the mummies and papyri were taken over by Emma, the Prophet's widow, but by then she had re-married. On the anniversary of the Prophet's birth, the 23rd of December, 1847, Emma Hale Smith married a forty-three-year-old non-Mormon, "Major" Lewis Crum Bidamon, a native of Virginia. (Buddy Youngreen, *Reflections on Emma, Joseph Smith's Wife*, p. 40.)

A little over a year after the death of her former mother-in-law, Emma Smith Bidamon sold the mummies to Mr. A. Combs. Following is a copy of the note of the sale dated May 26, 1856, and found by Dr. Atiya at the Metropolitan Museum:

Nauvoo City May 25/56

This certifies that we have sold to; Mr. A. Combs four Egyptian Mummies with the records of them. These Mummies were obtained from the catacombs of Egypt sixty feet below the surface of the Earth, by the Antiquarian society of Paris and forwarded to New York & purchased by the Mormon Prophet Joseph Smith at the price of twenty four hundred dollars in the year Eighteen hundred thirty-five they were highly prized by Mr. Smith on account of the importance which attached to the record which were accidentally found enclosed in the breast of one of the Mummies. From translations by Mr. Smith of the Records these Mummies were found to be the family of Pharo King of Egypt. they were kept exclusively by Mr. Smith until his death & since by the Mother of Mr. Smith notwithstanding we have had repeated offers to purchase which have invariably been refused until her death which occurred on the fourteenth of this month.

(signed)
L. C. Bidamon
Emma Bidamon (pencil:) former
Nauvoo   wife of Jos. Smith
Hancock Co, Ill May 26   Joseph Smith (pencil:) son of
Jos. Smith

(*Saga*, p. 290.)

Surprising Discovery by Non-Mormon Scholar

On November 27, 1967, an announcement stunned and surprised Latter-day Saints. Before this date, and since 1871, members of the Church thought the mummies and papyri had burned in the Great Chicago Fire of 1871:

New York—A collection of papyrus manuscripts, long believed to have been destroyed in the Chicago Fire of 1871, was presented to the Church of Jesus Christ of Latter-Day Saints (Mormon) here today by the Metropolitan Museum of Art.

The rediscovery of some of the papyrus (and bill of sale) was immediately assumed to be the original papyrus used by Joseph Smith in translating the book of Abraham as found in the Pearl of Great Price. The story of the rediscovery is best told in the words of Dr. Aziz Suryal Atiya, professor at the University of Utah and a world-recognized scholar and researcher of Egyptian and Arabic manuscripts (and not a Latter-day Saint):

> I was writing a book at the time, one that I had started while a professor of world Christianity and eastern Christianity, and I went to the Metropolitan Museum of Art looking for documents, papyri, pictures, and illustrations to serve the book. It must have been in the early spring of 1966. I really forget the date. My book was ready for the press, and I was looking for supplementary material.
>
> While I was in one of the dim rooms where everything was brought to me, something caught my eye, and I asked one of the assistants to take me behind the bars into the storehouse of documents so that I could look some more. While there I found a file with these documents. I at once recognized the picture part of it. When I saw this picture, I knew that it had appeared in the Pearl of Great Price. I knew the general format of the picture. This kind of picture one can find generally on other papyri, but this particular one has special peculiarities. For instance, the head had fallen off, and I could see that the papyrus was stuck on paper, nineteenth century paper. The head was completely in pencil, apparently by Joseph Smith, who must have had it when that part fell off. He apparently drew the head in his own hand on the supplementary paper. Also, the hands of the mummy, raised as they are, and the leg, raised as it is—usually the mummies lie straight forward—are very peculiar. This papyrus is Egyptian, true enough, but what it stands for, I really don't know.
>
> Now when I saw this, I began to search further. I saw more pieces of papyri stacked together and suspected that Providence had assisted. Another document was found with these documents, signed by Joseph Smith's wife, his son, and someone else, testifying that these papyri were treasured and owned by Joseph Smith.
>
> In 1918, a Mrs. Heusser came to the museum and informed the officials that she had some papyrus, but an understanding was not reached until 1947. They were then acquired by the museum, and then the museum changed curators of Egyptian antiquities and the whole subject was forgotten.
>
> When I saw these documents, I really was taken back. I know the Mormon community, what it stands for, its scriptures, etc., and I said at once that these documents don't belong here. They belong to the Mormon Church. Well, of course, the people in the museum are good friends of mine, and I tried to tempt them into ceding the documents to the Church. I informed my good friend Taza Pierce, who is executive secretary of the Salt Lake Council for International Visitors, and we discussed the manner in which I should acquaint the Mormon community of the find. She suggested I see President Tanner, and she was the intermediary who arranged and attended our first two meetings. Thereafter, I met directly with President Tanner, who had said the Church was very, very interested and would do anything or pay any price for them. Since that time, we worked quietly on the possibility of their transference to the Church.
>
> In these kinds of things, I never push. I take my time. With some kindly persuasions and discussions, the museum ultimately put a memorandum on the subject to the board of trustees of the museum. This took a long time to come to that step. The Board discussed the matter at very great length, greater length than you might think, and in the end they thought that since the museum had papyri of this nature in plenty, why should they keep these documents from the Church?

When their generous decision was made, it was telephoned to me by the curator, and he wrote to me also. Then we had a lull in the situation, because the curator had to go to Egypt for a month in order to arrange final steps for the transference to the Metropolitan Museum of another treasure, in which I also had a hand. It concerns a great temple that is being presented by the Egyptian government to the American nation in recognition of the contributions America has made toward the salvage of the Abyssinian monuments.

When the curator came back, he reported very nicely about the subject and said, "The decision has been taken; your Mormon friends are going to get these papyri. So, you go to your friends and the President of the Church and make the necessary arrangements for a ceremony."

Of course, President Tanner was just as excited as I was. He reported to President McKay, who was very enthusiastic about the project also. We then decided the way in which the ceremony would be conducted.

I felt very honored and very, very pleased to be in the center of the picture with such a distinguished person as President Tanner and Mr. Thomas P. F. Hoving, who is director of the museum. He's a very important man, as is his assistant and vice director, Dr. Joseph Noble. He's a very fine man. All of them were there, and to my surprise I found that the papyri were prepared in a very fine box for safekeeping.

But during the morning of that day I made it a point to go in at an early hour, long before the meeting of these magnates, in order to make sure that the papyri were there—not only the papyri, because what is of importance is the document that accompanied the papyri. It was a faded thing, in nineteenth century hand. I found that the museum had photographed it. Well, of course, they had tried to photograph it before, but it wouldn't show because it was very faded blue paper. Now they used infra-red and ultra-violet photography to get the text out, so that now the photograph is very much better than the original.

I was enchanted about the discovery of the papyri, which had been in the hands of Joseph Smith, but the discoveries were not ended there. On the morning of handing over the papyri, I began looking them up and down, up and down, and lo! I found on the back of the paper on which the papyri were glued writings and maps and an enumeration of townships and material of the highest value to Mormon history, made, I think, by Joseph Smith's own hand. Three of the backs were full of notes and maps, which have to be studied by the specialists. I am not a specialist of that, but I have an eye for original manuscripts, and these papyri documents are not fakes; they are original Egyptian papyri of a pre-Christian era. They could be from 3000 B.C. to 300 B.C.—over 300 B.C., at any rate. That is my estimate. The era will have to be decided by the specialists.

I know the kind of ink the Egyptians used and the difference between the genuine and the fake. Papyrus writings were usually placed with mummy—papyri of many kinds—but essentially the "Book of the Dead", which would give the mummy safe passage to the world beyond. The papyri were sometimes colored. You will find papyri like this with blue, gold, and red colors. This was not out of the ordinary. With regard to the ink used, it was generally made out of soot and glue, and that is why it was eternal. I think these scrolls are written in that kind of ink. Usually the priests did the writing—they were more skilled. They used reed pens, and had to sharpen the reed and split it in the middle.

The Egyptians had the papyrus plant, and they used to split it into thin layers and put the layers criss-cross on one another, pound them with a wooden hammer, and then glue them together. They cut them to suit the purposes of the documents they wanted to write. Usually long strips were used to make scrolls, and this one was made in that fashion.

In order to protect the papyrus, which becomes brittle with age—for instance, the head of the person fell off simply because the papyrus was brittle—Joseph Smith probably thought that the best thing for its protection was to glue it on paper. When I first discovered these documents, I was so excited about the Egyptian writings that I did not look on the back of the paper, but when I returned to the museum, I noticed the writing on the back by Joseph Smith. These writings may not turn out to be of very great importance; however, any footnote one can get in the restoration of Mormon history is valuable.

The exciting part, which has proved beyond doubt that this was the papyri that was in Joseph Smith's hand, was established by that document signed by his widow. When I saw that, I had it transcribed and a copy typewritten to show to President Tanner.

Do you know that this discovery appeared in the Egyptian press on the day following the ceremony? On the first page of the most important paper! You would be surprised at the attention that was given to this discovery, and apparently the Egyptians were very pleased about the revealing of these documents. I consider it a great honor to have been able to make this discovery. Great discoveries are always accidental, and this one was as accidental as any discovery I have made—and probably more exciting than all of them. It was an honor to have been able to persuade such an august body as the Metropolitan Museum to present it to another body as august as the Mormon Church. I feel flattered to have been able to do what I did. (*Saga*, pp. 333-337.)

Papyri Given to Church Scholar

After the Church received the papyri discovered by Dr. Atiya, they were given to one of the Church's best scholars in ancient languages and the Egyptian language in particular—Dr. Hugh Nibley, Professor of Religious Instruction at Brigham Young University. His challenge was to translate the papyri and determine if these were the original papyri used by Joseph Smith in translating the book of Abraham.

For almost six years we waited for his book to come out on the Joseph Smith papyri. In 1973, the author wrote to Dr. Nibley to see if he would reply as to the status and progress of his work. Following is the letter he wrote in reply to my inquiry:

March 3, 1973

Dear Brother Johansen,

I have delayed answering your letter because I thought there might be something interesting to report. The Reading Committee has had my book on the J.S. Papyri for over a month now, and I have heard nothing from them. The thing is 600 pages long, so no wonder. However, I can assure you that things are well and under control.

Let me point out just one thing here: It has been assumed by everyone that the J.S. Papyri X and XI, known as the Sen-sen or Book of Breathings, was the original document from which Joseph Smith pretended to derive the Book of

Abraham. May I point out just one objection among a hundred to this absurd thesis? The Prophet said that the original MS of the Bk of Abraham was (1) "In a state of perfect preservation", (2) that it was "beautifully written", and (3) that it contained rubrics. J.S. Mss X and XI were, it can be easily shown, in very poor condition when they reached Kirtland; of all the Papyri, very badly written even to the most amateurish eye, and never contained the tiniest speck of red ink; ergo, they cannot possibly be the J.S. Book of Abraham. People overlook little things like this. I can only ask for your patience.

> Yours,
> (Signed)
> H. Nibley

Message of the Joseph Smith Papyri

Professor Nibley's book, *The Message of the Joseph Smith Papyri*, was finally read and approved by the Church Reading Committee and published by Deseret Book Company in Salt Lake City, Utah, 1975. It is highly recommended to any who wants to read, in detail, results of the translation and extensive research done by Dr. Nibley.

In bold print, and in the first line of chapter one of the book, is this message: "What manner of document? What the Book of Breathings is Not. NOT THE SOURCE OF THE BOOK OF ABRAHAM." Brother Nibley goes on to reiterate: "Is the Book of Abraham a correct translation of Joseph Smith Papyri X and XI? No, the Book of Breathings is not the Book of Abraham!" (P. 2.)

> . . . And there can be no doubt whatever that the manuscript he was describing was and is an entirely different one from that badly written, poorly preserved little text, entirely devoid of rubrics, which is today identified as the Book of Breathings" (p. 3).

The papyri found by Dr. Atiya (and turned over to the Church and, consequently, to Dr. Nibley) have been identified by Dr. Nibley as the "Book of Breathings" and not the source for the book of Abraham—at least according to his research. If this is the case, we still do not have the original scrolls of papyri from which Joseph Smith translated the book of Abraham.

What do we have? What is the "Book of Breathings"? Nibley points out that it is a "Funeral Text—but not an ordinary funeral text . . . Our Joseph Smith Book of Breathings (funeral text) is one of a very special and limited and uniquely valuable class of documents clustered around a single priestly family of upper Egypt in the first century A.D." (p. 3). ". . . They were temple texts used in the performance of ordinances, 'an inventory of the holiest mysteries,' the saving ordinances, which were carried out or witnessed by both the living and the dead" (p. 6). "It is not only a funerary text but a 'book of the living' for conducting initiation here on earth" (p. 7). "Its importance was overlooked because of the nature of its composition—

a few notes dashed off 'in a very concise and sometimes obscure form' by a priest, to serve as a prompter during certain ceremonies'' (p. 11). "The Egyptians did not read from the large and ornate scrolls in their ceremonies, but only from small pages held in the hand like notecards; moreover, the texts were 'perfectly familiar' to the learned reader who needed the notes only to jog his memory with minimal jottings as he went through long ceremonies. . . . The hastily scribbled and highly personalized writing was for one man's eyes alone; the text was found clutched to the owner's breast in death as his most treasured possession, and indeed the document itself informs us that it is a highly secret and personal thing of immense value to the owner and to no one else. . . . What we have in the Joseph Smith Papyrus, then, is the most intimate and private version of a 'final codification of the religious and magic literature that was transmitted down from the predynastic time,' skillfully summarizing and epitomizing the whole Egyptian religious heritage in such a manner as to preserve the original concepts virtually unchanged (p. 11).

Joseph Smith Papyri Displayed in Temples

Brother Nibley points out that "it is an interesting coincidence that from the first the Joseph Smith Papyri were displayed in a place of honor in the temple, first in Kirtland and then in Nauvoo'' (p. 13). "Thus, though, as we have seen, the Book of Breathings does not contain the text of the Book of Abraham, it does have direct ties with the three Facsimiles which Joseph Smith interprets as relating to Abraham and which belong to just such ordinances as Abraham is supposed to be involved in'' (p. 14). "What the Egyptians were looking for was not unlike what the Mormons call an 'endowment' . . . no people were more willing to invest their means and energies in obtaining an endowment—a hope and a promise—than the Egyptians'' (p. 4).

As Latter-day Saints, we believe that the temple ordinances are as old as the human race, that some aspects of the ordinances were given to Father Adam and Mother Eve. They are part of the "new and everlasting covenant, even that which was from the beginning'' (see D&C 22:1; D&C 131:1-4; D&C 132). Since the gospel was given in its fullness to Adam and Eve the revealed religion, including the temple ordinances, has passed through alternate phases of apostasy and restoration which have left the world littered with scattered fragments of the original structure. Some are more or less recognizable but some are badly damaged and out of proper context. The temple endowment of The Church of Jesus Christ of Latter-Day Saints was not built up of elements brought together by chance, custom, or long research; it was revealed to the first prophet of this dispensation, Joseph Smith.

> It is a single, perfectly consistent organic whole, conveying its message without the aid of rationalizing, spiritualizing, allegorizing, or moralizing interpretations (Nibley, p. xii).

To what extent the papyri scrolls of Abraham and Joseph acted as a catalyst in bringing about the temple endowment revealed to Joseph Smith, we do not know. That some aspects of the Egyptian endowment were very similar is a truth.

The Egyptian Endowment

What about the Egyptian rites? What are they to us? Brother Nibley says:

> They are a parody, an imitation, but as such not to be despised. For all the great age and consistency of their rites and teachings, which certainly command respect, the Egyptians did not have the real thing, and they knew it . . . they were like a people in the dark searching for a key to truth; and having found not one but many keys . . . retained all lest perchance the appropriate one should be discarded. (P. xii).

But, Brother Nibley goes on: "If the Egyptian endowment was but an imitation, it was still a good one" (p. xiii). How good was the imitation?

Following is a summation of the research of Professor Hugh Nibley on the Egyptian endowment and the excellent material published in his 305-page book entitled *The Joseph Smith Papyri*, referred to earlier. One should not attempt to "digest" for someone else such an excellent work; however, the work is such an exciting capstone to the study of the Pearl of Great Price that it seemed appropriate to conclude this book with more than just a passing reference to Dr. Nibley's book. For the convenience of the student, the writer has noted the page numbers in parentheses where the source material is located in Dr. Nibley's work. Certainly anyone who desires to go more fully into the Egyptian endowment should read for themselves his entire work. They should also see and study the sources of his scholarship by noting the voluminous bibliography he draws on to verify his study.

The early Egyptian temples were the center for the study of the cosmos and the relationship of mankind thereto. It was at the temple that the heavens were closest to the earth. The temple was an earthly sanctuary, but carefully oriented to the celestial order, thereby becoming the connecting link between man and diety. Two stately pylons, which stood at the front of each temple, were so arranged that the sun would rise exactly between them at both the vernal equinox and the autumnal equinox. By this means the rites of the temple were timed in perfect coordination with the motions of the cosmos and, at a set moment each year, the temple basked in the full splendor of the sun's celestial glory.

One of the purposes of the temple was to capture the sun's light which the Egyptians believed was a source of knowledge and power. Thus their structures were designed as scale models of the universe, and the pylons were made in such a way as to direct the light inward and downward into the depths of the structure. Stone slabs were placed so that they formed narrow apertures through which the sunlight would pass along the walls of the otherwise dark interior: a brilliant contrast of light and darkness; an illumination of marked-off areas at set times to suggest God's presence in a fallen world (p. 154). The Egyptians, being sun worshippers, believed that the sun's light was a source of knowledge and power which, once understood, the initiate could use to become deified. These universal principles, by which godhood would be obtained, were revealed through the temple ritual (pp. 104, 153-154, 157).

Many have speculated and studied and tried to determine the exact purpose for which the great pyramids in Egypt were built. They were not primarily tombs: most of the kings or Pharaohs were buried in the Valley of the Kings near Thebes, hundreds of miles from the pyramids. Though the Egyptians never tried to make any two temples, tombs, texts, vignettes, or reliefs exactly alike (p. xiii) it is the contention here that the pyramids were, indeed, temples.

The Egyptians felt that the temple held the keys by which they could learn the secrets of obtaining eternal life and permanently secure it for themselves; however, it was not on a merely individual basis. Their idea of progression after earth life included the family so provision was made to have the initiate's family sealed to him in the next world (p. 142).

In order to receive these blessings, the initiate had to obey certain laws such as renouncing all bad passions and desires, consecrating himself to the work and showing willingness to sacrifice all things necessary (pp. 124, 214). In this way, his own desires and deeds would be increasingly identified with that of god and godhood. All movement in the temple was toward this goal. The closer one approached diety by penetrating deeper and deeper into the temple, the higher the law he must be willing to live. Thus there was a continual narrowing of the gap between his nature and that of god until, in the holy of holies, they actually merged (pp. 92, 161).

The one word which most nearly expressed what the temple was about was "Sensen": that is, "Breathing." But the Egyptian verb "to breathe" meant much more than merely taking a breath. It was indicative of the most intimate and close association between parties—to join the company of, and become one with, the gods—to fuse or have an indwelling relationship with them (pp. 9, 92). Thus the temple was the house of power and life. Knowledge was the secret of controlling the power and gaining eternal life (p. 155).

Before the initiate could enter the temple, he had to go through a purification ritual in an annex outside the temple. This ritual consisted of two parts (pp. 98-99). First, the ceremonial cleansing from abomination so the initiate would not pollute the temple (p. 93). Further, the ceremony insured that each part of the body, by virtue of remaining pure and intact, would never again lose its proper function (p. 106). The areas washed and blessed were: the eyes to see, the ears to hear, the mouth to speak, the legs to walk, the mind to think and remember, and the groin to procreate (pp. 107, 111). The whole was symbolic of a rebirth and a partaking of godly power, or a reuniting of the body with power forever (pp. 67, 106).

(Incidentally, Moslems go through a similar washing before they enter a mosque to pray and to worship. Hindus and members of other religions also have ritualistic washings and purification of the body.)

The second part of the Egyptian ritual was the coronation by which one was anointed a priest and king. This was a very sacred part of the ceremony (pp. 98-99). Again, various parts of the body received particular attention. Oil or ointment was placed on the head, cranium, brow, eyes, ears, lips, shoulders, arms, heart (breast), stomach, buttocks, thighs, legs, feet and toes, in that order (p. 112). Once this was complete, the candidate received a white ceremonial garment, thus showing that he was properly cleansed and empowered to be instructed in the mysteries of becoming a god (p. 93). Along with this he received a new name. This he had to remember in order to live forever. The name was guarded, for to possess knowledge of another's name was to have some power over him. This applied even to the gods, for to grasp the meaning of the name was to understand the nature of the being (p. 141).

Once this was accomplished, the initiate entered into the temple proper. The ceremony was not static but progressed from room to room, the order being ever deeper penetration into the temple and its teachings. (P. 115.) The first area of the temple was the hall of the two *Maats*. *Maat* was a female diety who symbolized every principle of social order and the entire concept of godhead. The presence of *Maat* was necessary at the moment one entered the temple to guarantee that one was a bona fide candidate for eternal glory and qualified to enter the holy place. *Maat's* presence signified that all was correct and in order (pp. 116-117). (Equivalent to a temple recommend.)

The first part of the temple ritual took the form of a mystery play complete with stage, props, and actors. In the hall of *Geb* and *Shu* the creation of earth and man was enacted (p. 126). The characters involved in the creation were *Thoth* and *Atum*, but they were working under the direction of a higher god to whom they were to continualy report their progress (p. 132).

It was *Atum* who had the major role in the play. In the heavens he was known as the god *Re*, but when he descended to earth his name was changed. Its meaning: creator, collective sum of all other beings, all embracing. More extended, it meant: sum totality—the combining of all preexistent beings into one archetype who then represented all beings who came after. Scholars have noted the god *Re's* close identity with Adam (pp. 133-134).

The creator of man *Atum* is *Ptah*, but again he was only an agent working under the direction of an even greater god known as *Amon*. He was the supreme god, source of all power. He was also the hidden one, the one with whom the fallen world cannot associate (p. 134).

Atum was created asleep. *Ptah* and *Amon* awakened him by giving him the breath of life (p. 148). He was instructed, then introduced to the lady he called the mother of all (p. 151).

The next stage of the ritual took place in a beautiful garden. There they paused and partook of refreshments. The garden was the home of the *Ished* tree. When they ate of its fruit their nature was changed. Things were not as they were before (p. 176). A further complication: the female companion had altercations with a serpent which represented corruption and destruction. For its deeds in trying to defeat the woman by preaching false doctrine, the serpent was deprived of its arms and legs to symbolize that it would never be able to rise in full power and might again, that its vulnerable head was made easy prey for the foot of man (pp. 179-180).

All those involved were then forced to take a long and dangerous journey. Fire and sword kept the serpent from the garden, but not the man. He was eventually to overcome all things and return to that blissful state. When he did return, there would be no serpent to ruin the tranquility (pp. 181-198).

As the people passed from room to room they symbolically underwent a change of nature, dramatized by changing the costume along the way (p. 165). As the initiate and his company began the long and dangerous journey back to glory, they donned special clothing for protection because their eternal life was in danger. Knowledge was revealed to them along the way by divine beings sent from the gods. *Atum* became the guide and all were to follow him (pp. 190-194). The purpose was to overcome the adversary which was done by escaping his power and by cleansing themselves of all legal and moral problems (p. 209).

Transition from one stage to another was done by passing through narrow gates which represented rebirth. Also, the progression was shown by mounting steps, thus symbolically going from a lower level of order to a higher. However, the initiate was not allowed to go through the gate unless certain formulas, creeds, and passwords were known (pp. 215-217). It was during this stage of the endowment that a puzzling practice was engaged in: the ritual woundings, or blows, struck upon the body of the candidate. These served to remind him that he was in real danger of losing his life unless he was careful. However, so sacred was this that what went along with it and what the wounds meant could never be divulged, ever (pp. 217-228). The candidate had to promise that he would not do certain things.

He was not to be lightminded, speak evil, be contentious, hard-hearted, or impure, etc. (pp. 218-220).

The climax of the ritual was the divine embrace when the initiate was clasped to the breast of *Amon*. This part of the ceremony was weighted with meaning and was the goal of all the consecration (p. 241). It represented the accepted return of the candidate and, through it, there was an infusing of power by which he was joined to the sun-god *Re* and received everlasting dominion (p. 243-244). It was not a sign of affection, but of communion between two beings (p. 243). It symbolized indissolvable togetherness, an enduring relationship between god and man and the actual binding of the two (p. 244).

The embrace also had the features of a recognition rite. The candidate was expected to give, to the priest, certain passwords in response to certain questions put to him. In part of the ritual, a specific formula was given which had to be repeated back exactly. This formula is not written out anywhere, but it was shown by the use of three symbols: *Ankh, Was* and *Djed*. These, however, do give a clue to what the rite was all about. *Ankh* was the navel string. It was associated with the backbone and represented life, durability, stability, and protection (pp. 250-251).

The last ceremony took place at a veil; not a small one, but a large, theatrical veil. It symbolized the separation between time and eternity and was believed to open on an uninterrupted passage devoid of all obstacles; thus, eternal progression (p. 245). There were four elements associated with the veil, which were also on the garments worn by the initiate. They followed the same pattern (pp. 246-247).

Once the candidate had received the embrace, he could be united with the gods in the gods' realm: the veil was parted and he stepped through. The ceremony ended in a blaze of glory, for the candidate stepped out into a court onto which was reflected, from the pyramid, the full power of the sun thus symbolizing the joining of the candidate with *Re* (pp. 147, 253). Using the splendor of the sun reflecting off gold-painted, huge surfaces of the pyramids at noonday would have been a dazzling celestial representation—and a spectacular physical as well as spiritual climax for the participant in the Egyptian temple endowment.

It may be an understatement to say that "If the Egyptian endowment was but an imitation, it was still a good one." Latter-day Saints who have been through the temple might well be amazed at similarities between the temple endowment and the Egyptian ceremony, as translated by Brother Nibley from the "Book of Breathings," which were part of the papyri which came into Joseph Smith's hands and which were re-discovered by Dr. Atiya.

Whether Abraham and Joseph of old shared with the Egyptians the fullness of the gospel including the temple endowment while they were on their "missions" in Egypt, we do not know.

What happened to the papyri from which Joseph Smith translated the book of Abraham? We do not know.

Why do we not have further extracts from the book of Abraham? We do not know.

Why do we not have the papyri or the translation of the "Book of Joseph of Old"? We do not know.

Whether Joseph Smith received the revelation on the temple endowment in these latter days partially from the stimulus or catalytic effect of the Egyptian papyri he was translating, we do not know.

> We believe all that God has revealed, all that He does now reveal, and we believe that He will yet reveal many great and important things pertaining to the Kingdom of God (9th Article of Faith, Pearl of Great Price).

We also believe a living prophet is in the world today; a prophet for this world, as much a prophet as were Adam, Enoch, Moses, Noah, Abraham, Joseph or any other of the ancient prophets. We believe there is a prophet to the Church and to the world today as much as Joseph Smith was a prophet in the opening of this dispensation.

President Kimball's historical revelation from the Lord giving the full blessings of the priesthood and the temple to benefit all people "without regard for race or color" (see D&C Official Declaration—2, June 8, 1978) reopens a vast field of labor for missionary work, both for the living and the dead. In a very real sense, we who are Abraham's seed are being called again to go "back to Egypt"—to the vast continent of Africa and its descendants of the ancient Egypt—to *all nations* of the earth with the fullness of the gospel of Jesus Christ, including the blessings of the temple and the endowment for the living and the dead.

> He inviteth them all to come unto him and partake of his goodness; and he denieth none that come unto him, black and white, bond and free, male and female; and he remembereth the heathen; and all are alike unto God, both Jew and Gentile (2 Nephi 26:33).

Summary of Chapter Fourteen

1. After the death of Joseph Smith, the mummies and papyri were understood to have belonged to the prophet's mother, Lucy Mack Smith, for a time.

2. When Lucy Mack Smith died in May, 1855, the mummies and papyri were assumed by Emma, the prophet's widow, who by then had re-married.

3. Emma Bidamon, former wife of Joseph Smith, sold the mummies and papyri to a Mr. A. Combs May 26, 1856.

4. Dr. Aziz Atiya, professor at the University of Utah, discovered some of the papyri along with the bill of sale of the mummies at the Metropolitan Museum of Art in New York City, in 1966.

5. The Metropolitan Museum (through Dr. Atiya's efforts) gave the papyri to the Church who, in turn, lent them to Dr. Hugh Nibley of Brigham Young University.

6. Professor Nibley's challenge was to translate the papyri and to determine whether these were the papyri used in the translating of the book of Abraham.

7. In 1975 Dr. Nibley's book, *The Message of the Joseph Smith Papyri*, was published by Deseret Book Company, Salt Lake City, Utah.

8. In bold print, in chapter one of Dr. Nibley's book, is this message: NOT THE SOURCE OF THE BOOK OF ABRAHAM.

9. The papyri, now in the hands of the Church, is apparently a "Book of Breathings" or Egyptian "Funeral Text."

. 10. It is, however, not an ordinary "Funeral Text," but, according to Dr. Nibley, it is a temple text and, in short, contains an Egyptian endowment.

11. The Egyptian endowment found in the papyri "if but an imitation, is still a good one, " according to Professor Nibley.

12. The following are a few of the still unanswered questions about the Egyptian papyri:

- Where, then, is the papyri from which Joseph Smith translated the book of Abraham?
- Why do we not have the further extracts promised from the book of Abraham? Or do we have some of them in the LDS temple endowment?
- Where are the papyri containing the writings of the ancient Joseph who was sold into Egypt? Why do we not have the translation of these writings which were on the original papyri?
- How much (if any) of the LDS temple endowment came from the stimulus or catalytic effect of the Egyptian papyri?

13. Many more of Abraham's seed, who have the priesthood and the true gospel, may yet be called "back to Egypt," back to the vast continent of Africa to teach the fullness of the gospel, including the blessings of the temple and the temple endowment.

The Holy Temple Endowment and Its Relationship to the Egyptian Papyri

Introduction and Review

The Pearl of Great Price is indeed a "Jewel among Scriptures." It is a strange compilation in that part of it, namely the book of Moses, came through Joseph Smith climbing "an exceedingly high mountain" with Moses and Enoch. That is, he was able to see by revelations from the Lord the great things that these ancient prophets saw. As we have seen the stimulus, or catalyst, for Joseph Smith's writing of the book of Moses in the Pearl of Great Price came as a result of his work on revising, or translating, the Bible. This revelation is properly found in the Joseph Smith Translation of the Bible as part of the preface to beginning Genesis.

The book of Abraham is even more unusual, perhaps, in that Joseph Smith seems to have had no prior knowledge of this record—no vision, no angel, no voice of the Lord foretelling him about the arrival of Mr. Chandler and the mummies, and the Egyptian papyri. Yet it is purported that Joseph's answer to Michael Chandler, when he was asked if he could translate the ancient papyri, was, "Yes, with the Lord's help" (Seminaries and Institutes of Religion Church History Sound Filmstrips, episode #5, "How We Got the Pearl of Great Price").

Joseph Smith said, "I gave him [Mr. Michael Chandler] the interpretation, and like a gentleman, he gave me the following certificate:

Kirtland, July 6, 1835

This is to make known to all who may be desirous, concerning the knowledge of Mr. Joseph Smith, Jun., in deciphering the ancient Egyptian hieroglyphic characters in my possession, which I have, in many eminent cities, showed to the most learned; and, from the information that I could ever learn, or meet with, I find that of Mr. Joseph Smith, Jun., to correspond in the most minute matters.

Michael H. Chandler
(Traveling with, and proprietor of,
Egyptian Mummies.

(*History of the Church*, 2:235.)

Orson Pratt, in a talk delivered at the Thirteenth Ward on Sunday, August 25, 1878, and reported in *Journal of Discourses*, 20:64-65, said:

> The prophet took them and repaired to his room and inquired of the Lord concerning them. The Lord told him they were sacred records, containing the inspired writings of Abraham when he was in Egypt, and also those of Joseph, while he was in Egypt; and they had been deposited with these mummies, which had been exhumed. (See also *Saga of Book of Abraham*, pp. 158-159.)

The Prophet Joseph Smith was thus very anxious to obtain the papyri. Orson Pratt continues:

> Mr. Chandler told him that he would not sell the writings unless he could sell the mummies, for it would detract from the curiosity of his exhibition; Mr. Smith inquired of him the price which was a considerable sum, and finally purchased the mummies and writing, all of which he retained in his possession for many years (*ibid.*).

The writings from these papyri were very important to the Prophet Joseph Smith as they ought to be to every Latter-day Saint and every seeker for truth. The book of Abraham in our present Pearl of Great Price is only part of the translation from these papyri which came into Joseph Smith's possession in 1835. More was promised, but never forthcoming. (See *Times and Seasons*, Feb. 1843, cited in *Saga*, p. 250.)

The writings of Joseph of old who was sold into Egypt, and which ought to be a part of the Pearl of Great Price, were apparently never fully translated. A few words of Joseph of old, which may have come from the papyri, are given in the Joseph Smith Translation of the Bible (see JST, Genesis 50:24-37; also 2 Nephi 3 in the Book of Mormon). These are all the writings of Joseph of old that we presently have.

The papyri from which Joseph Smith translated the book of Abraham, and the writings on the papyri of Joseph of old are, apparently, still lost. The November 27, 1967 collection of eleven Egyptian papyri, which were ceremoniously presented by officials of the Metropolitan Museum of Art in New York City to President Nathan N. Tanner of the First Presidency of The Church of Jesus Christ of Latter-day Saints, and which are widely known as the Joseph Smith Papyri, ARE NOT (according to Dr. Hugh Nibley of BYU) the source for the book of Abraham (Nibley, *Message of the Joseph Smith Papyri*, p. 1).

The existing papyri apparently are not the source of the book of Abraham. The mystery of the source remains. The discovery of the Joseph Smith Papyri is important, however, because they were part of the original scrolls sold by Mr. Chandler to the Prophet and, later, by Emma Bidamon, former wife of Joseph, to Mr. Combs and thence to the museum in New York. (*Saga*, p. 290.)

The existing papyri are important because they contain "An Egyptian Endowment" (see title of *The Message of the Joseph Smith Papyri—An Egyptian Endowment*, by Hugh Nibley).

According to Nibley, they are:

> Temple texts used in the performance of ordinances, 'an inventory of the holiest mysteries,' the saving ordinances, which were 'carried out or witnessed' by both the living and the dead (*Message*, p. 6).

The final chapter is an attempt to look briefly at the origin and development of the Holy Temple Endowment of The Church of Jesus Christ of Latter-day Saints and to show that there seems to be a relationship between the Egyptian papyri, especially that portion identified as the Joseph Smith Papyri, and the Holy Temple Endowment used in the temples of the Latter-day Saints. If this is true, then this is one more "pearl"—one more "jewel" in this marvelous scripture of the latter days.

Bible Contains Little on Endowment

The Bible contains almost no information concerning the Holy Temple Endowment. The Doctrine and Covenants, which deals with most of the Latter-day Saint principles and practices in some detail, treats the subject of the endowment only in general and scanty terms. The earliest reference to the endowment in this dispensation came from God in a revelation given through the Prophet Joseph Smith at Fayette, New York, on January 2, 1831, only nine months after the organization of the Church. The Saints were commanded to go west and gather at the Ohio Valley. "There," said God, "I will give unto you my law; and there you shall be endowed with power from on high" (D&C 38:32).

The nature of the power was not revealed. During the next ten years the Lord, in his revelations to the Church, repeatedly referred to an "endowment." He commanded the Saints to build a house for him in Kirtland: He told them it should be after the manner and according to plans which he would reveal unto the Church. The purpose of this house was revealed in these words:

> Yea, verily I say unto you, I gave unto you a commandment that you should build a house, in the which house I design to endow those whom I have chosen with power from on high (D&C 95:8).

Need for an Endowment

God revealed to the Prophet that "it is expedient in me" that the first elders of the Church receive an endowment in the house; that Zion could not be redeemed until the elders had received the "great endowment," and that the missionaries must receive this endowment before they were fully prepared to go unto all the world to teach the gospel and build up the Church (D&C 105:11-12, 33).

Thus the Lord had revealed the importance of the endowment without disclosing its nature. The Saints were left to anticipate, to hope for, and to await with eagerness the bestowal of the promised endowment.

How much the Prophet himself knew of the endowment at this time is not clear, but it undoubtedly exceeded what he had revealed to his associates. Joseph Smith seems to have received insights and inspiration on this as he did other doctrines; that is, "line upon line, precept upon precept, here a little and there a little; and blessed are those who hearken unto my precepts, and lend an ear unto my counsel, for they shall learn wisdom" (2 Nephi 28:30).

Subscription for Kirtland Temple and Chandler's Visit Coincide

On June 25th, 1835, there was a meeting in Kirtland to subscribe for the building of the temple. It is very interesting to note that a week later, on July 3rd, Michael H. Chandler came to Kirtland to exhibit his Egyptian mummies. On July 5th, two days later, the Prophet wrote in his journal:

> Some of the Saints at Kirtland purchased the mummies (four of them) and papyrus, and with W. W. Phelps and Oliver Cowdery as scribes, I commenced the translation of some of the characters or heiroglyphics and much to our joy found that one of the rolls contained the writings of Abraham, another of the writings of Joseph of Egypt (*The Journal of Joseph*, compiled by Leland R. Nelson, p. 88).

Was it just happenstance that the meeting to subscribe for the building of the temple, and the coming of Michael Chandler to Kirtland with the scrolls of Abraham and Joseph, occurred within the same week?

Did the manuscript of the book of Abraham play a "catalystic" role in helping the Prophet Joseph Smith receive the endowment for the temple? In the days, months, and even years that followed before the book of Abraham appeared in print in March of 1842, the entries in the *History of the Church*, and some of the available accounts in the prophet's journals, tell a fascinating story—a story of constant concern with the message that was there—or the message behind the message. Following are just a few of the journal entries of the Prophet Joseph as he often spent his spare time, or precious time, translating the scrolls:

> (July 1835) The remainder of this month, I was continually engaged in translating an alphabet to the Book of Abraham, and arranging a grammar of the Egyptian language as practiced by the ancients.
> (October 1, 1835) This afternoon I labored on the Egyptian alphabet, in company with Brothers Oliver Cowdery and W. W. Phelps, and during the research, the principles of astronomy as understood by Father Abraham and the ancients unfolded to our understanding, the particulars of which will appear hereafter.
> (October 7, 1835) This afternoon I re-commenced translating the ancient records. . . .

(October 19, 1835) At home. Exhibited the records of antiquity to a number who called to see them.

(October 24, 1835) Mr. Goodrich and wife called to see the ancient [Egyptian] records, and also Dr. Frederick G. Williams to see the mummies. Brother Hawkes and Carpenter, from Michigan, visited us and tarried over night. . . .

(October 29, 1835) We examined the mummies, returned home, and my scribe commenced writing in my journal a history of my life.

Another part of the entry under October 29th has considerable significance: "Brother Warren Parrish commenced to write for me, at fifteen dollars per month. I paid him sixteen dollars in advance out of the committee's store."

Two weeks later, November 14, 1835, on Saturday, a long overlooked revelation to the Prophet Joseph Smith is recorded. It is for the benefit of Warren Parrish and is entitled "Revelation to Warren Parrish":

. . . It shall come to pass in his day [Warren Parrish's day], that he shall see great things show forth themselves unto my people; he shall see much of my ancient records, and shall know of hidden languages; and if he desires and shall seek it at my hands, he shall be privileged with writing much of my word, as a scribe unto me for the benefit of my people; therefore this shall be his calling until I shall order it otherwise in my wisdom. (*History of the Church*, 2:311.)

Warren Parrish thus became the apparent appointed scribe for the book of Abraham.

(November 7, 1835) Exhibited the alphabet of the ancient records to Mr. Holmes, and some others. Went with him to Frederick G. Williams to see the mummies.

(November 19, 1835) Went, in company with Dr. Williams and my scribe, to see how the workman prospered in finishing the House of the Lord. I returned home and spent the day in translating the Egyptian records.

(November 20, 1835) We spent the day in translating the records and made rapid progress.

(November 24, 1835) In the afternoon we translated some of the Egyptian records.

(November 26, 1835) Spent the day in translating Egyptian characters from the papyrus, though severly afflicted with a cold.

With these few entries, the mention of "translating" in terms of the papyri ceases until 1842. However, there are many entries of the Prophet's showing the mummies and papyri, for example:

(December 12, 1835) Spent the forenoon in reading. About twelve o'clock a number of young persons called to see the Egyptian records. My scribe Warren Parrish exhibited them. One of the young ladies who had been examining them, was asked if they had the appearance of antiquity. She observed, with an air of contempt, that they had not. On hearing this, I was surprised at the ignorance she displayed, and I observed to her, that she was an anomaly in creation, for all the wise and learned that had examined them, without hesitation pronounced them ancient. (*History of the Church*, 2:329-330.)

Completion of Kirtland Temple

The Kirtland Temple, built according to the plans and specifications which the Lord had revealed to Joseph Smith, was completed and dedicated on March 27, 1836. The dedicatory prayer had been revealed by the Lord to Joseph, and he dedicated this first house of the Lord in this dispensation. (D&C 109.) In the days following the dedication, a great spiritual outpouring occurred within the temple and with the people. Such an outpouring of the Spirit can be properly called "an endowment." During a sacrament meeting in the temple, a week after the dedication, the Lord caused a pillar of light to rest upon His house while angels came into it and a heavenly choir was heard joining with the Saints as they sang praises to their Lord and God.

After receiving the sacrament, the Prophet and Oliver Cowdery went behind the veil to pray. Here the Lord Jesus Christ appeared and spoke to them, telling them that he had "accepted this house" and that "the hearts the keys, powers, and authority which they held under Christ. These prophets included Moses, who restored the keys of the gathering of Israel, and Elijah, who conferred the keys and powers of the holy priesthood. (D&C 110:11-16.)

Following the appearance of Jesus Christ, there came a succession of the ancient prophets who had stood at the head of former gospel dispensations, each conferring upon the Prophet Joseph Smith and Oliver Cowdery the keys, powers, and authority which they held under Christ. These prophets included Moses, who restored the keys of the gathering of Israel, and Elijah, who conferred the keys and powers of the holy priesthood. (D&C 110:11-16.)

Meaning of the Word "Endowment"

The word "endowment," even in the commonly accepted definition as given in the dictionary, has for one of its meanings "to enrich." What an endowment this was, then, to have the great keys, powers and heavenly manifestations given to the Prophet. How would the Lord fulfill his promises of old to gather scattered Israel and build up his earthly kingdom without providing and "endowing" his elders with the keys and powers to gather his people from among the nations of the world? What would family life be, on earth or in heaven, without the "endowment" of the keys and powers to seal wife to husband and children to parents to bind them into an eternally happy family?

In addition to these overall and world-blessing "endowments," the Lord had prepared an individual and personal "endowment" to be given to his Saints. The nature of this endowment was not recorded in detail in the scriptural records and would be known only to those who were worthy to receive it.

Endowment Not Fully Revealed in Kirtland

Certain of the initial ordinances of the personal endowment were received by many in the Kirtland Temple. Some of the brethren recorded in their journals and bore witness at general conferences of the Church, that they had received the endowment in Kirtland. (John K. Edmunds, *Through Temple Doors*, p. 64.) However, the language of a revelation given to the Prophet in Nauvoo on January 19, 1841, is rather clear evidence that the priesthood ordinances and endowment, as we have it in the temple today in its fullness, had not been fully revealed, nor given, at Kirtland:

> Verily I say unto you, let this house be built unto my name, that I may reveal mine ordinances therein unto my people;
> For I deign to reveal unto my church things which have been kept hid from before the foundation of the world, things that pertain to the dispensation of the fulness of times.
> And I will show unto my servant Joseph all things pertaining to this house, and the priesthood thereof. (D&C 124:40-42.)

Also in earlier verses, in this same section of the Doctrine and Covenants, he said:

> For there is not a place found on earth that he may come to and restore again that which was lost unto you, or which he hath taken away, even the fulness of the priesthood.
> For a baptismal font there is not upon the earth, that they, my saints, may be baptized for those who are dead—
> For this ordinance belongeth to my house, and cannot be acceptable to me, only in the days of your poverty, wherein ye are not able to build a house unto me. (D&C 124:28-30.)

The language in this revelation precludes the possibility of the total personal endowment having been revealed or practiced in its fullness in Kirtland.

Facsimile of Egyptian Scrolls Related to Temple Endowment

It is very clear, however, that some of the facsimiles from the book of Abraham, which the Prophet was translating in Kirtland, contained writings related to the endowment of the temple—whether this meant the Kirtland Temple or the Nauvoo Temple is not known. In Joseph Smith's explanation of Facsimile No. 2 from the book of Abraham, found in our present Pearl of Great Price, "Explanation of the Foregoing Cut," with regard to figures 8-20, states:

> Contains writing that cannot be revealed unto the world; but is to be had in the Holy Temple of God.
> Ought not to be revealed at the present time.
> . . . Will be given in the own due time of the Lord.

It is very interesting to note that the Prophet had such reverence for the scrolls and mummies that they were housed, at times, in the Kirtland Temple. The top floor—west room at the end of the hall in the Kirtland Temple— was called the "translating room." It is most likely that the Prophet translated part of the book of Abraham in these quarters. (See *Saga*, p. 199.)

In the latter part of 1836, Elder Wilford Woodruff returned to the Saints after two and a half years service as a missionary. He had not seen the Kirtland Temple nor the mummies nor the papyri. The same day that he returned to Kirtland, he visited the temple and viewed the Egyptian artifacts. His account is recorded in his journal under the date November 25, 1836:

> After walking into the pulpits, erected for the Priesthood and viewing the curtains all bespeaking grandure [sic], solemnity of order that nothing short of wisdom from God could invent. We then visited the upper rooms and there viewed four Egyptian Mummies and also the Book of Abraham written by his own hand and not only the heiroglyphics but also many figures that this precious treasure contains are calculated to make a lasting impression upon the mind which is not to be erased. Many other important views I was privileged within the upper story, the school rooms, belfry, etc., all indicating great architecture and wisdom.

Toward the latter part of 1837, under the date of November 2, the following entry is recorded in the *History of the Church:*

> The Church voted to sanction the appointment of Brother Phineas Richards and Reuben Hedlock, by the Presidency, to transact business for the Church in procuring means to translate and print the records taken from the Catacombs of Egypt, then in the Temple.

It is the author's contention that the book of Abraham played a greater role in the coming forth of the endowment than is generally understood. It is certain that the papyri played at least a catalystic role in helping the Prophet Joseph Smith receive the endowment. If Joseph Smith did not receive the endowment in the papyri, he did receive great stimulus from the papyri. There is evidence that some of the Abraham papyri contained at least a "very good imitation of the temple endowment." As the manuscript of the book of Abraham was being translated, further light and knowledge on the subject of the endowment was revealed to the Prophet's inquiring mind.

Temple Endowment Given in Joseph Smith's Store

Joseph Smith did not wait until the Nauvoo Temple was completed before he began to share, with others, the endowment in its fullness. He recorded, in his journal, that he dedicated a room for sacred purposes above his brick store in Nauvoo. In this room, he said, "I keep my sacred writings, translate ancient records, and receive revelations." (*History of the*

Church, 5:1.) In that room, on May 4, 1842, he revealed and bestowed the Holy Endowment upon certain of his brethren:

> I spent the day in the upper part of the store . . . in council with General James Adams, of Springfield, Patriarch Hyrum Smith, Bishops Newel K. Whitney and George Miller, and President Brigham Young and elders Heber C. Kimball and Willard Richards, instructing them in the principles and order of the Priesthood, attending to washings, anointings, endowments and the communication of keys pertaining to the Aaronic Priesthood, and so on to the highest order of the Melchizedek Priesthood, setting forth the order pertaining to the Ancient of Days, and all those plans and principles by which one is enabled to secure the fulness of those blessings which have been prepared for the Church of the First Born, and come up and abide in the presence of the Eloheim in the eternal worlds. . . . In this council was instituted the ancient order of things for the first time in these last days. (*History of the Church*, 5:2 [and footnote].)

Elder B. H. Robert's footnote to the Prophet's journal entry states:

> This is the Prophet's account of the introduction of the Endowment ceremonies in this dispensation, and is the foundation of the sacred ritual of the temples (*History of the Church*, 5:2 footnote).

For a time after the introduction of the endowment, it was bestowed upon others of the Saints in the upper room of the Prophet's store. Then it seems to have been discontinued pending the completion of the Nauvoo Temple. The Lord had already stopped the performance of baptisms for the dead which he had permitted the Saints to perform initially in the Mississippi River in the days of their poverty. The Prophet, in a doctrinal sermon delivered at a general conference at Nauvoo, October 2, 1841, announced to the assembled Church:

> There shall be no more baptisms for the dead, until the ordinance can be attended to in the Lord's House; and the Church shall not hold another General Conference, until they can meet in said house. For thus saith the Lord. (*History of the Church*, 4:426.)

Even though the Prophet Joseph Smith was martyred before the completion of the Nauvoo Temple, the Saints—with gun in one hand to protect them from their enemies and building tools in the other hand—dedicated workers "in the midst of trials, tribulations, poverty, and worldly obstacles, solemnized in some instances, by death," persisted in the construction of this second latter-day temple. Through their heaven-blessed labors, on October 5, 1845, the Saints met in the new house of the Lord in general conference.

Endowments in Nauvoo Temple

Brigham Young records that on Wednesday, December 10, 1845:

> At 3:45 p.m., we completed the arrangements of the east room, prepar-
> atory to giving endowments . . . four twenty-five p.m., Elder Heber C. Kimball
> and I commenced administering the ordinances of endowment . . . continued
> [through] the night until three-thirty a.m. on the 11th. (*History of the Church*,
> 7:539.)

The endowment work continued with little interruption until February,
1846. Persecution intensified. The endowment work continued with great
intensity also. It was reported that the Saints were about to be massacred if
they did not leave Illinois immediately. Thus on Sunday, January 11, the
"General Council" of the Church met and arranged to make an early start
west. The following day one hundred forty-three persons received their
endowments in the temple, and Brigham Young wrote:

> Such has been the anxiety manifested by the saints to receive the ordinances
> [of the temple] and such the anxiety on our part to administer to them, that I
> have given myself up entirely to the work of the Lord in the Temple night and
> day, not taking more than four hours sleep, upon an average, per day, and
> going home but once a week (*History of the Church*, 7:567).

Then on Tuesday, February 3, 1846, Brigham Young announced that
no further endowment ordinances were to be administered in the temple.
He writes:

> Notwithstanding that I had announced that we would not attend to the
> administration of the ordinances, the House of the Lord was thronged all day,
> the anxiety being so great to receive, as if the brethren would have us stay here
> and continue the endowments until our way would be hedged up, and our
> enemies would intercept us. But I informed the brethren that this was not wise,
> and that we should build more Temples, and have further opportunities to
> receive the blessing of the Lord, as soon as the saints were prepared to receive
> them. In this temple we have been abundantly rewarded, if we receive no more.
> I also informed the brethren that I was going to get my wagons started and be
> off. I walked some distance from the Temple supposing the crowd would dis-
> perse, but on returning I found the house filling to overflowing.
>   Looking upon the multitude and knowing their anxiety, as they were
> thirsting and hungering for the word, we continued at work diligently in the
> House of the Lord. Two hundred and ninety-five persons received ordinances.
> (*History of the Church*, 7:579.)

While some of the Saints were crossing the Mississippi with their
wagons, others remained to receive their endowments in the face of death.
Five hundred and twelve persons were endowed on Friday the sixth, and,
"according to G. A. Smith's journal, upwards of six hundred" were endowed on February 7th (*History of the Church*, 7:580).

On Sunday, February 8th, Brigham Young wrote:

> I met with the Council of the Twelve in the southeast corner room of the
> attic of the Temple. We knelt around the altar, and dedicated the building to
> the Most High. We asked his blessing upon our intended move to the west; [we]

also asked him to enable us some day to finish the Temple, and dedicate it to him, and we would leave it in his hands to do as he pleased; and to preserve the building as a monument to Joseph Smith. We asked the Lord to accept the labors of his servants in this land. We then left the Temple. (*History of the Church*, 7:580.)

This seems to have ended the giving of the endowments in the Nauvoo Temple. No less than 5,634 endowments were reported in Brigham Young's journal. So far as the records reveal, all of those endowments were for the living; no endowments were performed in behalf of the dead before the dedication of the St. George Temple.

An attempt was made to rent or sell both the temple at Kirtland and the Nauvoo Temple, but not a penny on the cost of these two buildings was ever recovered. They remained with the "conquerors" as did the dwellings and farms of the Saints—as spoils of victory. (Cecil McGavin, *The Nauvoo Temple*, p. 118.)

Defiling of Nauvoo Temple by Mobs

With the city practically vacated by its founders, there was no force to repel the mob and protect their vacant buildings that had not been sold. The Saints were not able to keep the enemy from taking possession of the Nauvoo Temple. For a season a gang of mobbers took possession of the temple, making it their place of rendezvous. Cecil McGavin reports the defiling of the temple in these words:

> They carried into the beautiful new building their couches and beds, cots, tables, barrels of liquor, playing cards and other gambling devices with which to entertain themselves in the big building. At night they would play cards as they drank whiskey and filled the rooms with tobacco smoke, while they cursed and profaned in the House of the Lord.
>
> Since they did not make their habitation in the basement rooms they used the font as their lavatory, making it a foul smelling cesspool. These impious intruders would play their games of chance far into the night, perhaps hurling their empty bottles against the freshly painted scenes on the smooth walls of the rooms.
>
> Far into the night their drunken brawls continued in the house that was built for God. Men would climb to the belfry and ring the giant bell that had been purchased by the Saints in England and sent to Nauvoo. The silence of the City of Joseph was often broken by the tolling of the bell during the long night.
>
> . . . Inside the temple these wicked intruders set up what they called a "Judicature of Inquisition," before which many of the old, infirm Mormons were tried in a court that smacked of profanity and prejudice. Many of the faithful who were unable to leave the city because of their poverty were tried by this mock tribunal in the House of the Lord, many of them being condemned to be taken down to the river and baptized in the name of "old Joe Smith and the temple." (McGavin, *The Nauvoo Temple*, pp. 125-126.)

In spite of the fact that in the spring of 1846 most of the faithful members of the Church, who had lived in Nauvoo, were at the wayside stations in Iowa or at the rendezvous on the Missouri. Even though the temple was defiled by the mobsters, it was decided to send a few of the brethren back to Nauvoo to dedicate the temple officially.

Dedication of Nauvoo Temple

The brethren who returned for the dedicatory service were Elders Wilford Woodruff, Orson Hyde, John M. Bernhisel, and three of the brothers of Brigham Young—Joseph, John, and Phineas. They were not unmindful of the fact that many mobsters were in the city and that there might be trouble from the reckless element that had moved into Nauvoo. For this reason, the visiting brethren decided to hold a private dedicatory service the last night of April just in case the enemy should be on hand to prevent the public service that had been advertised for May 1st, 1846.

During the darkness of night the visiting brethren and a few of the local brethren quietly went into the temple and witnessed its private dedication. Elder Joseph Young offered the prayer of dedication in the presence of a few friends.

Elder Wilford Woodruff has written of this private service in the Nauvoo Temple:

> In the evening of this day I repaired to the Temple with Elder Orson Hyde and about twenty other Elders of Israel. There we were all clothed in our priestly robes and dedicated the Temple of the Lord, erected to His most holy name by the Church of Jesus Christ of Latter-Day Saints. Notwithstanding the prediction of false prophets and the threat of mobs that the building should never be completed or dedicated, their words have fallen to the ground. After the dedication, we raised our voices in a united shout of "Hosanna to God and the Lamb!" After offering our prayers we returned to our homes, thankful for the privilege enjoyed in our evening services. (M. F. Cowley, *Wilford Woodruff*, p. 247.)

The following day the temple was officially dedicated with, surprisingly, not the slightest unfriendly gesture from the "new citizens."

Nauvoo Temple Destroyed

Two and a half years after the first of the exiles fled from the city of Nauvoo, the temple was destroyed by fire. About 3:00 o'clock in the morning the fire was discovered by some of the citizens, but much of the building was ablaze by that time, and the fire spread so quickly that it was utterly impossible to save even a fragment of woodwork from the new building. In a few hours every splinter of woodwork was destroyed leaving only the charred, hot walls of stone standing naked on the hill. Then, in 1849, a tornado swept through the area and knocked down some of the walls. Community officials met and decided to tear down the other walls to avoid any serious accident should they fall on someone. (McGavin, *The Nauvoo Temple*, p. 153.)

When Brigham Young heard that the temple had been burned and that the walls had fallen in, he said:

> I would rather see it burnt up than see it in the hands of devils. I was thankful to see the Temple of Nauvoo on fire. Previous to crossing the Mississippi, we had met in the Temple and handed it over to the Lord God of Israel, and when I saw the flames, I said, "Good, Father, if you want it burned up."
>
> I hoped to see it burned before I left but I did not. I was glad when I heard of its being destroyed by fire, and the walls having fallen in, and said, "Hell, you cannot now occupy it." When the temple is built here, I want to maintain it for the use of the priesthood, which is our right privilege. I would rather do this than to build a temple for the wicked to trample under their feet. (*Journal of Discourses*, 8:203.)

First Endowments in Utah Territory

The first historically recorded endowment in Utah Territory was administered on Ensign Peak on October 21, 1849. During a general conference of the Church on October 6, "it was moved and seconded that Elder Addison Pratt, James Brown, and Hiram H. Blackwell, go to the Society Island to preach the Gospel." The motion was carried and preparations were made for their departure. Addison Pratt had not received his endowments. Since it was the will of the Lord that the elders receive the endowment before going forth to preach the gospel and build up the kingdom, Elder Pratt was taken to Ensign Peak to be given the endowment. Brigham Young says of this incident: "Addison Pratt received his endowments on Ensign Hill on the 21st, the place being consecrated for the purpose." (B. H. Roberts, *A Comprehensive History of the Church*, 3:386.)

The first under-roof endowments in the Salt Lake Valley were given in the "Old Council House," which was the first permanent public building erected in Salt Lake City. It stood on the southwest corner of the intersection of South Temple and Main Streets. Building of the structure began on February 26, 1849, and completed in December of 1850. Under instructions from Brigham Young, Heber C. Kimball on the 7th of July, 1852, resumed the administration of endowment ordinances to the Saints in it, a privilege that had been suspended since the expulsion of the Saints from Nauvoo. (*History*, 4:13.)

On May 5, 1855, the Endowment House, built at the northwest corner of Temple Square, was dedicated and superseded the Old Council House as the endowment sanctuary. It remained for thirty-four years then it was taken down by order of Wilford Woodruff, in the spring of 1889, because of rumors that plural marriages, contrary to the law of the land, were being solemnized in the building. (*History*, 4:15.)

St. George Temple First in Utah Territory

On April 6, 1877, twelve years before the demolition of the Endowment House, the St. George Temple was dedicated. It should be noted that certain parts of the temple were dedicated on January 1, 1877, and immediately after that endowments began in this, the first temple completed in the Territory of Utah. For the first time, in this temple, on January 9, 1877, the ordinance of baptism for the dead was administered. Two days later, on January 11, Brigham Young announced in the temple during an endowment session "that this was the first time that endowments had been administered for the dead (of which there was any record) in this dispensation." (Letter of David H. Cannon, President of the St. George Temple, addressed to President Joseph F. Smith, Oct. 21, 1916—quoted in Edmunds, *Through Temple Doors*, p. 73.)

Wilford Woodruff Assigned to Write Temple Endowment

On April 8, Brigham Young appointed Wilford Woodruff to preside over the temple as its first president and charged him with the responsibility to "write all the ordinances of the Church from the first baptism and confirmation through every ordinance of the Church." (*Temple Doors*, p. 73.) Brigham Young, Jr., was appointed to assist him in this writing project. Wilford Woodruff states that George Q. Cannon also "assisted some in this writing." It appears that as the writing progressed it was periodically presented to President Young for his approval.

When the writing of the endowment was finished to the satisfaction of Brigham Young, he said to Wilford Woodruff, "Now you have before you an ensample to carry on the endowments in all temples until the coming of the Son of Man." (*Temple Doors*, p. 74.)

President Edmunds concludes his chapter on The Holy Endowment with this great observation:

> There are, in the endowment, truths that I have not yet comprehended, vistas of learning that I have not yet seen, and fields of wisdom and understanding which I have not yet even entered upon, much less explored and brought into possession. Considering the new light and understanding that continually comes to me as I serve in the house of the Lord, I feel that the endowment is a subject that I shall not exhaust in this life, but that which I know will ever be to me a "Pearl of Great Price." (*Temple Doors*, p. 78.)

Summary of Chapter Fifteen

1. The standard works of the Church contain very little concerning the Holy Temple Endowment.

2. Some of the facsimiles of the book of Abraham contained information related to the temple endowment.

3. The book of Abraham played a greater role in the coming forth of the temple endowment than is generally understood.

4. If Joseph Smith did not receive the endowment through the Egyptian papyri, he did receive information and stimulus for the endowment from them.

5. The Prophet had such reverence for the Egyptian papyri and mummies that he housed them for some time in the Kirtland Temple.

6. Joseph Smith did not wait until the Nauvoo Temple was completed before he began to share with others the personal endowment.

7. In the upper room of the Prophet's brick store in Nauvoo, the personal endowment in its fullness was first given.

8. Even though the Prophet Joseph was martyred, the Nauvoo Temple was completed and dedicated. Many personal endowments were received by the early Saints before they came West.

9. The temple at Nauvoo was lost to the Church, desecrated by mobs, later burned, and then destroyed by a tornado.

10. The first endowment in the Territory of Utah was given on Ensign Peak above Salt Lake City to Elder Addison Pratt on October 21, 1849.

11. Before the Salt Lake or St. George Temples were completed, endowments were performed in the "Old Council House" and the Endowment House in Salt Lake City.

12. The first temple completed in the territory of Utah was the St. George Temple in Southern Utah.

13. The St. George Temple was the first temple to have endowments administered for the dead (of which there is any record) in this dispensation.

14. Wilford Woodruff, Brigham Young, Jr., and George Q. Cannon were charged by President Brigham Young to write all the ordinances of the Church in 1877, including the temple endowments.

15. This writing of the temple endowment became the ensample to carry on the endowment in all the temples until the coming of the Son of Man.

Selected Bibliography

Book of Jasher. Translated from Original Hebrew into English. Salt Lake City: J. H. Parry and Company, 1965 printing.

Clarke, Adam. *Bible Commentary of Genesis-Esther*. New York: Abingdon Press.

Clark, James R. *The Story of the Pearl of Great Price*. Salt Lake City: Bookcraft, 1962.

Corbett, M. N. *The Harp of Ethiopia*. Freeport, New York: Books for Library Press, 1971.

Deseret News Church Almanac. Salt Lake City: *Deseret News*, 1983.

Frankl, Viktor E. *Man's Search for Meaning*. New York: Washington Square Press, 1971.

Documentary History of the Church. Salt Lake City: Deseret Book Company, 1978 ed.

Hymns. Salt Lake City: Deseret Book Company, 1972 ed.

Kimball, Spencer W. *The Miracle of Forgiveness*. Salt Lake City: Bookcraft, 1969.

Lao Tzu. *Tao Teh King*. New York: F. Unger Pub. Co., 1958 ed.

Lund, John L. *The Church and the Negro*. Austin, Texas: Paramount Pub. Co., 1967.

Lundwall, N. B. *A Compilation Containing the Lectures on Faith*. Salt Lake City.

Matthews, Robert J. "A Plainer Translation." *Joseph Smith's Translation of the Bible*. Provo, Utah: Brigham Young University Press, 1975.

McConkie, Bruce R. *Doctrinal New Testament Commentary*, Vol. III. Salt Lake City: Bookcraft, 1977 ed.

Nibley, Hugh. *Abraham in Egypt*. Salt Lake City: Deseret Book Company, 1981.

Pratt, Parley P. *Key to Science of Theology*, 5th ed. Salt Lake City: Deseret Book Company, 1883.

Peterson, Mark E. *Abraham, Friend of God*. Salt Lake City: Deseret Book Company, 1979.

Skousen, W. C. *The First Two Thousand Years*. Salt Lake City: Bookcraft, 1953.

Smith, Joseph Fielding. *Teachings of the Prophet Joseph Smith*. Salt Lake City: Deseret News Press, 1951 ed.

———. *Man, His Origin and Destiny*. Salt Lake City: Deseret Book Company, 1954.

———. *Essentials in Church History*. Salt Lake City: Deseret Book Company, 1953 ed.

Talmage, James E. *Jesus the Christ.* Salt Lake City: Deseret Book Company, 1961 ed.

Todd, Jay. *The Saga of the Book of Mormon.* Salt Lake City: Deseret Book Company, 1969.

Youngreen, Buddy. *Reflections of Emma*, Joseph Smith's Wife. Orem, Utah: Grandin Book Co., 1982.

Index

A

Abel, hearkens to voice of Lord, 83-84; brings firstlings of flock, 83-84; killed by Cain, 85

Abraham, gazed at heaven through Urim and Thummim, 13, 40, 43; was tenth generation from Noah, 15; flees Ur of Chaldees, 16; genealogy of, 116, 117; mission to Egypt, chapter 12; early life of, 118; taught gospel by Noah and Shem, 118; tells of origin of Egypt, 119; delivered by angel, 120-121; called to a strange land, 120-121; ordained by Melchizedek to priesthood, 121; received endowment, 121, 122; left Ur for Egypt, 123; receives Egyptian language and cultural background, 123; his approach to teaching Egyptians, 124; teaches about creation of earth, 124-125; goes to Egypt, 126; invited to stay in Egypt, 127; teaches deeper aspects of gospel, 124-125; his stay comes to a halt, 128, 129; respected for wisdom and teachings, 129

Adam, first man of all men called, 40; on other worlds, 40; literal child of God, birth of, 52-53; understood gospel in pre-earth life, 66; given free agency, 55-56; confronted by Lord in Garden, 57; to be priesthood holder and represent the Lord in the home, 59; blessed with work, 59; kept from Tree of Life, 60, 64, 65; broke Word of Wisdom, 63; not to die until gospel taught, 67; he fell that men might be, 63; had no knowledge of purpose on earth for a time, 70; called upon Lord, 71-72; lived 930 years, 71; learns principle of obedience and sacrifice, 72-73; Enoch knew and was ordained by, 75; learns gospel line upon line, 75-76; asked why baptism, 75; told to teach his children the gospel, 76; is baptized, 79; ordained to higher priesthood, 79; is Michael the archangel, 79; teaches Eve, 81; testimony of, 82; his children reject the gospel, 82; prays for a child who will not reject, 83-84; patriarchal order instituted in days of, 99; Abraham tells of, 84; Enoch tells how gospel was given to, 102; Atum in Egyptian temple rites compared with, 155-156.

Apostacy, parable about, 20-21; Isaiah prophecies of, 21; first explained, chapter 8, 81; Enoch sees, 109.

Articles of Faith, written by Joseph Smith at request of Mr. Wentworth, 13-14; James E. Talmage wrote book on, 14; presented for sustaining vote, 27-28; as scripture, 28-29

Atiya, Dr. Aziz Suryal, Professor of University of Utah, researcher of Egyptian and Arabic manuscripts, discovered Joseph Smith Papyri, 146-147, 150-151.

Atonement, need to comprehend, 67; see meaning of blood sacrifice, 74-75; Son of God atoned for original guilt, 75-77; Enoch sees effect of, 108-109; suffering of Savior for, 108

B

Babbitt, Almon, stayed at Nauvoo as Trustee-in-Trust for Church, 146

Baptism, taught to first people on earth, 20; Adam asks why, 75; analogy of birth to, 76-77; by water (baptism) we keep the commandment, 77-78; Adam is baptized, 79; eight souls saved by water, 94-95, 112-113; of earth, 105; Noah taught, 112-113; for dead, 168

Bidamon, Emma Smith (see also Emma Smith), sold papyri to Mr. Combs, 161

C

Cain, rejects gospel and becomes a son of perdition, 15; hearkens not, 83-84; why offering rejected by Lord, 84; becomes angry, 84; who made Cain angry? 84-85; kills Abel, 85; blames everyone but himself, 85; punishment given to, 86; strange story of, 86; men punished for own sins, not Cain's, 88; genealogy of for six generations, 88; originated "Secret Combinations," 88-89; posterity of, 91.

Cannon, George Q., assisted in cannonizing Pearl of Great Price, 27; assisted in writing temple endowment, 173

Celestial kingdom, celestialized, celestial, all trees are Trees of Life in, 66; Enoch sees, 104; God lives in, 35-36, 49, 66; real promised land is, 34

Chandler, Michael H., came to Kirtland, Ohio, 16, 140, 146, 160-161; received papyri from his uncle Lebolo, 140; exhibits mummies and papyri, 141; gives opinion on Joseph Smith's translation of papyri, 127, 142-143

full endowment, 165-166; meaning of some facsimiles only revealed in, 161; Nauvoo Temple, 168; attempt to sell Kirtland and Nauvoo, 169; defiling of Nauvoo Temple, 170; Nauvoo Temple dedicated, 171-172; fire destroys Nauvoo Temple, 172; St. George first in Territory of Utah, 173

Terah, Abraham's father, became idolater, 119; raised Sarai as a daughter, 129

Times and Seasons, newspaper of Saints in Nauvoo, published writings of book of Abraham, 143; promised more extracts of book of Abraham, 144

Tower of Babel, 116

Tree of knowledge of good and evil, placement so Adam and Eve could act for themselves, 62; necessary in newly created earth, 62; maybe tree of this telestial world, 125

Tree of life, Adam and Eve kept from, 60; antidote to tree of knowledge of good and evil, cherubim and flaming sword to keep from, 64; why the Lord kept Adam and Eve from, 64-65; explained in book of Revelation, 65; Lehi saw vision of, 65; perhaps are real trees, 66

Tubal Cain, an instructor of every artificer in brass and iron, 91

U

Ur of Chaldees, 118-119; Abraham leaves, 122

Urim and Thummim, Abraham saw heavens through, 13; God's world like, 35, 48-49; Abraham beheld stars by use of, 123

W

War in Heaven, came about because of contrast of two pre-earth leaders, 45; has changed to earth, 45

Woodruff, Wilford, describes seeing mummies and papyri, 167; assigned to dedicate Nauvoo Temple, 171-172; appointed to preside over St. George Temple, 173

Y

Young, Brigham, said when man fell, earth fell into space, 24, 27, 50, 52, 61, 137, 146, 168, 169, 171; said Cain's mark is flat nose and black skin, 86; describes giving endowments in Nauvoo Temple, 168-169; tells of seeing temple on fire, 171; tells of Addison Pratt receiving endowment on Ensign Peak, 172; appointed Wilford Woodruff to preside over St. George Temple and write ordinances for temples, 173

Young, Joseph, dedicatory prayer, Nauvoo Temple, 171

Z

Zion, Lord calls his people, 103; city of holiness, even, 103-104; Enoch establishes, 103; to look down from heaven, 106-107; "Golden City" of, 107; Enoch sees Latter-day gathering to, 110; taken to heaven, Enoch sees, 103-104, 110